IFS seems to be expanding now, lots of practitioners and trainings and a certain "hey this works" buzz gathering around it. I can't remember how I heard about it, but I'm very glad I did. I've always been interested in therapies which employ the concept of "parts"/"subpersonalities"/"ego states," but have never felt I got beyond a certain point with the concept. IFS has, so far, proven to be the missing key I needed. It takes parts therapy past anything else I've tried for dynamic psychological self discovery and healing.

Jay Earley's book is for the beginner who wants to practice IFS, including completely alone, which is highly feasible. As such it goes slowly, explains carefully, and contains a lot of encouragement for the initially unsure. It is however far from lacking in experienced wisdom, and I will testify you can do wonderful stuff with it and nothing else. The system is incredibly user-friendly but it's also extremely deep. You know you are dealing with the real stuff of the psyche—the sudden shifts, the realizations, the sheer off-the-cuff creativity, the insights given by each part painting a truly personal and dynamic picture, yet fully in control. Yes, I really would say IFS has managed to come up with the right systems-based, loose-but-accurate formula to induce such experiences deliberately, yet organically, without any hint of being mechanical or stiff.

The main thing about IFS is that it works, and works by honouring systemic processes and knowing just what to do with them, after having plainly worked very hard to arrive at this ingenious and soulful understanding. I really do recommend it to anyone who wants to work on themselves in a deep yet safe manner, because I think you'll find it effective, and fascinating. This excellent book will form a great gateway. I have never been more impressed with any therapy system.

—Jason Wingate

Enormously hopeful and empowering, this book illuminates the process of Internal Family Systems (IFS) as a method of self-therapy that centers on the revolutionary principle that all of us have a Self. Presenting a view of the human psyche with this calm, compassionate, curious Self at the center, Jay Earley takes the reader step-by-step through a method of self-exploration which views overwhelming emotion and dysfunctional behavior as stemming from parts that are doing their best to help the person survive. Earley's writing is beautifully organized and clear, as compassionate and respectful as the process he is teaching, and the reader is supported and encouraged at every step. Anyone wishing to live a fuller, richer, more meaningful life, or help others do so, needs to read this book.

—Ann Weiser Cornell, PhD, author of *The Power of Focusing* and
The Radical Acceptance of Everything

The non-pathologizing and empowering aspects of the IFS Model find their ultimate expression in Dr. Earley's book, *Self-Therapy*. Exercises, illustrations, and session transcripts supplement this detailed approach for individuals to safely work alone or with a peer to transform their inner worlds dominated by outmoded beliefs to lives filled with love, compassion, and connection. Therapists, too, will appreciate this clear map of the inner territory of the psyche and will find this book a valuable and accessible resource for their clients.

—Susan McConnell, senior IFS trainer

Jay's classes have been life-transforming for me, and this wonderful book is a support for Self-leadership. I often feel heartfelt gratitude at finding myself standing strong after having been guided by Jay through my inner tangle of parts.

—Elizabeth Russell, Florida

Jay has a great talent for making complex things easy to understand. The vignettes are very useful in seeing how IFS works in real life, and the help sheets are particularly valuable when you work on yourself.

—Sandy Therry, M. Couns., Perth, Western Australia

Dr. Earley's clinical competence and passion for teaching IFS provide an invaluable, user-friendly companion for students and practitioners alike. His clear descriptions, outlines, illustrations, exercises, and transcriptions offer a thorough and systematic contribution to the understanding and application of this magical model for transformation and healing.

—Laura S. Schmidt, MA, LMFT, Spokane, WA

Self-Therapy was a big help to me in the beginning when I didn't have much knowledge of IFS or myself. The transcripts were intriguing because I looked at other people's experience in the book and recognized my parts. This helped me to realize that I'm not the only one with these difficult feelings. In my journal I wrote out the answers to each of the questions for my parts, and this brought it all together for me.

—Mindy Lamberson, Des Moines, Iowa

I read all the time, and *Self-Therapy* was exceptionally clear without being repetitious. It goes into much more detail than other IFS books, but it doesn't feel dense or overwhelming. I found it so intriguing that I just wanted to keep reading. It is much clearer than most psychology writing and very accessible for the general public.

—Linda McLyman, M.S., leadership consultant, Syracuse, NY

Self-Therapy is an invaluable resource, an absolute must for all therapists who want to move their clients beyond tolerable recovery to a more thorough process of healing. It is a gift to those of us who want to offer a gentle excavation of wounds resulting in a beautiful new landscape.

—Cheryl Ades, LCSW, Louisville, KY

Jay presents an exceptionally clear explanation of the IFS model. He provides "user friendly" directions on how therapists and clients can use the process. I can apply it directly from this book.

—Kevin J Miller, PhD, Florham Park, NJ

Jay has a very thorough understanding of IFS and an uncanny ability to break it down into small enough chunks to make it accessible to novices while still making it stimulating for experienced IFS practitioners. *Self-Therapy* demystifies therapy and empowers people to work on themselves to expand and heal their lives.

—Kira Freed, M.A., LPC, CLC, Tucson, AZ

The inside of the psyche is so hard to describe, and Jay does a great job of making it accessible. The illustrations really helped me to get a visual notion of the concepts. *Self-Therapy* describes each idea in many different ways, so that something sticks for each person. It really adds to the professional IFS literature.

—Kathy Grace, M.A., LPC, Chapel Hill, North Carolina

Self-Therapy

A *Step-By-Step* Guide to
Creating Wholeness and Healing Your Inner Child
Using IFS, A New, Cutting-Edge Psychotherapy

———— • ————

Second Edition

———— • ————

Jay Earley, PhD
Foreword by Richard C. Schwartz, PhD

Pattern System Books
Larkspur, CA

Pattern System Books
140 Marina Vista Ave.
Larkspur, CA 94939
415-924-5256
www.patternsystembooks.com

ISBN 13: 978-0-9843927-7-3
LCCN: 2009933156

Illustrations Copyright © 2009 by Karen Donnelly, except for those on pp. 20, 24, 161, 162.
Cover Design by Kristeen Wegner

Printed in the United States of America

Contents

Acknowledgements

I am deeply grateful to Dick Schwartz for creating such a brilliant method of therapy, which has changed my life and the lives of so many of my clients and students. I also appreciate the trainers who, along with Dick, have taught me IFS and helped me to grow as a person, a therapist, and a trainer—Michi Rose, Cece Sykes, Toni Herbine-Blank, and Susan McConnell.

I have learned so much about the human psyche and about IFS from my therapy clients, the students in my IFS classes, and the participants in the IFS training programs I have helped to lead.

Amanita Rosenbush, my editor, taught me a lot about how to write a self-help book and made my writing clearer and more lively. Amanda Sawyer read the entire manuscript and gave me helpful suggestions to improve it. Kira Freed did a fine job of proofreading to put the book in final form. Karen Donnelly produced wonderful illustrations to bring the parts and the psyche to life.

My wife, Bonnie Weiss, LCSW, is my partner in life and also in practicing and teaching IFS. She supported me through the entire project, not only emotionally, by also by providing her professional perspective on the content of the book and the writing. She also created the many composite illustrations by arranging Karen's drawings in a meaningful way.

Foreword

One way to judge a model of psychotherapy is by the kind of people it attracts. The fact that Jay Earley wrote this book is high praise for the IFS model because he was an accomplished writer and thinker, steeped in systems thinking, long before encountering IFS. Jay's passion has been to introduce IFS to a lay audience in such a way that people can work with their parts on their own—without the need for a therapist. He has been pursuing this goal with great success through his teleconference classes for several years. Through those experiences, he developed the structure of this book.

Another way to judge a model of psychotherapy is by whether it fosters dependence on the therapist or empowers people to trust themselves. This book can help you bring a new sense of compassion and healing to yourself without having to be in therapy. Through Jay's user-friendly description of IFS, you will begin to change how you do "self talk," or internal dialogue. As you relate to even your most shameful emotions and impulses with curiosity rather than judgment and with caring rather than disgust, you will find that these parts of you are not what they seem. They are valuable inner resources that have been distorted by difficult life experiences. Even more uplifting, you will learn that you have a core, an essence, that is untouched by life's traumas. What IFS calls the Self is in every one of us; it is a source of wonderful qualities from which we can lead our inner and outer lives. In this way, the book releases our self-concepts from the pathological and pessimistic way we have been taught to view ourselves. It proposes a new, optimistic, and edifying vision of the mind and shows how easily it can change and heal.

This book does even more than that. Yet another way to judge a psychotherapy is by whether it merely teaches people to cope with their extreme emotions and beliefs or actually transforms those emotions and beliefs. Through well-described experiential exercises and examples of actual IFS sessions, you will be able to enter your inner world in such a way that your extreme parts begin to heal. Rather than just coping with them, you welcome them and transform them into valuable resources. You are also encouraged to form partnerships with friends in which you accompany each other on these inner journeys, which can deepen your friendships.

This may all sound too good to be true, and for some readers it will be. There will be some who cannot achieve this kind of change on their own and will need to find a therapist to help them. My twenty-seven years of experience using this model, however, tell me that many people can do a great deal of work on themselves without a therapist. They may not be able to unburden all their exiles, but they can reverse the atmosphere of their inner worlds from one of self-loathing to self-love and Self-leadership. Also, people who are in therapy will find the book a useful guide for their between-session work on themselves.

Therapy is too expensive in both time and money for many people. I'm grateful that this book allows IFS to extend its reach to those who would not otherwise have access to it.

Richard C. Schwartz, PhD, creator of IFS, author of *Internal Family Systems Therapy, The Mosaic Mind,* and *You Are The One You've Been Waiting For.*

Introduction

I have been practicing psychotherapy as a psychologist for thirty-five years. During that time, I have studied and learned many approaches, but when I discovered Internal Family Systems Therapy (IFS), a new model developed by pioneering psychologist Richard Schwartz, it radically improved the effectiveness of my work with clients. IFS was so good that I switched over to practicing it almost exclusively, and it has enabled my clients to access their issues quickly and incisively and to make deep and lasting changes. Of course, I still rely on all the learning and experience I gained from my long years of doing therapy, but IFS completely transformed the way I practice. And as I continue to use the model, I keep gaining a deeper appreciation for how profound it is. Recently I was impressed with how it helps my clients approach their psychological issues with both maturity and emotional openness, a relatively rare combination for people who haven't completed therapy.

A good therapist is always working on themselves and continuing to grow. IFS has enhanced and deepened my own self-exploration. I have participated in various therapies, growth methods, and spiritual practices for over forty years, and IFS has taken this work to another level. It has allowed me to precisely target the issues I pursue and to keep track of the structure of my psyche with greater clarity. There were times in the past when I would avoid deep pain in myself without realizing it. IFS helped me to see when I was doing this and showed me how to approach these painful places in a safe way so I didn't have to avoid them. I now know exactly what needs to happen to heal my pain and free my stuck patterns. The most important thing I have gotten from IFS is a breakthrough in relating to myself in a loving and respectful way. Even though I had already made strides in this direction with other forms of growth work, IFS showed me how to love every aspect of myself in a specific way.

In addition to my therapy practice with individual clients, I have been teaching classes in which participants learn how to use IFS in working on themselves and doing peer counseling with each other. Since I love IFS so much, I want people to be able to use it for their own enrichment without necessarily having to go into therapy. I have taught hundreds of people the IFS Model, and most of them have used it successfully for psychological healing and growth. Many students continue on their journeys of personal development after the classes by working on their own or with partners they met in the class.

This book, *Self-Therapy*, is based on these classes. It shows you in detail how to use the IFS approach to work on troubling issues in your life and resolve them. This includes uncovering and understanding what is going on in your psyche—your unconscious motivations, blocks, and inner conflicts. You get to know yourself at a deep level—your hidden places of pain and the power and love that is within you but has been disowned. You learn how to heal the hurt, fear, and negative beliefs that most of us carry like old luggage. The IFS process will transform problematic parts of you into resources of inner wisdom, spontaneity, self-support, and openness. It will help you improve your capacity to relate to people, be successful in your work, and be happy and contented in your life.

Introduction to Second Edition

It has been such a joy to open my email these days. I continually get messages from people who tell me they have read *Self-Therapy* and it has changed their lives. They tell me that they've tried different therapies over the years, and IFS is the approach that has worked best for them. I've been told that my book is so clear and detailed that it has really helped them to make significant breakthroughs. This type of feedback has made the two and half years I spent writing the book all worth it.

Then why produce a second edition? There are a couple of reasons.

For the last year, I have been working on a web application based partially on IFS. Some of the material from *Self-Therapy* was put into that program but in a more interactive form. In the process of adapting it to that use, I had to go over it in detail, and I made a lot of specific improvements. I want this book (and my readers, of course) to benefit from that effort.

The other reason came from an unexpected source. A publisher approached me with an offer to publish *Self-Therapy*. (The first edition was self-published.) At the end of our discussion, I decided to retain the book in self-published form, but out of that meeting came some very good ideas. They pointed out that I hadn't introduced the notion of "parts" sufficiently at the beginning of this book. I assumed that all of my readers were comfortable with this idea and went ahead from there. In this edition,

I have added a section at the beginning of Chapter 1 that introduces parts to people for whom this may be a foreign concept.

Meanwhile I continue to write books on IFS to extend its benefits for readers. I have published a new book that utilizes the material from *Self-Therapy* in working with that most difficult kind of part—the Inner Critic. It is called *Self-Therapy for Your Inner Critic* and is co-written with my wife, Bonnie Weiss.

I will soon be publishing a book on how to work with "polarized parts" using IFS. This is a vital part of the IFS method which I couldn't fit into this book due to space limitations. I am now happy to rectify that by releasing *Resolving Inner Conflict*.

I hope that all these books will help you to engage in deep psychological healing and transformation so your life becomes satisfying, creative, and joyful.

Chapter 1

Personal Healing and Growth the IFS Way

———————— • ————————

We humans sometimes have painful feelings or destructive impulses that cause difficulties in our lives. This is often the reason a person decides to seek help through psychotherapy. Let's look at some examples:

Joe frequently blows up at his wife, Maureen, over little things. A fight erupts and it escalates until he is yelling at her. She becomes frightened and ends up crying. Joe then feels terrible about himself: "How could I have done such a thing? I don't want to hurt Maureen. I wasn't myself." Joe judges himself harshly for this behavior, but that doesn't stop it from happening the next time.

Sometimes Meg finds herself having a difficult day. She gets in a little trouble at work; or her beloved dog gets sick. Then she sits down and eats an entire cake or a box of cookies. She doesn't even think about what she is doing at the time, but right afterwards she feels horrible. "I have been trying to lose weight and this just makes matters worse. I feel so ashamed. What was going on that I stuffed myself like that?"

Many people, like Joe and Meg, are troubled by emotions or impulses that don't make sense to them. They try to handle these irrational feelings by fighting with their impulses or criticizing their emotions. This might work for a little while, but in the long run, it is ineffective. And as I'll explain, it actually backfires.

1

This book presents a new way of understanding how the mind works. It is based on a powerful form of psychotherapy called Internal Family System Therapy (IFS). When you comprehend the makeup of the human psyche from an IFS perspective, it opens up a whole new way of dealing with difficult feelings, which has proven to be highly successful with a wide range of people.

These problematic emotions and desires really come from parts of us, sometimes called "subpersonalities." These "parts," as they are known in IFS, are like little people existing inside of us—each with its own unique feelings, motivations, and view of the world.

For example, Joe has an Angry Part that blows up at Maureen for a very specific reason. When they get into fights, she sometimes taunts Joe in a shaming way. This triggers a young child part of Joe who was humiliated as a kid, and that part starts to relive the childhood shame all over again. Then his Angry Part comes to the rescue. It gets enraged at Maureen as a way of protecting Joe from feeling that shame. If Joe took some time to get to know his Angry Part and the Ashamed Child it protects, he could shift this whole dynamic so he wouldn't get enraged in these situations.

When Meg's boss criticizes her, she becomes very afraid for her job even though there really isn't any chance of her losing it. This fear is much more intense than is warranted because her boss's behavior reminds Meg of some scary events from her childhood. This current-day event triggers a Frightened Child Part in Meg that is holding onto a childhood fear from many years ago. Meg's Overeater Part becomes concerned that Meg will be flooded by this fear. It causes her to stuff herself with food for comfort and to keep her from feeling the child's fear.

Joe's Angry Part and Meg's Overeater are each trying to protect them from the pain of their child parts. These aren't just irrational feelings or out-of-control impulses. They are like little persons inside of them who are doing the best they can to cope with discomfort and pain.

When we understand this, we see that it doesn't help to try to fight with these parts, or suppress them, or judge them. They are just trying to help and protect us in their own (distorted) ways. In fact, if we get into battles with our parts, they will fight back, and if we try to disown them, they will feel even more lonely and worthless than they already do.

However, if we treat them like little beings inside of us who have our best interests at heart, we become open to a brand new way of relating to our feelings. We can get to know them, understand what drives them, and actually befriend them. When this happens, these parts will change, so they don't have to overeat or flip out in rage anymore. They can relax and act sensibly.

We can also nurture and heal those wounded kid parts that are hidden behind the rage or overeating. When they feel accepted and loved by us, they can feel whole and good about themselves, and this will change our self-esteem in a profound way.

I used to get very sad and lonely whenever my wife, Bonnie, was away for more than a day. If she traveled for a weekend or, God forbid, a week, I would feel bereft and depressed. Once I learned IFS, I realized that these feelings were coming from a Deprived Child Part of me who was left alone in an incubator for weeks after I was born prematurely, and then didn't get enough nurturing from my mother.

By doing IFS work with this part, I realized that I could take care of him and comfort him when Bonnie was gone. I even helped him to get in touch with what he really needed at those times. He needed love from me and encouragement to be in touch with his (my) body and its aliveness. After a while, this child part felt held, soothed, and connected to me, and he also felt in touch with his senses and his body. This completely resolved my loneliness issue. These days I no longer have those debilitating feelings when Bonnie is gone.

The human mind isn't a unitary thing that sometimes has irrational feelings. It is a complex system of interacting *parts*, each with a mind of its own. It's like an internal family--with wounded children, impulsive teenagers, rigid adults, hypercritical parents, caring friends, nurturing relatives, and so on. That's why this new therapy approach is called Internal Family Systems Therapy.

If you embrace all of these wounded and protective parts inside of you as "real beings" who deserve compassion, understanding, and love, you can transform your psyche and create the joyful life you have always wanted.

You don't have to worry. I'm not suggesting that you are a multiple personality, like Sybil or Tara or others you may have seen on TV or in the movies. As you will see in this book, we are all multiples, but not in an extreme way that you might think. The human psyche is just naturally a family of subpersonalities.

IFS is not the first system of therapy to recognize this. Carl Jung saw it a century ago, and other therapy approaches have been built around this notion. In fact, recently there has been a spate of therapies popping up that work with subpersonalities. IFS is simply the latest and most sophisticated of these methods. And it has produced some amazing results for people who use it.

A Detailed Example

Let's look at a more detailed example of parts. Sandy wanted to take on a creative video project, but she couldn't seem to get started. First she had to clean up her office, and that seemed to take forever. Then she found herself working out on the treadmill. *Okay*, she thought, *now I'm ready to go.* But instead of going to her office, she headed for the kitchen. Half an hour later, she was preparing a three-course meal. After a few days like this, she acknowledged to herself that she was avoiding the project. This procrastination made her feel vaguely negative about herself; she was undoubtedly lethargic and stuck. Sandy had a long-standing pattern of procrastination and depression, and now it was back.

Self-help books were somewhat useful; they gave her tips on mobilizing herself, rallying support, making decisions, and thinking positively. But these approaches ignore the crux of the problem. There is a part of Sandy that *doesn't want* to work on her video project. She calls it the Busy Part. It keeps her busy with other activities as a way to avoid the video project, even though that project is her highest priority. The Busy Part is unconscious but nevertheless has the power to stop her from succeeding.

Actually, the Busy Part has such power *because* it is unconscious. Since Sandy doesn't know about it, she has no way to interact with it. A hidden part has extra influence because it can't be addressed. It is like someone speaking ill of you behind your back. Rumors begin to fly, but you don't have any idea where they came from, so you can't confront the source.

If Sandy went into conventional therapy, she would probably uncover the Busy

4

Part, and she might try to convert it or overcome it. She would certainly see it as her enemy. However, this approach won't work very well because it ignores the very real fears and motivations of this part. Sandy might explore where the Busy Part came from in her childhood, but this usually involves analytically understanding her history, and real change rarely comes from intellectual insight alone.

If we ask why the Busy Part operates the way it does, we see that several parts of Sandy are involved in her procrastination. Sandy was ridiculed by her peers at certain times in her childhood when she did something that made her publically visible. Now whenever she attempts to accomplish something that could make her visible again, an Embarrassed Child part is triggered, like an echo from her past. The Busy Part is not really Sandy's enemy at all. It is just trying to protect the Embarrassed Child; it is afraid she will be ridiculed again if Sandy tackles this video project.

There is also another force at work here. A third part of Sandy pushes her to work hard and criticizes her when she doesn't. It is constantly on her case to "get working and be productive." All this self-criticism is grinding her down, making the child part feel hated and worthless.

So the Busy Part starts rebelling against this Pushy/Critical Part. It doesn't want Sandy to be dominated by harsh judgment, so it distracts her with other activities. However, she can't enjoy them because this Pushy

5

Part keeps yelling at her in the background, punishing her for not working on the project.

Sandy's Psyche

Busy Part

Pushy Critical Part

Embarrassed Child

These parts are all extreme and are in serious conflict with each other. Sandy feels like a ship in a storm, buffeted here and there, without a center from which to understand herself and move forward. What she needs is a way to integrate those parts into a caring, cooperative whole so she can feel good about herself and accomplish things.

Even if all three parts were uncovered in traditional therapy, the change would need to come through a developing relationship with her therapist, which can be expensive and time-consuming to establish. Many people want to feel better but don't want to spend a decade on a therapist's couch to do it. In this book, I will introduce you to Internal Family Systems Therapy (IFS), developed by psychologist Richard Schwartz. IFS is an approach that helps you find your center, pinpoint the parts of you that are causing difficulties, heal them, and unify them. IFS is not only a powerful form of therapy, it also lends itself especially well to self-therapy and peer counseling. This book shows you how to use IFS for self-healing.

Using IFS, Sandy would learn how to access her true Self, which is a port in the storm, a place of strength and compassion, and the source of internal healing. Her Self would connect with each of Sandy's three parts in a loving way that allowed them to trust her. Following the IFS procedure, she could help them release their fears and negative beliefs, allowing their natural strengths to flourish. They would learn to cooperate with each other and support the unfolding of her life in wholeness. She could then move ahead with her video project passionately and without reservations.

Unlike many forms of therapy, IFS doesn't pathologize people. When we have problems in life, IFS doesn't see us as having a disease or deficit. It recognizes that we have the resources within us to solve our problems, though these resources may be blocked because of unconscious reactions to events in the past. IFS is designed to be self-led. It empowers you to take charge of your own growth because your true Self, not a therapist, is the agent of healing and wholeness. This makes IFS a natural vehicle for self-therapy.

IFS approaches the psyche with respect and acceptance. You learn to relate to yourself with compassion and caring. IFS has what you might call a spiritual perspective, not because it subscribes to any religion or spiritual practice in particular, but because it embodies spiritual qualities such as love, wisdom, and connectedness.

IFS is also user friendly. Most people find it easy and natural to understand themselves as made up of various alive parts, and this gives them surprising insight into their psychological dynamics.

The IFS View of the Human Psyche

IFS provides a new and startling view of the human psyche. Mostly we think of ourselves as having sensible emotions and taking practical, rational actions. Of course, we recognize that occasionally irrational feelings like rage or fear pop up. We realize that sometimes we don't act in our own best interest, like when we can't discipline ourselves to live a healthy lifestyle. This kind of behavior upsets us because we see it as a deviation from what should be a unitary, sensible personality. When these aberrations happen a lot, we think there must be something wrong with us.

As I have explained, IFS sees human beings as complex systems of interacting "parts," which are natural divisions of the personality. Suppose one part of you is trying to lose weight, and another part wants to wolf down a ton of sweets. When you crave that piece of cake late at night, it isn't just a desire that comes up from time to time. There is an entity inside you that repeatedly needs a sense of sweet fullness. It has reasons why it feels it must have that dessert. It might need to push down anger or fill an unbearable sensation of emptiness. This part has memories that drive these needs—for example, feeling emotionally hungry as a child.

You may hear a different inner voice saying "Eat a piece of celery instead," or "You should be ashamed of how you gorged yourself!" You may think of these as just thoughts that pop up, but they come from another part of you whose job is to control your eating. It could be concerned with your waistline or your health. It might believe that you won't be loved if you aren't thin. And it may have memories of being ridiculed for being overweight in grade school.

But these are simple concepts that only begin to touch on the richness and complexity of our inner life. Our inner family may include a lonely baby, a wise mentor, an angry child, a stern mother, a calm meditator, a magician, a happy animal, a closed-off protector, and so on.

These parts inside us are frequently shifting and changing. One of them takes over for a while, and we act and feel a certain way. Then we enter a new situation, and another character comes to the fore. Usually we view these changes as no more than slight shifts in mood or perspective, but, in fact, each shift marks the emergence of an entirely new subpersonality.

Each part gets activated at certain times. When I am in a large group of strangers, a part of me feels shy and wants to withdraw. When a supervisor criticizes you, a part of you may be thrown off balance and feel utterly incompetent. When Jill's husband acts arrogant, a part of her wants to strangle him. When you get rejected by a lover, a part of you may feel devastated, like an abandoned child. When you feel threatened by a powerful person, a headache may come on because a part is clamping down on the muscles in your head to defend against terror. Any feeling reaction, thought sequence, behavior pattern, or body sensation can indicate the presence of a part.

Some of our parts are in pain, and others want to protect us from feeling that pain. Some try to manage how we interact with people. Some are locked in battles with each other. And all this is going on largely outside our awareness. All we know is that sometimes we feel content and sometimes we are anxious, depressed, frustrated, or confused, and we don't know why. We hold a simplistic view of ourselves that can't penetrate to the richness and turmoil within.

Many people spend their whole lives thinking that this surface view is all there is to them. They never taste the juice or sit with the pain, and they don't plumb the depths of themselves. Underlying this cast of characters, every human being has a true Self that is wise, deep, open, and loving. This is who we truly are when we aren't being hijacked by painful or defensive voices. The Self is the key to healing and integrating our disparate parts through its compassion, curiosity, and connectedness. It is also the natural leader of our inner family, a guide through the adventures of life.

Yet if the Self is truly at the center of each of us, you may be asking, why don't we know it better? Because over the years we have experienced hurts, trauma, and grief, which have burdened us with shame, fear, and negative beliefs. These events have prompted some of our inner characters to take over in a desperate bid to protect us from harm. They blot out our pain, and, in the process, the light of the Self gets dimmed or lost. We don't see what's really happening because they cover over much of their activity as they construct a conventional life for us.

IFS can help you access your Self, and from that place of strength and love you can connect with your troubled parts and heal them. Your parts are naturally endowed with qualities such as joy, freedom, perceptiveness, and creativity, but these have been lost because of childhood wounds. The Self can help heal these wounds and allow these parts to reclaim their natural strengths and goodness. They can come to trust you to lead, if you do it from Self. They can learn to work together with each other as a harmonious inner family that supports your flowering in the world.

When you really understand this view of the psyche, you see yourself in a whole new light. You perceive your depth and beauty. You reclaim your true nature as a garden of healthy, effective, vital plants growing in the deep, rich soil of the Self. This perspective also changes how you see other people and the world. You realize that even the most destructive person is driven by parts that are doing their best to protect him or her. You see that everyone has a loving Self, even if it is deeply buried. You understand that at our deepest level we are all connected, and peace and harmony may indeed be possible in the world.

Positive Intent

Experience with IFS shows that every part has a positive intent for you. It may want to protect you from harm or help you feel good about yourself. It may want to keep you from feeling pain or make other people like you. Every part of you is trying to help you feel good and avoid pain. This is how we are constructed biologically, and our psyches work the same way. Since some parts keep us stuck in negative patterns and have a destructive impact on our lives, it may be hard to imagine how they could be trying to help. The answer is that despite their best intentions, these parts don't always act wisely; they take extreme stances or behave in clumsy and primitive ways. However, if you look under the surface, you discover that they are always doing what they think is best for you. They may have a distorted perception of situations and an exaggerated sense of danger, but their intent is always positive.

For example, Joe has a part that makes him close his heart and lose interest in women whenever a relationship turns intimate and moves toward commitment. At first, he didn't approve of this Closed-Hearted Part of himself and wanted to get rid of it because it was preventing him from finding love. However, when he looked deeper through IFS therapy, Joe found that this part was trying to look out for him. It was terrified that he would be taken over by a woman and lose himself, which is exactly what happened with his mother. When he was a child, being close to a female meant being controlled by her. So this part protected him in the only way it knew how, by withdrawing. It said, "I just want to keep you safe. I don't want this to happen to you again." Joe's Closed-Hearted Part shut him down because it saw danger that wasn't there. It distorted the present based on the past.

Even if a part sees the present accurately, it may have a faulty strategy for helping you. Many parts know only one way to act, which may be something that worked fairly well in your family forty years ago when you were a child. However, in today's adult world, this strategy is ineffective, short-sighted, or immature. A protective part often has no finesse or flexibility. It only knows how to do one thing, regardless of the situation. Like the proverbial man with the hammer who sees everything as a nail, a part only knows how to pound on things.

Bill has a part that is judgmental and competitive with other people in a way that is not consistent with his true values. He always felt that this part was reprehensible and ought to be locked away. However, once he got to know it, he discovered that it was actually trying to do its best for him. It wanted to protect him from feeling worthless and help him feel valuable and important instead. The part tried to achieve this in the only way it knew—by feeling superior to others. It didn't realize that there could be other ways for Bill to feel valuable—by connecting with others, by valuing himself, by doing meaningful things in the world. It knew only one strategy—judging others as inferior.

We are often afraid to get to know our parts or embrace them because we fear that this will give them power to sabotage our lives. What if they take over and cause even more problems? Joe was afraid that if he got to know his Closed-Hearted Part, it would take over and he would have no chance of loving a woman. However, with IFS he got to know this part and understand its positive intent without letting it take over. In fact, embracing a part is a step toward healing it.

This approach is fundamentally different from the way we ordinarily relate to our parts. Usually when we become aware of a part (or a feeling or behavior pattern), the first thing we do is evaluate it. Is it good or bad for us? If we decide it is good, we embrace it and act from it. If we decide it is bad, we try to get rid of it. We tell it to go away or attempt to bury it. However, this approach doesn't work. You can't get rid of a part of your psyche. You can only push it into the unconscious, where it will continue to affect you without your awareness.

In IFS, we do something altogether different and radical. *We welcome all our parts with curiosity and compassion.* We seek to understand each one and appreciate its efforts to help us, without losing sight of the ways it is causing problems. We develop a relationship of caring and trust with each part, and then take steps to heal it so it can function in a healthy way.

We can relate to our parts in this way because we all have a true Self that is open, curious, and compassionate. The entire IFS approach is based on working with your parts from this place. When we approach our parts with curiosity and the desire to know who they truly are, they reveal themselves to us. When we relate to our parts with compassion, they trust that we care about them, and they open up even their deepest places of pain and shame for healing. However, you may not trust that you can do this. You may ask, "What if I don't feel curiosity and compassion toward my parts?" And frequently we don't at first. However, IFS has innovative methods for accessing Self, with its qualities of curiosity and compassion, and returning to it when we become sidetracked.

IFS Results

In my experience, IFS is not only incredibly effective but also quite efficient in helping people change. When clients come to me for relief from specific psychological problems, we can often accomplish this in a month or two, sometimes even in a couple of sessions. These are a few of the issues that were solved in a brief time using IFS: depression over aging and being alone, difficulty in asserting oneself at work, a tendency to fly off the handle in marital disputes, anxiety about meeting new people.

If you have psychological issues that are deep seated or if you want comprehensive personality transformation, the work will take longer—possibly a year or two. However, in that time, you can make profound changes in matters that deeply affect your life: how you feel about yourself, how you relate to people, and the way you function in the world. Here is one client's story.

When Robert first came to me for IFS therapy, he felt very alone in the world. He had had only one experience of love in his life, but that girlfriend had rejected him a couple of years before, and he was still yearning for her. He longed for intimacy and a deep sensual connection with a woman but believed he could never have it again. He felt desperately lonely and unlovable. He wanted to have friends and community in his life, yet he experienced himself as an outsider in groups and organizations. It seemed that everyone else was included and he was always left out. He thought he was incapable of relating to others in a way that would make a genuine connection. Deep inside he believed that there was something so fundamentally wrong with him that people wouldn't be interested in being close to him. Consequently he shied away from contact with people and stayed walled off in his room most of the time.

Unwittingly, Robert contributed to his own isolation by the way he related to people. When he did interact with someone, he did it in a dour, wooden, intellectual manner that came from a part of him that expected to be rejected. This part kept him in his head and away from his emotions in an unconscious attempt to protect him from being hurt when he was snubbed. He also thought that his intellect was the only thing he had to offer people. Of course, this closed-off approach only contributed to making people less interested in him, thereby confirming his fears.

After a year and a half of IFS work, all that has changed. He became aware of how he was keeping people away through distancing and intellectualizing, and he has now changed the way he relates to others. His sense of humor comes out frequently, and he can smile and connect with people in a friendly way. He has begun to feel like an integral part of groups he is involved with. Through our work, he healed the part that believed he was unlovable. Now he basically feels good about himself, and he expects most people to respond to him positively. He started dating his old girlfriend again, and she was so delighted with the way he had changed that she was eager to rekindle their relationship. They are now happily connected and planning to get married.

What You Can Get from This Book

This book is designed to help you learn the following:

1. How to understand your psyche from the IFS perspective. What drives your behavior? What makes you avoid people or situations? Where do your emotional reactions come from? What is the nature of your inner conflicts? What are your parts? What impact do they have on your life? How do they relate to you and each other? You will end up with a detailed map of your psyche.

2. How to work with and relate to your parts on a daily basis as they get activated in your life. How to recognize when a part is activated. How to connect with it and help it relax. This will help you to deal with situations in a calm, effective, open way. It will also foster more internal cooperation and integration.

14

3. How to do an IFS session with yourself in order to explore yourself, understand and connect with your parts, discover their history, and heal them.

4. How to be a more effective client when working with an IFS therapist or when doing IFS peer counseling with a friend who is also reading this book.

5. If you are a therapist, how to use IFS in your work with people.

Since IFS uses a structured method for therapy, it is easy to teach as a step-by-step procedure in this book. We illustrate each step with a transcript of an IFS session so you can see how it actually works in vivo.

How to Use the Book

You can learn much about yourself by just reading the book, even if you don't choose to do the exercises. When you really understand what it means to be a loving Self surrounded by a system of parts, it transforms the way you understand yourself and other people. Whenever you run into a technical term that you don't understand, consult Appendix C for its definition.

However, if you do the exercises as you read the book, this will ground the concepts in your direct experience of your inner family. This takes it out of the intellectual realm and connects to your feelings, your body, and your imagination.

To get the full benefit of this book, I recommend you do IFS practice sessions on a regular basis. This will teach you to do self-therapy in a deep and transforming way. These can be done on your own, but most people find it easier to do these sessions working with a partner in peer counseling, especially at first. So after you have read enough of the book to be ready to dive into the work, find a friend who will also read the book and hopefully become serious about learning the method. The two of you can schedule times to do IFS practice sessions as you read. You take turns with one of you acting as listener/facilitator while the other one works on himself or herself. Your ability to do self-therapy will be enhanced by all that you learn from working with a partner.

Being in IFS therapy is a profoundly life-changing event for most people. This book can't be a complete substitute for that experience because nothing can replace the connection with and guidance from a competent, caring professional who is an expert in IFS. However, this book teaches the IFS model in enough detail to do full IFS sessions on yourself, especially with the support of a sensitive friend. In this way, you can gain many of the benefits of this powerful model. How far you will be able to go in this direction depends on many factors—your previous experience working on yourself, your degree of openness and creativity, and your dedication to the practice.

Some people find that this book isn't enough by itself for them to do IFS sessions on their own. If you are one of them, don't feel bad; you're not alone. Take our IFS Courses or find yourself an IFS therapist. (See Appendix B.) Even if you don't engage in full IFS self-therapy sessions, you can still gain a great deal through understanding your psyche from the IFS perspective, learning to connect with your parts, and grasping how psychological healing occurs.

Who Can Benefit from the Book

If you fit one of the following groups, Self-Therapy might be helpful to you.

1. People who want to work through a wide variety of troubling personal issues—low self-esteem, procrastination, anxiety, shyness, depression, isolation, and so on. Any problem that is psychological in origin can be transformed using this approach.

2. People looking for personal growth of various kinds. It can help you increase confidence, accelerate your career success, deepen your ability to relate to others, enhance your intimacy, and develop your spiritual awareness.

3. People who are considering entering therapy. This book will acquaint you with the IFS approach so you can decide whether to choose an IFS therapist to work with.

4. People who have had bad experiences in psychotherapy and are reluctant to try again. There are many different forms of therapy. Even though your previous therapy wasn't effective, you can still be successful with the right approach and therapist. This book will give you an idea of how powerful therapy can be with IFS. If it feels like a fit, you can choose to engage in self-therapy or find an IFS therapist to work with.

5. People who can't be in therapy. Is it hard to find a good therapist nearby? Is it difficult for you to afford therapy? Are there other reasons

why therapy doesn't work for you? This book will permit you to get some of the benefits of therapy by working on your own and with a partner.

6. People who are in therapy with an IFS therapist. This book will give you a detailed understanding of the IFS model, which will enhance your ability to work in sessions and give you the capacity to do IFS sessions on yourself at home. This will make you more effective as a client, speed up your therapy, and help you become more Self-led in your life. I have found this to be true for those clients of mine who have taken my IFS classes, so I recommend the classes to all my clients. Since this book is based on my classes, it should serve the same function.

7. Psychotherapists. Even though the book is written for the general public, it contains a wealth of information useful to clinicians. A detailed description of the IFS approach will permit you to experiment with using IFS in your practice, either by itself or as a complement to the approaches you currently employ. The book is so detailed that it constitutes a manual for the IFS method. If you fall in love with it, as I did, you may want to get professional training in the model.

8. IFS therapists. This book contains a review of what you have learned in your IFS training but organized in a somewhat different way. The details of the procedure outlined in the book may help you to deepen your understanding of the model. The many transcripts may enhance your comprehension of how IFS works. You may also want to encourage your clients to read this book to enhance their ability to do IFS work.

Safety

The IFS model is very respectful of the pain or trauma that we all carry. Despite the fact that IFS goes deep into the psyche in powerful ways, it never tries to barge past defenses or dive quickly into deep issues. It is respectful of the parts of us that protect us from pain and only works with our deep issues after getting permission from all relevant protective parts. Therefore, it is fairly safe to use on your own. Most people can do the exercises in this book and the practice sessions without problems.

However, this book is not a substitute for psychotherapy. Some people have experienced so much pain and trauma in their lives that their internal systems are sensitive, reactive, chaotic, unstable, or strongly conflicted. If you have this kind of internal family, doing IFS work could trigger intense emotional or physical reactions. You could become panicked or depressed when trying to work with your parts. The work could activate headaches, allergies, or other psychosomatic reactions. It could prompt you to engage in addictive or dangerous behavior. You might feel spaced out and confused in the middle of a session or afterwards.

If you sense that responses like this could happen to you, it probably isn't safe for you to use IFS without the guidance of a psychotherapist. If you aren't sure, you can try the work in this book very carefully to find out, but if you have any unusual or intense reactions, it is a sign that you should be working with a therapist. Don't take this lightly by trying to push on. Take care of yourself and wait until you can do this work with professional guidance. A psychotherapist can help you to approach the work in a safe way and can provide the support you need to be successful. If any difficult reactions crop up, your therapist will know how to handle them.

If you are dependent on a parent, guardian, or spouse who couldn't tolerate your changing the way you relate to him or her, doing IFS work on your own might not be advisable. It would be better for you to do IFS under the guidance of a therapist, who could also work with important people in your life.

The Center for Self-Leadership has a listing of trained IFS therapists organized by geographic location at www.selfleadership.org.

Summary

In this chapter, you learned about the power of the IFS perspective on the human mind and how our psyches are made up of parts, each one doing its best for our welfare. You know about the true Self, the place of grounded compassion that is the agent of internal healing in IFS. You have seen how to use the book and who can benefit from it. In Chapter 2, we explore these ideas in more detail.

Chapter 2

Your Internal System

Summary of the IFS Model

This chapter introduces you to the IFS model, developed by psychologist Richard Schwartz, and gives a quick overview of how it works. As mentioned in Chapter 1, IFS sees the human psyche as divided into subpersonalities, or parts.

The Power of Subpersonalities

The concept of parts in IFS corresponds to ideas from other forms of psychotherapy—for example, defenses, psychic forces, self-images, introjects, and schemas. However, these concepts are normally seen as just mechanical or biological descriptions of how the psyche operates. Parts, or subpersonalities, may operate in similar ways, but they are alive and personal. They do what they do for reasons of their own, and they have relationships with you and with each other. For example, suppose you are using the defense of repression, which makes a certain memory unconscious. IFS recognizes that a protective part is purposely excluding that memory from your awareness for a reason. Perhaps it is afraid that the memory would cause you to be overwhelmed by pain.

Parts are entities of their own, with their own feelings, beliefs, motivations, and memories. It is especially important to understand that parts have motivations for everything they do. Nothing is just done out of habit. Nothing is just a pattern of thinking or behavior you learned. Everything (except for purely physiological reactions) is done by a part for a reason, even though that reason may be unconscious. For example, if you get distracted at a certain point while exploring yourself in therapy, this is probably not an accident. A part wants to distract you because it is seeking to avoid something.

Understanding the psyche in this way gives you a great deal of power to change your inner world for the better. Since parts are like little people inside you, you can make contact with them, get to know them, negotiate with them, encourage them to trust you, help them communicate with each other, and give them what they need to heal. When you do, you will have an enormously increased capacity for understanding and transforming your psyche—for achieving wholeness.

You may treat the idea of subpersonalities as simply a useful metaphor for viewing the psyche, which it is, but it is much more than that. If you treat the components of your psyche as real entities that you can interact with, they will respond to you in that way, which gives you tremendous power for transformation. Are they actually real? I believe so, but I invite you to read this book, do the exercises, and make up your own mind.

IFS is the latest in a long line of therapy methods that work with subpersonalities. Early methods were Jungian analysis, Psychosynthesis, Transactional Analysis, and Gestalt therapy. More recent approaches are hypnotherapy, inner child work, Voice Dialogue, Ego State Therapy, John Rowan's work, and others. IFS is the latest and most sophisticated of these methods. And many forms of therapy that don't explicitly work with subpersonalities nevertheless use concepts that are quite similar, such as "schemas" in Cognitive-Behavioral Therapy.

IFS represents an advance over these other methods in a number of ways. It recognizes the power and importance of the Self and bases the therapy on relating to your parts from Self. The IFS method takes you deep inside yourself while still remaining alert and in charge during a session. It doesn't just work with parts in isolation; it has a sophisticated understanding of the relationships between parts that guides the therapy method. As you will see, the most important relationship is between those parts that *protect* us from pain and those child parts that are *in* pain. The problems that occur within the human psyche are largely structured around the need to protect ourselves from pain. Since the IFS approach is organized around this, we can have respectful sensitivity to our pain and defenses while pinpointing our work with laser-like efficiency.

Roles

Each part has a role to play in your life; it brings a quality to your psyche and your actions in the world. Each tries to advance your interests in some way (even if sometimes it has the opposite effect). Some parts govern the way you handle practical tasks in your life. Some protect against external threats or internal pain. Some are open and friendly with people. Others hold unresolved fear or shame from your childhood. Some are performers; others solitary thinkers. Some care for people, while others affect the way you feel about yourself. And so on.

Many parts perform roles that are healthy and functional. They make sure your life works well. They may help you connect with people or get work done. They may help you assert yourself or comprehend the world. Many parts have positive qualities that enhance your inner experience and external life, and allow you to cope with difficulties that come your way. They may manifest charisma or humor. They may bring you creativity, aliveness, joy, or peace.

Other parts, however, have taken on more extreme roles in a desperate attempt to protect you from pain, vulnerability, or harm. In IFS, an *extreme role* amounts to any action, feeling or thought that is dysfunctional. Quite simply, a part playing an extreme role causes problems in your life; it hampers it at best and cripples it at worst. It can act in ways that are self-defeating or create conflicts with people. It can cause you to have distorted perceptions, inaccurate beliefs, or obsessive thought patterns. It can flood you with pain or body tension—anything that cuts you off from the richness of life.

Many extreme parts protect you even when it isn't necessary, thereby causing you to act in abrasive ways that offend people or distance you from them. Some overdo it by pushing you to be perfect in all things, like a demanding parent. Others distort your perceptions of people or situations so that you believe they are threatening, causing you to act defensively or

21

controlling and overbearing. Some parts have intense emotional reactions, while others close you off to all feelings.

Many parts play roles that are a mix of healthy and extreme. Their normally healthy approach turns extreme at certain times. For instance, I have a part that handles the details of my life with clear organization and efficiency. That's fine. It isn't fine is when it does this in a mechanical, driven way that takes the joy and presence out of my life. I don't want to sacrifice aliveness just to get things done.

IFS focuses on parts that play extreme roles in order to heal and transform them, which is what you will learn to do in this book. There are two kinds of extreme parts—protectors and exiles.

Protectors

The job of *protectors*[1] is to protect you from feeling pain. They try to arrange your life and your psyche so that you are always in a kind of comfort zone and you never feel hurt, shame, or fear. They attempt to protect you from hurtful incidents or distressing relationships in your current life that could bring up buried pain from childhood. Since this can be intense, protectors are keen on preventing it from being activated. Some protectors block off pain that is arising inside you so that you can't feel it at all. Others try to arrange your external world so that nothing happens to trigger pain in the first place. And some do both. Protectors are the parts you usually encounter first when exploring yourself because they are most accessible to everyday consciousness.

Even though protectors are ostensibly focused on your current life, most of them are strongly influenced by events and relationships from your childhood. There is a residual fear of events from long ago that involve abandonment, betrayal, judgment, or abuse. Protectors don't realize that you aren't a child anymore. They don't realize that you have many more strengths and resources now, and you usually aren't in danger as you were in the past. They try to avoid any situation that is similar to what you experienced as a child. It's a little like the Jews' motto about the Holocaust: "Never again!"

---

[1] IFS distinguishes between two types of protectors—proactive managers and reactive firefighters—but there isn't space to go into that distinction in this book.

Protectors employ a wide variety of strategies. I have a part that closes off my emotions by being extremely intellectual. Another part of me hardens my heart in order to forestall vulnerability and heartache. Some people's parts go into denial and pretend that everything in their life is all right when it isn't. You might have a part that projects your feelings onto other people so you don't have to face them in yourself. In standard psychological language, these protectors are called "defenses."

Some protectors distract you from pain. Some people drink to drown out pain; others go shopping or work excessively. Any form of addiction can be used in this way, as long as it anesthetizes you. For example, many of us have protectors who eat to ward off pain. When we are rejected, judged, or ignored, a protector pops up and heads for the refrigerator. It wants to divert our attention from the pain through the pleasure of food. It wants to soothe us and fill us up to make us feel better about ourselves.

Some protectors criticize you and control you to try to make you into a "good boy or girl," or they may push you to be productive and successful so no one can have reason to judge you. The infamous "inner critic" does this. In Chapter 1, we saw that Sandy has a Pushy Part that criticizes her to get her to work hard and avoid procrastination. It is trying to prevent her from being ridiculed the way she was as a child.

Some protectors help you be successful or popular to build up your confidence and self-esteem. They see a hole deep inside you where you feel deficient, and they want to compensate for it with accolades from others. Some try to make you into a loveable person so people will like you; that way they won't hurt or abandon you. Others attempt to arrange your life so all of your needs are filled, which wards off an inner emptiness.

Darlene has a protector that religiously looks after the needs of other people at the expense of her own. It believes that the most important thing in life is making sure that other people are comfortable and feel good about themselves. The problem is that she neglects herself. As a child, Darlene didn't get the love and nurturing she needed from her mother because her mother was often upset and depressed. As a result, Darlene felt empty and needy. However, she put aside her feelings and did her best to make her mother feel better. Darlene had a good heart and couldn't bear to see her mother suffer, so she worked tirelessly to nurture her and take care of her. She reversed roles with her; she became the caretaker and her mother the child. But little girls need a mother. Who was there to take care of Darlene? The only time she received love from her mother was when she was caring for her. So Darlene's protector learned that the way to get love was to give and give. Now, in Darlene's adult life, this part propels her to tirelessly take care of others in an attempt to get some love to fill her inner emptiness.

As we have seen, parts play a wide variety of protective roles. Some try to control every situation to ward off unpredictable threats. Some rebel against authority in order to preserve our autonomy and keep us from being dominated by others. Some try to please other people so they can win their approval. Others are charismatic performers whose job is to obtain admiration from people. Some are self-effacing and quiet to avoid being judged. You might have a protector that avoids intimacy for fear of being engulfed or abused by someone close to you. You might have an angry protector that makes sure you don't accept blame for problems. Or one that deadens your feelings so you're not vulnerable to the slings and arrows of the world. The list goes on and on.

Exercise: Learning about Protectors

Think about two of your protectors. For each one, write out answers to the following questions:

- What is its role in helping you manage your life and interact with the world?
- How does it relate to other people?
- How does it protect you from pain?
- What is its positive intent for you?
- What is it trying to protect you from?

You may not have answers to all these questions. As you read further, however, you will learn much more about how to understand your protectors. This is just a beginning step. Keep these notes and add to them later.

Exiles

Exiles are young child parts that are in pain from the past. While protectors try to keep us from feeling pain, exiles are the parts in pain. They are the ones the protectors are trying to protect us from.

Exiles are often stuck at a particular time in childhood, at a specific age. They are literally two years old, or five or seven, and they exist in a situation from that time in your life. They are frozen at that time because something difficult or traumatic happened then, and you didn't have the inner resources or the external support to handle it. Therefore, it was overwhelming for you and the fallout couldn't be processed and metabolized. There will be an exile (perhaps more than one) that experienced this painful event and is stuck there.

Let's look at a traumatic example. Lisa has an exile that is stuck at age three. One day, her father went out of control and hit her repeatedly, which was terrifying and overwhelming for a three year old. And she didn't have a strong enough connection with her mother that she could go to her for help. In fact, there was no one she could turn to for support and understanding. So the incident couldn't be processed, and the part of Lisa that experienced that abuse was frozen at the point in time when she felt frightened and powerless. When Lisa contacts that exile, it looks like a three year old and feels terrified in just the way that a toddler does. It curls up in a ball and moans for someone to help it.

Exiles aren't always stuck at a single place. There can be a series of childhood incidents, even a situation that went on for a number of years or all through your childhood. For example, Sam has an exile that is stuck in his relationship with his mother. Throughout his early years she was indifferent to his needs, and this exile constantly felt needy and unloved. There was no single incident. This exile took on pain from Sam's entire relationship with his mother.

Exiles often take on the beliefs or the feeling tone of your family. If your family life was chaotic, you will probably have an exile that feels jumbled inside. If your family treated each other with cold silence most of the time, you may have an exile that feels as though it lives in the Arctic. Exiles can also be affected strongly by incidents that were beyond your family's control. Perhaps you were caught in a war zone and went through traumatic and violent events. Or you had an illness that kept you bedridden and in pain for months. Maybe your mother had surgery that took her away from you at a crucial time. Perhaps your family was stuck in poverty, or you were deeply affected by prejudice.

Whatever the cause, exiles can exhibit a wide variety of painful emotions. Some feel lonely and abandoned, others abused or betrayed. Others feel ashamed of themselves because of something they did or because of what they believe is an intrinsic flaw. Some are afraid of being intruded upon or taken over by others. Many feel desperate for the nurturing and love they didn't receive when they were young. Some feel that their very survival is at stake and are terrified of dying. Some feel powerless and under other people's control.

In addition to painful emotions, exiles have negative beliefs about you and about the world. You might have one that believes you are intrinsically unlovable and no one will want to be close to you. You might have an exile that believes it is responsible for your mother's pain, as Darlene does. Some exiles believe they are inadequate and therefore can't be successful at anything they try. There are exiles who believe that the world is intrinsically dangerous. These are global viewpoints that cannot be pierced by logic.

Because exiles hold pain from your past, they are pushed away by protectors. They are exiled from your inner life and kept in dark dungeons away from the light of consciousness. An exile is usually caught in its own little world and is unaware that you have grown up and developed the capacity to take care of yourself, make friends, be independent, and perhaps start your own family. All it is aware of is a certain painful situation from your early life. Whenever something happens in the present that is similar, it reactivates that pain, which comes bubbling up toward the surface. Then your protectors go into high gear to prevent you from having to feel it.

For example, let's say you worked hard in math in the fifth grade. You rushed home with a B+, which was better than anything you had achieved before. You thought for sure that your father would congratulate you for your achievement. You stood in front of him, full of hope for applause and approval, as he read the paper. Instead, he crumbled up the report card and threw it at the wall, then yelled at you for falling short. He told you that he never stooped to a B in math when he was in school and he can't believe you're his child sometimes. His words were no less than a knife through the heart. You were standing there, but you wished you could disappear. This incident caused one of your exiles to feel worthless; it ended up believing that no matter what you do, you aren't good enough.

Now you are an adult performing well in your job, and your boss calls you into his office. He tells you that a proposal you wrote wasn't done properly, explains why, and asks you to rewrite it. He isn't particularly judgmental, mostly matter of fact. He just wants you to redo the proposal. However, that worthless-feeling exile is still there, hidden away in your unconscious, and it gets triggered by your boss. It perceives him as being harshly critical of you, and its worthlessness start to come up. That old feeling of never being good enough starts to arise. However, before you are even consciously aware of this, a protector takes over to prevent you from feeling that excruciating pain. There are many possibilities for what such a protector might do. One protector might get furious at your boss to distract you from the pain and to put the blame on him. Another protector might go out of your way to please your boss so he will like you and give you praise in the future. A third protector might cause you to go home and have a few drinks to dull the pain. All of these are in service of protecting you from that old humiliation that is emerging.

Another common occurrence: You have an exile who was harmed in the past—for example, physically abused by your brother, who was a bully.

Whenever you are in a similar kind of danger, the fear of that exile will be triggered, and a protector will step in to protect you from being harmed again, even if there is no real danger now. For example, your husband comes home one night annoyed because traffic made him miss the beginning of Monday Night Football. He stomps around the house in a cranky mood. This triggers the fear of the exile that was beaten up by your brother. Even if your husband is only mildly angry and it isn't aimed at you, a protector might step in and cause you to immediately withdraw from him. Your husband has no idea why you are pulling away, and incidents like this create distance in the marriage.

Exiles aren't always kept hidden. Sometimes they take over our consciousness despite the protectors. Then we may feel sadness, fear, shame, insecurity, or need, like a child.

Exercise: Learning about Exiles

Think about two of your exiles. For each one, please write out the answers to the following questions:

- What emotions does it feel?
- What pain does it carry?
- What is it afraid of?
- What negative beliefs does it have?
- What situation or relationship is it stuck in from childhood?
- What current situations tend to trigger it?
- What protectors come up when that happens?

It is fine if you don't have answers to all these questions yet.

The Self

Fortunately, human beings are not simply a collection of parts. We are so much more than that. Our true Self is mature and loving, and has the capacity to heal and integrate our parts.

In the early days of the development of IFS, Richard Schwartz was learning the model through feedback from his therapy clients. He had learned about parts, and when he worked with a client, he would often ask a protector to step aside so they could go deeper with a piece of work. Then another protector would emerge, and he would help the client to get that one to relax, too. This would continue until eventually a different kind of presence would emerge. Dick would ask his clients what part that was, and they would say, "Well, it's not a part exactly. It has a different quality to it. It doesn't feel like all my other parts." Then he would say, "Well, if it's not a part, what is it?" And they would answer, "Well, I don't know, it's just me. It's who I really am." When the clients expanded on what they meant, they would usually say something like, "When my parts have all stepped aside, what is left is me." And once this "me" was accessed, the therapy would flow effortlessly because now the person's energy was freed up. It felt like a surfer who was in "the zone," catching a wave and riding it smoothly and easily.

And so Dick learned about the *Self*.[2] This was wonderfully transformative, and a deeper level of the power of IFS was unleashed.

We all have a core part of us that is our true self, our spiritual center. When our extreme parts are not activated and in the way, this is who we are. The Self is relaxed, open, and accepting of yourself and others. When you are in Self, you are grounded, centered, and non-reactive. You don't get triggered by what people do. You remain calm and unruffled, even in difficult circumstances. The Self is so much larger and more spacious than our parts and is not frightened by events that would scare them. The Self has the strength and clarity to function well in the world and connect with other people. When you are in Self, you come from a depth of compassion, enabling you to be loving and caring toward others as well as yourself and your parts. The Self is like the sun—it just shines.

The Self is connected to the deeper ground of being that spiritual teachings speak of, sometimes called God. It has access to a kind of higher wisdom and understanding that can guide you in dealing with the larger questions of life. It allows you to be fully present and embodied in each moment with aliveness and depth. It is an inexhaustible fountain of love.

Most of us have had glimpses of the Self, experiences that give us an idea of what is possible. However, our extreme parts are frequently so prevalent that they obscure it. When a part is strongly triggered, it tends to take over and push out the Self. We identify with the part, feeling as if we have *become* it, and have little or no access to the wondrous qualities of the Self.

To return to an earlier example, when your husband comes home from work in a cranky mood, a part of you gets triggered and takes over, and you withdraw from him. Your normal ability to be caring and reasonable, which comes from your Self, isn't available at that moment. Most of us have at least a few parts activated much of the time, so we rarely have full access to Self. We may feel some openness and compassion, or other Self qualities, but not the complete depth and scope of the Self.

Much can be said about the Self, but for our purposes, the most important thing is that *it is the agent of psychological healing* in IFS. It is, by nature,

---

[2] The IFS concept of the Self has a counterpart in Voice Dialogue, Jungian analysis, and Psychosynthesis. However, it doesn't seem to exist in most other forms of therapy. Even methods that use the term "self" are usually referring to something different. On the other hand, many spiritual traditions do have an understanding that is similar to the IFS Self, called by a variety of names—for example, Essence, Buddha Nature, Atman, and Inner Light.

compassionate and curious about our parts. The Self wants to connect with each part and get to know it and heal it.

Let's look at four qualities of the Self that are particularly important for psychological healing. When you are in Self, you will naturally embody these qualities.

1. The Self is *connected*. When you are in Self, you naturally feel close to other people and want to relate in harmonious, supportive ways. You are drawn to make contact with them, to be in community. The Self also wants to be connected to your parts. When you are in Self, you are interested in having a relationship with each of your parts, which helps them to trust you, opening the way for healing.

2. The Self is *curious*. When you are in Self, you are curious about other people in an open, accepting way. When you inquire into what makes them tick, it's because you want to understand them, not judge them. The Self is also curious about the inner workings of your mind. You want to understand why each part acts as it does, what its positive intent is for you, and what it is trying to protect you from. This curiosity comes from an accepting place, not a critical one. When parts sense this genuine interest, they know they are entering a welcoming environment, and they aren't afraid to reveal themselves to you.

3. The Self is *compassionate*. Compassion is a form of kindness and love that arises when people are in pain. You genuinely care about how they feel and want to support them through difficult times. When you are in Self, you naturally feel compassion for others as well as yourself. Your extreme parts are reacting to pain; exiles feel it, and protectors try to avoid it. So compassion is really needed to hold, support, and nurture you while you take on very difficult material. When you are in Self, you care about the pain of your exiles and feel compassion for your protectors, which are driven to wall off your misery. Parts can sense the compassion of the Self, which makes them feel safe and cared for, so they want to open up and share themselves with you.

4. The Self is *calm*, centered, and grounded. This is especially helpful when you are relating to a part that has intense emotions. Intense grief or shame, for example, can be overwhelming if you aren't grounded in Self, and protectors will avoid a part that has emotions like this at all costs. But when you are centered in the calmness of Self, there is no need to avoid a part with intense affect. You remain in Self while the part shows you its pain. The calmness of Self supports you through the difficult work of witnessing and healing this part.

30

For all these reasons, the Self is the agent of psychological healing in IFS work. It helps you to heal and transform your parts so they become free of their extreme feelings and behavior, and can assume healthy roles in your life.

The Structure of the Psyche

The Self is also the natural leader of your internal system. It has the courage to take risks, the perspective to see reality clearly, the creativity to find good solutions to problems. The Self is balanced and fair, and sees what needs to happen in most situations. When you have healed your parts and they trust you, they finally allow the Self to lead. Ideally the Self is the one who makes decisions and takes action. It works together with your healthy parts and the parts that have been healed through therapy.

Parts provide a lot. They offer you the capacities and insights you need in any particular situation—spontaneity, humor, organization, perseverance, for example. But on their own, they lack a larger sense of direction. The Self provides that. The Self is the conductor of the orchestra, the one who brings in the woodwinds at the right time, tells the musicians when to play softly, cues the horn solo. It chooses the best course of action in each moment and calls on your healthy parts to contribute their gifts. Your parts trust the Self and count on it for wisdom.

This is the ideal situation, and it's how your psyche tends to operate after IFS therapy. However, most of us don't start here. Because of pain and trauma in our lives, and especially in childhood, our parts have taken over and shoved the Self into the background. When you were wounded at a young age, your Self wasn't developed enough to handle what life threw at you. You probably felt weak and vulnerable, completely defenseless, unable to grapple with the situation on your own. Your parts felt that no one was minding the store, so they had to protect you at all costs. They took over and did their best.

Being primitive and immature, your parts had to protect you in extreme ways because that was all they were capable of. You didn't have the experience and the inner resources of an adult, so your parts had to do what they could—shut you down completely, throw a tantrum, become overly pleasing—whatever seemed to work. In this way the Self got eclipsed, to a greater or lesser extent, and you have lived a life influenced or dominated by your extreme parts. But now that you are a resourceful adult living in a better situation, those extremes reactions are no longer needed. Through IFS therapy, you can learn to access your Self, heal those parts, and transform your internal system. There are two goals for IFS therapy: one, heal your parts so that their extreme roles are converted to healthy roles, and two, help them to cooperate with each other under the leadership of the Self.

This illustration shows the structure of an internal system before therapy. The exiles are hidden behind a curtain so you won't feel their pain. The protectors have taken over leadership from the Self and determine your feelings and actions. They don't trust the Self and therefore push it into the background, where it can't lead.

The Structure of the Psyche Before IFS Therapy

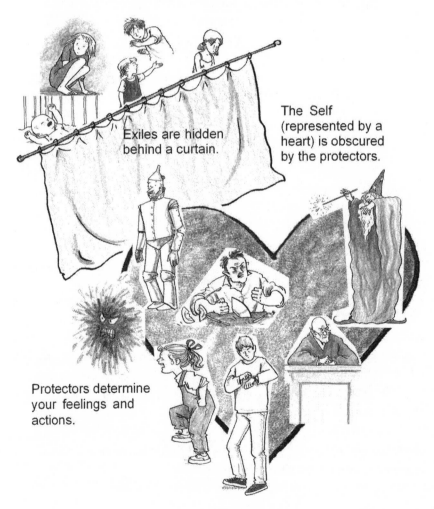

Exiles are hidden behind a curtain.

The Self (represented by a heart) is obscured by the protectors.

Protectors determine your feelings and actions.

The IFS Process

Let's now look at the IFS process of psychological healing. The most important aspect of this is learning how to stay in Self. IFS has many effective ways of doing this, which are covered in this book.

You begin a session by choosing a part to focus on, usually a protector. For example, let's look at Bill, whom we met in Chapter 1. He has a protector that is judgmental and competitive. This is distressing because these qualities are contrary to his better values. He believes in being cooperative, accepting, and inclusive. To some extent he is, but any time he is threatened or pushed to his limits, his judgmental protector crops up to take control. Often he is able to hide his judgments, but sometimes they leak out and offend people because he seems critical and harsh. At work, this behavior causes a great deal of dissension and hostility, which Bill genuinely hates, even though he is often the one causing it. Bill also wants a close and affectionate relationship with his wife, but this same protector can be derisive and mocking with her. The atmosphere in their home is not harmonious, and that is the one thing he most wants.

 Bill started out his IFS work with me by focusing on this particular protector because it was clearly the most disruptive. He called it, aptly, "the Judge." It wasn't easy for Bill to even approach working with the Judge because he was disgusted with it for not living up to his ideals. I knew that he wasn't in Self when he was disparaging of the Judge because the Self is never disgusted. This could only be another protector passing judgment on the Judge!

With some work, Bill was able to access Self, which allowed him to be genuinely interested in getting to know the Judge. Bill had grown up in a judgmental, competitive home, so The Judge modeled itself after his parents. It puts people down and acts superior to them to compensate for another part of him that feels worthless and scared. As Bill got to know the Judge, he understood why it acted as it did, and he came to appreciate its efforts on his behalf, even though they led to problems.

He asked the Judge for permission to work with the exile who felt worthless, which he called Little Billy. Getting to know this child proved invaluable. Little Billy showed him childhood scenes when he was hit by his impatient father for not doing a task perfectly or for not grasping a homework assignment quickly enough. Up until then, Little Billy had been hidden away in Bill's unconscious. Being locked in the basement of the psyche only increased Little Billy's feelings of worthlessness because he felt rejected by Bill.

As a result of childhood incidents, our exiles take on pain and negative beliefs, which, in IFS, are called *burdens*. Little Billy had taken on the burdens of worthlessness and fear. Burdens are not intrinsic to the part; they "land on" the part as a result of what happened in the past. The good news is that they can be released through IFS therapy.

Bill responded to Billy with compassion and caring from Self, and the part took this in, feeling cherished and valuable for the first time. With love from Bill's Self and with my direction, Little Billy took additional steps to release the burdens he had been carrying. He transformed into the healthy part he truly is, feeling adequate and competent for the first time, and also safe from harm. This allowed him to be playful, loose, and free as well.

The transformation went even further. Bill's judgmental protector could now relax since there was nothing to protect. It no longer needed to criticize people to compensate for Billy's pain. It let go of its protective role of judging people and took on a new role as a kindly supporter and mentor for people. This enabled Bill to respond to people in the way he had

always wanted, with openness and acceptance and a cooperative attitude. As a result, he became much more effective at work, and his fights with his wife decreased dramatically.

This description of the IFS process has been simplified for the sake of this introduction. There are, of course, many other difficulties and complexities that will be covered in the rest of the book. Though some of the steps in the IFS process are similar to procedures in other forms of therapy or spiritual work, IFS brings them together in a comprehensive process that is unique.

Transformation of the Psyche

The illustration below shows how the psyche transforms as a result of IFS therapy. All parts are now cooperating under the leadership of the Self. (The parts will also be transformed so they are performing healthier roles, but that isn't shown in the illustration.)

The Structure of the Psyche Transformed

The exiles are brought forward in front of the curtain.

The Self is now the center of the psyche.

All the parts are now cooperating with each other under the guidance of the Self.

Structure of the Book

In these first two chapters, you have been introduced to the IFS Model and learned about protectors, exiles, and the Self. You have seen something about how the IFS approach works to heal and transform parts and help them to cooperate in your best interests.

In the rest of the book, I teach a step-by-step procedure for doing IFS sessions. I also show how to work with parts in the moment when they become activated by the events of your life. Part I describes how to get to know a protector, which includes how to stay in Self. Part II explains the steps for getting to know an exile and releasing it from its burdens. Each chapter teaches one step in the overall process and includes exercises for practicing that step on your own or with a partner. The steps are illustrated with stories of people's IFS work and transcripts of IFS sessions. Some of the chapters also show how to work with parts in real time in your life.

I invite you to dig in and begin this great adventure of self-healing. Prepare to eliminate the pain you have lived with and lift yourself from the stuck places in your psyche. Now is the time to discover its riches.

Chapter 3

Taking an Inner Journey

Example of an IFS Session

———————— • ————————

This chapter takes you on a journey through a complete IFS session with a student from one of my IFS classes. The IFS process follows a trajectory towards healing that can sometimes be accomplished in a single session. I chose this session because it does complete this healing process for a number of parts. It will give you a feeling for the overall IFS procedure and what it can accomplish.

Christine[1] is a 50-year-old college teacher from the West Coast who is the youngest of three sisters. She is of British extraction but has lived in the U.S. for many years. She has engaged in many years of therapy and spiritual work, and she joined my class to learn more about how to heal psychological issues. You will be able to tell from the transcript that she is quite intelligent and able to access subtle experiences in herself with clarity. Prior to my class, she had done some therapy work involving childhood hospitalizations that seemed to cause repeated panic. She also had memories of her sisters running away and leaving her but hadn't yet worked on them.

Since she was in my class, she already knew a fair amount about the IFS Model, which helped her in this work. I chose this session because the

———————————————

[1] Christine (not her real name) gave permission to use this transcript. This is true for all the transcripts in the book.

work moves in a fairly straightforward way, which is helpful for this initial demonstration of IFS. Most sessions involve many more complications and sidetracks, which the IFS model is excellent at handling. Examples of these are shown later in the book.

Christine starts this session by bringing up an issue from her life that she wants to explore. My comments are in *italics*.

Christine: I would like to work on how I get confused and distracted sometimes. Most of the time I am quite clear and sharp, but every once in a while I get fuzzy and confused. This often happens in situations where I need to have my mental acuity.

Jay: Okay. It sounds like there is a part of you that becomes confused at times. Does that make sense to you?

C: Yes.

J: So let's focus on that confused part. How do you sense it in your body?

C: Well, when it happens I feel a slight dizziness and blankness in my head.

In IFS we don't analyze our parts—we contact them directly.

J: Mm hmm. Check and see if you are feeling separate enough from that part to get to know it.

C: Well, I'm not sure. I think so. Hmm. How would I tell?

J: Do you sense in yourself a clear place from which to connect with the confused part?

In order for the work to be effective, Christine must be in Self as she gets to know the part. This means she must be in a grounded, separate place from which she can relate to the part.

C: ... I'm having a hard time telling about that. (pause) What question did you just ask me?

J: It sounds like you may be blended with the confused part right now. So ask that part to separate from you so you can get to know it.

It seems pretty clear that Christine is confused right now. This probably means that the confused part has taken her over, i.e., "blended" with her. Therefore I have her ask it to separate so she can be in Self.

C: Okay ... Well, now I feel differently, more solid or something. And I actually see an image of the part as a cloud of smoke.

J: Good. Check to see how you are feeling toward this confused part right now.

C: I wish it would go away. I hate being confused.

J: Okay. That hatred and desire for it to go away are coming from another part of you. I understand why that part of you would want the confused part to go away—so you won't lose your sharpness—but approaching it from a place of hatred won't really work. Ask the hateful part if it would be willing to step aside so you can get to know the confused part from an open place.

Since Christine hates the confused part, I can tell that she is still not in Self, because Self doesn't hate.

C: Sure. That makes sense. It is willing to.

J: Good. How do you feel toward the confused part now?

C: Kind of curious about it, like why does it do this to me?

Christine has now accessed enough Self for us to move on to the next step—getting to know the confused part.

J: Okay. Invite that part to tell you or show you more about what it feels.

C: It says that it feels sleepy and dull. I can sense that it goes blank.

J: It feels dull and blank.

C: Yes. It says "I want to go to sleep. I don't want to be awake or conscious." Sometimes it can't answer people's questions.

J: Mm hmm. Ask the part what its name is or what it would like to be called.

C: I get the word Confuser.

J: Okay. We'll call it the Confuser. Ask it what it is trying to accomplish by being sleepy and confused.

I pose this question to discover the Confuser's positive intent for Christine.

C: It says, "I don't want to see something. I don't want to know something." This part has to just make unclarity and confusion, blandness. It wants to make sure that I don't know what is going on.

J: It creates confusion to protect you from whatever is going on .... You might ask the part how it creates confusion and not knowing.

C: Various things. It internally changes the subject, it takes my attention away, it looks or acts very agitated, so there is no settling or landing in one place. It draws attention to itself and therefore away from whatever else is there. All those ways. Now the part looks like a person who is making magic signs in the air to create confusion and distraction.

It is fairly common for the image of a part to change as you get to know it.

J: Okay. Ask the Confuser what it is afraid would happen if it stepped aside and allowed you to see things.

This kind of question serves a specific purpose. It tends to lead the inquiry toward the exile that is being protected.

C: What it says is: "What would happen is just unthinkable, unspeakable." It is so frightened, we can't even go there.

The Confuser backs up against the curtain and makes magic signs to prevent Christine from seeing what is behind it.

Christine's Self is curious to learn more about her hidden parts.

J: I see, so it is very frightened about this.

C: At a survival level.

J: Yeah. You might ask the Confuser how long it has been doing this job.

C: It feels like forever.

J: How does it feel about its job?

C: It's a completely impossible job, overwhelming. Yet it is unable to stop.

J: Yeah. See if there is anything else the part wants you to know about itself.

C: I feel clearly that it does want my love and respect and gratitude for suffering on my behalf.

Most parts want appreciation for performing their roles, but they rarely ask directly in this way.

J: And what's your response to that?

C: I do feel a lot of appreciation.

J: So really let the Confuser know that.

C: I feel I can't even express in words how much I appreciate the degree of dedication and desperation this part has shown in doing this job. (Christine is really moved.)

J: Yeah. So you really get it. And how is the part responding to you?

C: It's softening. And as it softens, I see one very clear thing. When I said earlier that it didn't know how to stop, that was because it had no connection with Self. There was nothing for it to release into, relax into. But now the Confuser is softening, because it does sense that I'm here.

This is very moving to me. Christine has really connected with the Confuser from Self, and it is beginning to trust her and relax. This is an important step.

J: Good. Ask the Confuser if it would be willing to show you a part that it is protecting with its confusion.

Most protectors can't completely let go of their roles until the exile they are protecting is no longer in pain, so we need to heal that part.

C: Oh! Now I'm getting a glimpse of a panic state behind the Confuser.

J: Check to see if the Confuser will give you permission to get to know this panicked part.

C: … Okay. It is not sure about this. It's very nervous.

J: You might ask it what it's worried about. What is it afraid will happen?

Since the protector has concerns about proceeding, we need to find out what these are so we can reassure it. Otherwise it won't give us permission to work with the exile.

C: The Confuser is afraid that the exile will come rushing up and swamp me.

J: You might invite it to signal us in some way if it feels that the exile is beginning to swamp you, because we can keep that from happening. This protector can actually help us by letting us know if that starts to happen, so you can return to Self.

IFS has techniques for helping a person stay in Self and not be flooded by an exile's emotions, which will be covered in a later chapter. I reassure the protector that this is possible and invite it to help her do that.

C: All right. It seems OK with that ... Now there are all sorts of judgments coming up. I will be too slow. I will go meandering all over the place and nothing will happen.

This first reassurance seems to have worked, and now the Confuser's other fears come out. This is good because it gives Christine a chance to reassure it about those as well.

C: I'm telling the Confuser that I can understand its concerns, but I don't think that will happen. We've tried things like this before, and I have shown myself to be helpful when given the chance. And you (Jay) are there as well to offer support, so I suggested to the Confuser that it's a chance to find new territory where it can relax and not have to work so hard.

Christine suggests that the protector has something to gain by allowing us to proceed—it would be able to relax.

J: Good. How is it responding?

C: OK, these images are so funny. The Confuser sort of sat back in a lawn chair and crossed its legs to watch what happens next. It's so funny. Oh goodness. (laughing)

The fact that the Confuser sits back indicates that Christine's reassurance has worked and it is giving permission to proceed with the exile. Her parts can trust her fairly easily. This is an indication of how much work Christine has already done on herself.

J: Good.

C: So here is the exile. She is very little and skinny, and quite frail. It's interesting because I'm tall and strong. But she is in a little dress, and she is quite vulnerable in her small, light, little body. She's all knotted up in her throat, and she's watching and on the edge of panic.

J: Mm hmm. You might ask this part what she would like to be called.

C: I guess just the Little Girl.

J: Okay, ask the Little Girl what she is so frightened of.

C: That she is going to be left alone in the dark and nobody will be there. It is so interesting. But now she is panicking, and it's too much for me.

The Little Girl's panic is blending with Christine and pulling her out of Self.

J: Let her know that it is Okay for her to be scared, but ask her not to flood you with it.

Being swamped is one thing the Confuser was afraid of, but we can take care of this by asking the exile not to flood her.

C: I'm Okay now. I don't feel too scared anymore. It's good that *she* is allowed to feel the panic, because otherwise she would go away.

This shows the importance of making it clear to the exile that asking it to separate doesn't mean it can't feel its emotions. If this exile felt that her emotions weren't allowed, she wouldn't have trusted Christine enough to stay around.

C: She likes that I'm here now. She actually sees that there is some-one (Self) here, and she is surprised. And as soon as that happens, she calms down and just wants to talk to me. She's not charged.

J: Mm hmm. She is more relaxed and open to you.

Now that the part isn't flooding Christine with her panic, Christine can be in Self and the Little Girl has someone to rely on, which allows her to calm down.

C: Yes, that's right.

J: What does she want to tell you?

C: How hard it has been for her. How she's had to do it all on her own, and she's really frightened. She didn't know what was hap-pening. Nobody was there. My impulse is to ask her what the situation was.

J: Sounds good.

C: . . . I can see how my mind jumps in and says it was in the hospital when I was a baby, but I'm not sure. I want *her* to tell me.

Christine has an intellectual idea of where the exile's fear comes from in her childhood, but to be sure it's accurate, she needs the information to come from the exile experientially, so she asks her. This also allows the work to proceed in the alive, embodied way that it needs to.

J: Good.

C: She is telling me it is dark and the lights are out. And nobody loves her. Nobody's there, so that means nobody loves her. There's no one to take care of her.

This is the childhood experience that created the burdens of fear and panic and the belief that no one loves her.

C: And so from the point of view of Self, when I hear that, I want to hold her. I want to sit her on my lap.

J: Go ahead and do that.

Christine has a wonderful spontaneous impulse to comfort the Little Girl. She is reparenting the part, which is an aspect of the healing process.

C: I'm struck by the little body that doesn't have tension in it. It's a very soft, undefended little body. And there's a weight, a heaviness in the heart, that she is carrying around ... Okay, the heaviness in the heart comes from hopelessness that nothing is going to get better. And she has to carry this burden all by herself because nobody else is there. *(pause)*

There it is. I can see the thread now. When nobody is there to pick her up, there is a contraction, a closing off, a walling off. There is fearful watching in the cells of the body. This heavy heart has formed over time. It's not one event that does it. It sort of chips away. The heaviness comes from her inability to change anything.

The heaviness in the Little Girl's heart is a response to many events over a number of years in Christine's early childhood in which no one was there for her when she needed comfort or holding. Gradually, the Little Girl grew hopeless about getting the care she needed.

J: And the thing that formed in the cells of the body, what was that?

C: The watchfulness, the alertness, guarding, protecting, and the closing off from the world. It's like a defense. It's a felt thing. Almost like a catch in the tissues. (pause) Now there is a sense of being frightened, caught in the dark by herself. That feeling is much younger; it goes way back. I'm getting a specific memory. She's flailing her arms and legs. Somebody is supposed to come and pick her up, but they don't come. Now I'm getting some vague memory of something dangling in a crib ... a hollow sound. There's a sense of trying to get somewhere, to get picked up. But no one is there.

J: She desperately needs to be picked up, but no one comes.

In the middle of witnessing the Little Girl's story, Christine has accessed an even younger part, which I will call the Baby, who has earlier memories

44

related to the feelings of aloneness and
*panic. We still don't know exactly when
this was or what the external circumstances were, but that is not necessary for
healing.*

C: Yes, it's interesting that I say that.
Because this is different from how
the Little Girl feels. I can't quite make
sense of that.

J: Well, sure. This younger memory is from a different part.

C: Oh, I see. The Little Girl comes later.

*The Baby has some very early memories of being stranded in her crib when
she really needed to be picked up and comforted. Christine seems to have
had experiences like this over the next few years, which left the Little
Girl, who is stuck at four years old, with similar feelings of being alone
and panicked, and also hopeless and guarded.*

C: Well, right now something is shifting by itself, I think. By feeling
both of them there, there is less charge. (pause)

J: Would you like a suggestion?

C: I would.

*Now that Christine has witnessed the story and feelings of both parts, she
can move on to healing them.*

J: Focus on the Baby, and bring yourself into that place where she is
all alone. See what she needs from you.

C: She wants me to pick her up.

J: Go ahead and do that.

C: She cries louder, and then she just clings. Now I'm nuzzling her
around the ears and she's just clinging to me. I see her bald head.
She's quite young and doesn't have much
hair, just soft down.

J: Can she sense you there?

Christine is reparenting the Baby. I ask this ques-
*tion to make sure that the Baby is receiving what
Christine is giving her.*

C: Very much so.

J: And how is she responding?

C: Softening, and now she's not crying. She's
feeling into me and resting into me. And now

there's a little burp. You know when a baby has been crying and there's a little aftershock going through her. I can feel it in her back.

Clearly the Baby is taking in Christine's reparenting.

C: Well, OK, I don't know if this is right or not, but what happened is that the Little Girl, with the little body and the heavy heart, wants to hold the Baby. So I'm going to let her do that.

J: Okay.

C: It's so sweet! The whole thing has now just shifted to this beautiful playtime. I just feel so much love. Not just from me to these little ones, but both of them are bathed in love. They're totally relaxed. (Sigh)

The reparenting seems to have gone well, so I suggest we move on to the next healing step—unburdening.

J: The Baby has taken on certain feelings, like panic and loneliness, as a result of being left alone in the dark. If it's appropriate, we can do an unburdening where she releases those emotions she took on. It's possible that some of them have already been released during this process, but it might be helpful to conduct an internal ritual to release them further. Check with the Baby to see if she would like to release them.

C: (laughs, cries) Okay, goodness.

J: What's happening?

C: There was a rush of sadness and pain, and then when I asked that question, she wanted to grow up so she could be with the Little Girl. It's like an accelerated growth thing without any blocks in the way. I felt a big rush of emotion coming up; it moved through my heart in my body.

J: And was that Okay?

C: Yeah. It felt good.

J: Good.

C: The Baby is happy.

This is very sweet. It seems that the Baby has had a spontaneous unburdening that came from my just mentioning the possibility of the ritual. Of course, this could only happen because of all the good work that had already occurred in this session. Now I have Christine check to see if the actual unburdening ritual is still needed.

J: I offered to do an unburdening ritual, and then this feeling moved through you. Now check to see if that is all that is needed or if the ritual would still be helpful.

C: The Baby is fine now, from whatever that rush was, but the Little Girl seems to need an unburdening ritual.

J: Okay, what burdens is that Little Girl carrying?

C: The heavy heart, the despair, the sense that things will never change, that she'll always have to carry the panic and fear of the baby.

J: First check to see if she is aware that the Baby is happy now.

I want the Little Girl to be aware that the Baby has been unburdened because that might allow her to let go of her hopelessness and her need to protect it.

C: Yeah. She wants to play with the Baby. That's interesting. Even though she's playing with the Baby, there's still a belief that she's got to look after it and carry that burden. Even though she's seen with her own eyes that the Baby is happy, she still thinks she can't let go of that heaviness and hopelessness.

J: Okay. Ask the Little Girl if she would like to release that heavy heart she is carrying and the belief that things will never change.

C: That's disorienting, because she believes that is who she is. Without that belief, she wouldn't be there.

J: Let her know that if she lets go of that belief, she can take on any other role she wants and be whoever she wants to be.

Parts aren't defined by the negative beliefs and emotions they took on in childhood, which IFS calls their burdens. They have their own potential that is intrinsic to them. That is why they can let go of a burden and take on a new role in the psyche. I explain this to the Little Girl.

C: Yeah, she wants to let go of that so she can play. She can see that that would be fun.

J: Good. Check and see how she is carrying that heavy heart and the hopeless belief—where she carries those in her body or on her body.

C: There is a weight around her heart, and the rest of it is almost like a heavy mantle that she wears over her head and back and shoulders. And she's not allowed to be joyful.

J: Okay. She can have those washed away by water, or blown away by wind, or she can give them up to the light, or put them in the earth, or have them burned up in fire, or anything else that feels right to her.

IFS has discovered that it is helpful to release a burden to one of the basic elements in nature—earth, fire, wind, water, or light. This signifies that the burden won't come back because it has been carried away, or transformed, by something elemental and powerful.

C: She wants them to be transformed so nobody else has to carry them. So … burning.

J: She wants to burn them in fire. So arrange that.

C: She wants to burn her little dress, as if that is the burden. That is so weird, but that is what she is saying. She wants another dress.

J: As this is happening, feel that burden leaving her body, and take as much time as she needs until it's all gone.

C: That's interesting. She felt quite disoriented and scared in the moment it was changing, but then I held her hand, and now she's got a new dress.

J: Are all those burdens gone now?

C: Yeah.

J: So notice what positive qualities are emerging in her now that the burdens are gone.

Now that the unburdening ritual has been completed, there is room for the exile to embody those positive qualities that are innate to it.

C: She's grateful. The two of them are actually looking up at the smoke from the burning dress as it blows away. So bizarre. Somebody in here is a bit embarrassed by all this, but these images are coming, so I'm just going to say them anyway … They're playing footsy with each other. I mean, I couldn't make that up. It's really happening. It's sweet. All the little feet.

J: That's wonderful. And the unburdening sounds complete, so now check with the Confuser. See if she is aware of the work you just did.

C: I remember she was sitting back in the lawn chair. Oh, this is a real English expression. She is gobsmacked.

J: What does that mean?

C: It means shocked, words taken away. But she's Okay.

J: Ask her if she still feels a need to create confusion.

C: (pause) No. She seems to feel like that isn't necessary any more.

The Confuser only needed to perform its protective role of creating confusion as long as the Little Girl and the Baby were in pain. It has been paying attention, so it realizes that role is no longer needed and it can now take on a new one.

J: Good. Ask her if she would like to have a different role in your psyche.

C: Well, let's see. She wants to be a kind of guide or mentor for the Little Girl, so she won't feel alone.

J: Great. See if any other parts want to say anything before we stop.

C: There is one part I've never met. She's in awe of the process and of what's possible when the other parts don't interfere, being able to create a beautiful thing. I can plumb the depths and access something without the usual limiting voices. That feels very strange to this part. The Self says, "Of course this can happen." But this part feels it has never seen these depths before. Thank you very much. It's been quite a journey.

What a wonderful session! The exile and protectors have been unburdened, and the protectors have let go of their protective roles and taken on new, healthy ones.

Summary

This transcript gives a beautiful demonstration of the healing power of IFS. It shows how giving respectful, caring attention to our parts permits them to open up deep places inside us—places that can be healed through their relationship with Self and the unburdening ritual. You may have many questions about how the details of this session relate to the IFS process.

These will be explained throughout the rest of the book as you learn how to do this kind of work on yourself.

I chose this session because it illustrates in a single chapter what is possible with IFS work. It is exceptional in that Christine encountered very few difficulties in the process. Few people have such smooth sailing. Often, more resistances and sidetracks must be handled to achieve this level of access and healing, and it usually takes more than one session, sometimes far longer. Don't be discouraged if the work you do on yourself doesn't go this smoothly. IFS is expert at handling the difficulties that arise, as will be explained in succeeding chapters.

Part I: Self and Protectors

The human psyche is organized around avoiding pain. That is the job of the protectors—to buffer you from suffering. These are hard-working parts that manage your life and your psyche so that you don't have to face your hidden pain. They take their job extremely seriously, believing that your well-being, and maybe your survival, depends on what they do. In order to heal and transform your psyche, it is necessary to access and heal the exiles that are hidden behind the protectors. However, in IFS we don't break through doors and rush toward the exiles. We respect our protectors' need for defenses, and we take our time getting to know them and gaining their trust. Only then will these gatekeepers relax and give us permission to work with the exiles.

The IFS process is actually quite efficient and penetrating, but, paradoxically, it does this by being careful and respectful of protectors, not through strong-arm tactics. Furthermore, protectors are important in themselves. Since exiles are pushed into the background, it is the protectors that are out front relating to people and acting in the world. It isn't enough to heal our exiles; our protectors must also be healed and transformed so they can drop their defensive roles, let their positive qualities emerge, and assume healthy roles in the inner system.

Consequently, we start most IFS sessions by focusing on a protector. Since they are the parts that are most conscious and easily accessible, it is natural to begin with them. However, the main reason is that, in IFS, it isn't appropriate to work with an exile until we have permission from any protectors who might not approve.

This book teaches the IFS method as a sequence of steps. The steps for getting to know a protector can be summarized as follows: In beginning a session, you access a number of protectors and then choose one to focus on, called the *target part*. You inhabit Self and get to know this protector, finding out its positive intent for you. You establish a trusting relationship with the protector and understand what it is trying to protect you from. This sets the stage for further work with the protector or for healing the exile it is protecting.

Here are the five steps in getting to know a protector, labeled P1-P5. "P" stands for protector. These steps constitute the content of Part I.

P1: Accessing a part

P2: Unblending from the target part

P3: Unblending from a concerned part

P4: Discovering a protector's role

P5: Developing a trusting relationship with a protector

These terms will be defined and explained in Chapters 4-8, which cover each of the five steps in detail. In reality, these steps may sometimes intertwine or occur in a different order. Sometimes it's necessary to refocus our attention on a different protector and therefore go back to the beginning of the steps. However, this is the basic order. Chapter 9 explains how keep your sessions on track by dealing with the various unexpected occurrences that can pop up along the way.

Chapter 4

Getting Acquainted Inside

Accessing Your Parts

———————— • ————————

Suppose you wanted to understand why your next-door neighbor has many strange visitors at all hours of the day and night. You could set up a telescope and watch him in his home. You could hire a detective to follow him and find out about his activities. You could create theories to explain his actions. However, there are limits to what you can discover by distant observation and intellectual guesswork. Yet this is the way we typically try to understand our psychological life.

On the other hand, you could go knock on his door, introduce yourself, and ask him to sit down and tell you about himself. You could reveal yourself to him and spend time with him as he goes about his life, and over time develop a friendship with him. You will learn much more about him this way. This is the IFS approach to our inner life. We get to know our parts in a personal, experiential manner.

Trailheads

Let's suppose you have an issue you would like to work on. How do you know what parts to explore? In this section, we will show you how to determine which parts are involved with an issue. In IFS, issues are sometimes referred to as trailheads. A *trailhead* is an experience or a difficulty in your life that will lead to interesting parts if you follow it. It can be a situation or person that you react to, an emotional or bodily experience, a pattern of behavior or thinking, a dream, or anything else that indicates parts to explore. We call it a trailhead because it is the beginning of a trail that can lead to healing. It usually involves both a life situation and your response to that situation.

A trailhead indicates the presence of a part (or parts) in an extreme role, where your behavior or emotional reaction is dysfunctional or problematic.

1. A part might misperceive the situation. For example, a part sees your boss as judging you when he is actually just trying to help you, because he reminds you of your judgmental father.

2. A part might overreact emotionally. For example, your boss might be moderately judgmental, but the part becomes extremely upset.

3. A part might take action that is extreme or inappropriate. For example, the part becomes angry or rebellious with your boss because it perceives him as judging you, and this behavior causes problems.

One of my trailheads is feeling shy in large groups of people I don't know very well. I tend to be withdrawn and not very expressive or open.

Here are some examples of trailheads from people in my classes:

1. A particular person at work who upsets me.

2. A situation in which I was afraid that whatever action I take, someone would feel hurt. I ended up feeling paralyzed because I felt like I had to choose between two people.

3. . Fear of flying on an airplane.

4. Difficult work projects. When some piece of a project is more complex and taking longer than I thought, I focus on it intensely for hours trying to get it done while ignoring my bodily needs, any awareness of myself, and any other tasks that need attention. I watch myself getting sucked in, but I can't pull away.

5. Controlling people. When I feel like someone's trying to control me, I withdraw and get away as soon as I can.

6. Thoughts about rejection. Sometimes when I feel rejected by someone, I obsess about it, trying to figure out what I did wrong and what I should have said instead.

When you are at a trailhead, there is at least one part activated and often more than one. For example, when I am in a large group of strangers,

I have at least three parts activated—one that is scared of being hurt, another part that wants to withdraw to protect me, and a third part that wants to reach out and talk to people despite the fear.

Identifying the Parts at a Trailhead

By examining your experience and behavior, you can make an initial identification of the parts that are involved in any trailhead you want to explore. There will be parts corresponding to feelings and body reactions triggered by that situation and thoughts and desires you have about it. There will also be parts that determine the way you behave in that situation. Let's look at each of these in turn:

Feelings. You are likely to have at least one emotional reaction to the trailhead situation, perhaps more than one. You may feel angry, sad, or afraid, for example. In addition, you may notice certain attitudes you have in that situation; you may feel judgmental, thoughtless, stingy, careful, zany, doubtful, or mischievous. Each feeling, emotion, or attitude indicates the presence of a part, except for those attitudes that come from the Self, such as being kind or centered. Furthermore, if you feel cut off from your feelings, that is probably caused by a part. For example, if you feel dead, closed, or cold in a trailhead situation, there probably is a part causing this.

Body Sensations. Most body sensations that come up in response to a trailhead are related to parts. The exceptions are purely physiological sensations (like a stomachache because of something you ate) and the bodily experiences of Self, such as feeling peaceful, open, or energetic. Parts can cause muscle tension, such as tightness in your shoulders or back. They can produce heat in your arms or cold in your belly. There are many possible body sensations—hardness, heaviness, nausea, emptiness, or holding, for example. You might experience them in certain places in your body or in your body as a whole. In addition, if there is a deadness or lack of feeling in your body (or a part of your body), that is also caused by a part that doesn't want you to feel.

Thoughts. Many thoughts that arise in response to a trailhead situation come from parts. This includes thoughts about people in the situation, "She is certainly intrusive," or about yourself, "That was a stupid thing to say." Many *patterns* of thinking also indicate parts—for example, obsessing

55

about a difficult conversation with your boss or having frequent judgmental thoughts about people. Even the absence of thought sometimes indicates a part. For example, if your mind suddenly goes blank, there is usually a part causing this, perhaps because it doesn't want you to continue with a train of thought that it considers dangerous.

Behavior. An action or pattern of behavior can indicate a part—for example, withdrawing or becoming pushy. The avoidance of behavior also indicates a part. For example, if you find yourself avoiding a phone call or a project you need to work on, that comes from a procrastinating part.

Desires. Certain types of desires come from a part. One part may want closeness or success. Another might want to be seen and appreciated. A third might want to be left alone. A lack of desire could also come from a part that doesn't think it is safe to want things.

Let's look at a more detailed example of a trailhead. When Betty visited her grown son's house, she felt that he was being verbally abusive to his son, and she was considering talking to him about this but kept hesitating. In order to explore this, I asked her to imagine bringing it up with him. Here is a list of the parts she accessed:

1. One part wants to avoid talking to her son about this. This was attended by a strangling feeling in her throat that was intended to stop her from speaking because she might otherwise make a mistake and cause her son pain.

2. A loving part cares about him and her grandson.

3. A part is sad and regretful because she hasn't communicated well before.

4. A part feels disappointed and embarrassed about how he treats her grandson.

5. A part is angry at him and protective of her grandson. It wants to say "How dare you?!" and push her son away.

6. A part is afraid of the angry/protective part, and that is reflected in her stomach feeling very disturbed. This part is afraid of being overwhelmed by the angry part and making hurtful statements to her son. This disturbed part kept her from being aware of the angry part for a while.

You can see from Betty's experience that many parts may be activated by a single trailhead, and they interact with each other in attempts to influence her feelings and behavior. This brings up the question of how you tell one part from another. If two feelings seem very different or if they are opposed to each other, they are clearly different parts. For example, Betty's love for her son and her anger at him are so opposite that they clearly come from different parts. If one part seems to be blocking or protecting against another, it means they are different parts. For example, her disturbed-stomach part blocked Betty's awareness of the angry/protective part for a while.

However, what if two parts seem similar? For example, the strangling feeling and the disturbed-stomach seem to have roughly the same attitude, so they might be coming from the same part or from two different parts. This can't be determined intellectually. Betty will only find out when she explores them in more depth.

Exercise: Identifying the Parts at a Trailhead

Choose a trailhead that you are interested in exploring. Using the approach described above, make a list of each of the parts involved with that trailhead. For each part, write the following if you can:

Name of part _____

What it feels emotionally _____

What it looks like _____

What it feels like in your body and where _____

What it says _____

How it makes you behave _____

What it wants _____

You haven't fully explored these parts, so don't be concerned if you don't know much about them. Just fill in what you do know. Add information to your description later as you get to know the part better.

In order to allow you to more easily write out the answers to this exercise and all the others in the book, I have created a Companion Workbook that you can download for free from my website www.personal-growth-programs.com. Mouse over Self-Therapy on the Books menu, and then click on Support for Self-Therapy.

Step P1: Accessing a Part

You begin an IFS session by accessing a part that you believe will be helpful to work with. It might be related to an important trailhead, or it might be causing you intense feelings at the moment. The emphasis in this chapter is on how to make simple contact with the part. Getting to know the part fully will be covered in succeeding chapters. Though these methods can be used for accessing any part, we will emphasize protectors because that is the overall focus of Part 1. It is best to close your eyes during this process and for the rest of any IFS session. I also recommend doing this work in a private room where you won't be disturbed by people, pets, phones, or computers. This cuts down on distractions and allows you to focus completely on the protector you are accessing.

Go inside and make contact with it experientially, through your emotions, images, body sensations, and internal voices. There are a variety of internal channels for accessing a part:

Feelings. You feel the emotion, attitude, or desire that characterizes the part, giving you a felt sense of it.

Body Sensations. You sense the bodily experience that goes with the part.

Images. You see an internal image that represents the part. This may arise spontaneously, or you may look for an image that represents the part. This could be an image of yourself with a certain body stance or expression, such as droopy or muscular. It might be an image of you at a particular age. It could also be an image of a famous person, a cartoon character, a mythical figure, or an animal. Images of parts can also be more abstract—for example, a wall, an ice chest, a brilliant sun, or a garden full of weeds.

Internal Voice. You hear the part speaking words silently inside. It might be speaking to you or to someone in your life, or even to another part.

Written Dialogue. You write a conversation between yourself and the part.

Speaking as the Part. You become the part and speak out loud voicing what the part has to say.

Direct Knowing. You just know about the part.

Sometimes the body sensation or image that you access isn't very clear at first. That is fine; it just means that you haven't fully accessed the part. As you proceed to get to know it (as described in Chapter 7), the part will become clearer.

To understand more fully how to access a part, let's look at an example from one of my IFS classes. Here is Julie's description of her experience.

Julie: I'm getting ready to end a relationship I've been in for a year. My boyfriend just seems too needy and demanding, and I've been acting like a control freak.

Jay: How do you feel that part in your body?

Julie: There is a kind of hardness to that part. I don't have any feelings toward my boyfriend. It's an overall sense of not having compassion. And it seems like a hardness because I'm not feeling soft and loving. I'm just kind of closed off, not connected, rigid. I don't feel my heart or anything below my head.

Jay: See if an image arises that corresponds to that part.

Julie: I see the Tin Man from *The Wizard of Oz*. I'm getting more of a connection to it now.

Notice that the image is male. It isn't unusual for certain parts to be the opposite gender of the person. It is well known in psychology that we all have qualities of both genders inside us.

In this example, Julie accesses the part using three channels. She feels a hardness in her body, a feeling of being closed off emotionally, and an image of the Tin Man. However, it isn't necessary to use many channels to access a part; just one is enough.

You may find that certain channels are easy and natural for you, and others are more difficult. For example, I am poor at visualization, so I don't get much useful information about my parts through images. However, I have good access to parts through sensing my body, feeling my emotions, and hearing my parts speak to me. Other people are great visualizers but don't have good access to body sensations. Furthermore, different parts may communicate through different channels. You will know intuitively which channel or channels to use with each part. IFS allows you to use whatever channels work best for you, unlike many methods of psychotherapy that work with only one channel.

Activation of Parts

How you access a part depends on whether or not it is activated at the moment, so we must first understand activation. At any given moment, there are one or more parts that are *activated* because of a situation you are in or are thinking about. Each activated part influences your feelings, your body, your thoughts, and your behavior. The rest of your parts are dormant but can be activated at any moment. For example, in this illustration, Julie's Tin Man part is in the activated space, and the rest of her parts are behind a curtain, dormant for the moment.

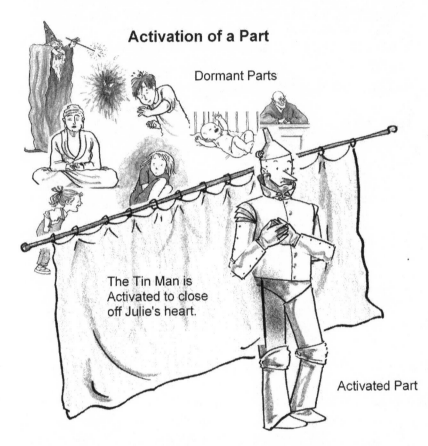

Activation of a Part

Dormant Parts

The Tin Man is Activated to close off Julie's heart.

Activated Part

(You may remember that Chapter 2 showed a version of the psyche with only exiles behind this curtain. This was a simplification. Actually, any protectors that aren't activated will also be behind the curtain.)

Parts become activated according to external situations or internal memories or thoughts. If you are relating to a person or dealing with an event that seems dangerous to one of your parts, it will activate and take over your psyche to protect you. For example, Julie's Tin Man felt that it needed to protect her from her boyfriend's demands. It was afraid that if her heart stayed open to him, she would be swallowed up by his neediness and she wouldn't be able to end the relationship. So it stepped out from the group of dormant parts, took over the activated space, and closed off her soft, loving feelings.

Activation of a Part by a Situation

Julie perceives her boyfriend as needy and demanding.

The Tin Man steps forward and activates to protect Julie's heart from her boyfriend

Activation and Access

When you decide to access a part, it may already be activated at that moment, or it may be dormant. Access is done a little differently in each case. If you decide to access a part that is currently activated, like the Tin Man, it is relatively easy to do. You just feel into your body and emotions, you listen for voices, and you notice images. Access is like shining the flashlight of consciousness on that part.

Accessing a Part

Julie's Self shines the flashlight of
consciousness on the Tin Man.

However, even if a part is not activated, you can still access it and work
with it. You just need to activate the part first. A good way to do this is to
remember a recent time when it *was* activated and imagine that you are in
that situation now. Notice what you feel inside as you imagine this, and
also pay attention to images or voices. Or you can remember what you
usually feel like when the part is activated. For example, if Julie wanted
to access her Tin Man, she could think about the last time she was with
her boyfriend and he was needy, and then remember what she felt inside.

Activating a Part in Order to Access It

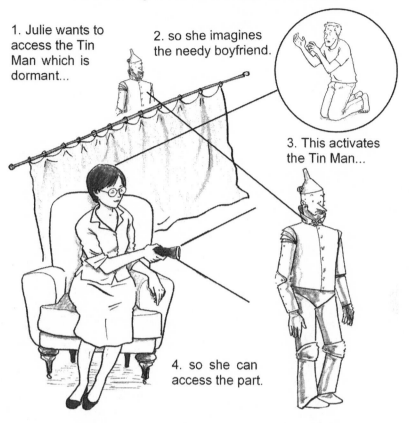

1. Julie wants to access the Tin Man which is dormant...

2. so she imagines the needy boyfriend.

3. This activates the Tin Man...

4. so she can access the part.

Activating a part in this purposeful way won't trigger it as fully as an external situation will, but it will activate it enough that you can access it. Sometimes it is actually easier to work with a part when it doesn't start out activated because the part's emotions won't be so intense that they flood you (see the next chapter for how to prevent flooding from happening).

Here is Jane's description of accessing a part that isn't activated at the moment:

Jane: This is a part that I encountered yesterday. I gave it the name of Deadbeat. It came up when my sister was judging me.

Jay: Remember what this part felt like yesterday when your sister was judging you.

I ask her to remember since clearly the part isn't activated at the moment.

Jane: (pause) Okay. Now I have a sense of it. I feel tightness in my neck, in the back of my neck up near my skull.

Jay: See if you have an image of that part.

Jane: A picture comes up of a skeletal head with big, bulgy, blackened eyes. It is mad, furious. It can hardly contain itself.

Jane has activated the Deadbeat Part through her memory of yesterday so she can access it now.

Exercise: Accessing a Part that Isn't Activated

Pick one of your parts that isn't activated right now. Imagine that you are in a situation in which the part is activated and notice how that feels. From that place, try accessing the part using each of the channels—feeling, body, image, and internal voice. Write down what you experience.

Name of part _____

What it feels emotionally _____

What it looks like _____

What it feels like in your body and where _____

What it says _____

However, remember that it isn't necessary to achieve access through all channels.

Accessing Parts from Current Experience

Often you start a session by accessing a part that you already know about, as in the previous examples in this chapter. However, sometimes you don't have a clear idea of what part to work with. You may be feeling something at the moment that seems important to explore, but you aren't clear about exactly which emotions or experiences are there; it might just be a muddle of feeling. IFS can help you sort this out. Frequently there is more than one part activated at any given time, so it is helpful to get a map of the territory by exploring your current experience to identify all the parts that are up. Then you can choose one to work with further.

Here is the procedure: Check inside, noticing your feelings, body sensations, images, and voices. One of these will probably come to your attention first. Use this experience to access a part. Then ask it to step aside so you can learn about the other activated parts. Then notice one of the other experiences and access the part that connects to it. Keep going in this way until you have accessed all parts that you find.

Georgia

Here is an example of accessing parts in this way. I asked Georgia to notice one part that she was aware of at the moment.

> **Georgia:** It started already when you were talking. It's a black sensation in my chest. And it is quite tense and rigid. And when I go more into it, there come these little shocks in my body related to fear.
>
> **Jay:** What does that part look like?
>
> **G:** Maybe there are two parts together. The fear seems to come from a part that is reacting to another part. The scared part doesn't seem to have this blackness itself. She seems like a little child, maybe four or five, and she is quite frightened.
>
> *She is correct that there are two parts activated, and she has now accessed one of them, the scared part.*
>
> **J:** Ask that part if it would be willing to step aside so you can access the other one.
>
> **G:** Now it has stepped away, and another part is here, an attacker. It seems as if it is outside me, standing in front of me. There's a pressure in my third eye (on the forehead).
>
> **J:** See if an image arises of that part.
>
> **G:** Male, huge, totally black, strong.
>
> **J:** Ask that part to step aside as well.
>
> **G:** I see an opening up in my third eye, light coming in. It seems to be comforting me in the face of the attack.

Georgia has accessed three parts that are up in that moment—a scared child, a black attacker, and a comforting light (which could be Self). This gives her a sense of the inner forces that are influencing her.

Walter

Here is Walter's experience of accessing parts in the moment:

> **Walter:** I notice poison oak burning on my neck. And I feel very irritated.
>
> *The burning sensation is not from a part. That is just his body's reaction to poison oak, purely physical. However, the irritation is probably a part's emotional reaction to the burning sensation, so I ask him to focus on that.*
>
> **Jay:** How do you sense the irritation in your body?
>
> **W:** It feels like a pressure in the trunk of my body.
>
> **J:** What does that part look like?
>
> **W:** It's like someone smashing things. It's feels good for him to be able to express how irritated he is.
>
> *The "him" that Walter is referring to is the part.*
>
> **J:** See what other parts are there.
>
> **W:** At the same time, there's a sense of not taking him (the irritated part) overly seriously. A sense of allowing, acceptance of what's so. I have poison oak, and there's nothing I can do about it. It feels more like relaxation.
>
> **J:** And what does that part look like?
>
> **W:** Fat Buddha just sitting.
>
> **J:** Check for another part.
>
> **W:** This is a part that I got in touch with this week. It's a striving part. There's something wrong that has to be fixed, like the poison oak, and I have to stay at it. I have to make sure that it turns out a certain way. I have to make an effort. I can't rest. Always figuring the angle, how to do it better.
>
> **J:** Where do you feel this part in your body?
>
> **W:** I feel it in my head, kind of a narrow focus. Type A, anal retentive, tight part. I don't like this part. It doesn't fit my self-image, which is more easygoing.
>
> **J:** Is there an image for this part?
>
> **W:** An accountant at his desk, frantically working on his papers.

Walter has also accessed three parts—a man smashing things, a Buddha part, and a frantic accountant. This gives him a feel for his inner landscape at that moment.

Accessing Parts Activated in the Moment

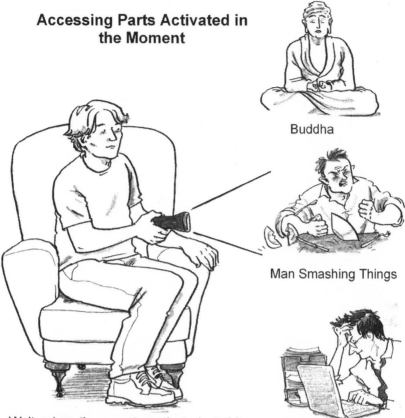

Buddha

Man Smashing Things

Frantic accountant

Walter has three parts activated at this moment, and he accesses them one at a time.

Exercise: Accessing Parts from Your Current Experience

Focus on your experience in the moment and access each of the parts you are aware of, one at a time. Use as many channels as you can. For each part, write down what you experience.

Name of part _____

What it feels emotionally _____

What it looks like _____

What it feels like in your body and where _____

What it says _____

Accessing Parts from a Trailhead

Earlier in the chapter, we discussed how to determine intellectually what parts are involved in a trailhead. When you begin to work experientially with a trailhead, you will become clearer about those parts and perhaps discover more. You can also start directly with an experiential exploration of the parts related to a trailhead. Here's how.

At any given moment, a trailhead may or may not be activated, just like a part. If it *is* activated, you will feel your reaction to it. When you want to explore a trailhead that isn't activated at the moment, imagine a recent time when that trailhead was active and notice how you feel inside. Or notice how you usually feel when that trailhead is activated. Then you can access all the parts related to it.

Check inside to notice the feelings, body sensations, images, and voices that are related to the trailhead. There will often be a number of experiences. Pick one that catches your attention and use it to access a part. When you have a sense of that part, ask it to step aside, then access the next, and so on.

Here is an example from Laura. She starts by describing the trailhead:

Laura: I'm staying in the house I built. I don't live there anymore since my ex and I split up. I'm traveling through the area, and my ex is gone and is letting me be here for a couple of days. This situation is stirring me up a lot.

The fact that she is "stirred up" indicates a trailhead.

Jay: Feel one of the parts related to this situation.

L: I'm feeling teary. I'm coming up for air just mentioning this, like I've been underwater. There's an impulse to speak, like a vibration all over my body, a tremulousness. Something wants to cry out, in a way.

J: Is there an image of this part?

L: What comes up is the Little Match Girl from Charles Dickens.

J: Okay. Check for another part.

L: I don't understand what part this is ... Well there's some feeling of strength here. A sense of being supported. I feel like my eyes are opening wider, and my head feels like it's listing a little. I'm hot and there's a vague sense of opening up, and a feeling in my body of mobilization for a fight, like an adrenaline rush.

J: What does this part look like?

L: A warrior with a helmet that comes to a sharp point, incisive, fierce. It wants to protect that little girl.

Laura has accessed two parts related to the trailhead of staying in her ex-husband's house. The warrior is, of course, a protector.

Exercise: Accessing Parts from a Trailhead

Pick a trailhead that is important to you in your life. If it isn't activated at the moment, imagine yourself in that trailhead situation or remember a recent time when you were. Notice what you feel in that situation. Access each of the parts you are aware of that are related to that trailhead, one at a time. Use as many channels as you can. For each part, write down what you experience.

Name of part _____

What it feels emotionally _____

What it looks like _____

What it feels like in your body and where _____

What it says _____

Focusing on a Target Part

Up till now, you've been learning how to access a part. Now you'll see how to use that ability to begin an IFS session. At the beginning of an IFS session, you may want to discuss an issue in your life or talk about some parts you are aware of. Pretty soon, however, this purely intellectual understanding ceases to be of much value. It is time to go inside and explore yourself experientially. Your goal will be to focus on one part to get to know in some depth (as you will learn how to do over the rest of the book). This is called the *target part*.

You have three options for going about this:

1. Start with a part you already know about and access it.

2. Access all the parts activated at the current moment and then choose one to focus on.

3. Start with a trailhead. Analyze it to see what parts are related to it and then choose one to access. Or access all the parts related to the trailhead experientially and then choose one.

Once you start working with a part, others may get activated that you must deal with. Sometimes you will continue to work with the original target part, and sometimes you will change your focus to one of them. This issue is discussed in detail in Chapter 9.

Noticing a Part in Real Time

It can be very useful to access a part in real time, at the moment when it is activated in your life. I use the term "real time" to refer to working with parts during the flow of your life as opposed to a scheduled IFS session.

At any point in the day when you notice that a part is activated, you can briefly access it and pay attention to how it is affecting you. This gives you information about how often it is triggered, under what circumstances, and how it affects your emotions, your behavior, and your life. For example, suppose your boss calls you into his office. Before he even says anything, you notice that your palms are sweaty and you feel anxious in your chest. This lets you know that a nervous part has been activated. You can briefly access it and find out that it is afraid of being judged by an authority figure. Or suppose you have to make an important phone call, yet an hour goes by and you realize that you've been busying yourself with other tasks instead of making the call. This lets you know that an avoidant part has been activated. You access it and find out that it is afraid of sounding stupid on the phone call.

Exercise: Noticing a Part in Real Time

Choose a part that is activated with some frequency in your life that you want to learn more about. _____

Over the next week, you will practice noticing when this part is activated. First think about which cues that will tip you off that it is activated. What body sensations, thoughts, or emotions will let you know it is up? For example, a tight stomach, revenge fantasies, or feeling teary like a child. _____

_____

What behavior will cue you that the part has taken over? For example, withdrawing from your partner, taking over a conversation, or eating too much. _____

What situations or people tend to activate this part? For example, meeting someone you are attracted to, giving a talk, or being disobeyed by your son. _____

When are these likely to occur during the next week? _____

_____

Set an intention to be especially aware of whether this part becomes activated during those times. Each time you notice the part is triggered, access it briefly and take down brief notes about it. If you can't stop at the moment to make notes, do it at your next break or as soon as you can. You want it to be fresh in your memory. At the end of each day, take a few minutes to review the day for moments when the part was activated. Add to your notes at this time. This daily review will also help you to keep this exercise in mind the next day.

Notes to take each time it happens:
Situation_____

How you experience the part_____
What about this situation triggered the part _____

Don't expect perfection. You probably won't catch all the times this issue is activated or be clear about what is going on each time. That is very difficult to do. You may be driving or trying to get a project finished or talking with someone, for example, so it may be difficult to be aware of much else. That is fine. Just do the best you can.

Summary

In this chapter you have learned how to access a protector experientially, which is the first step (P1) in getting to know it. You have learned how to determine what parts are related to a trailhead. You can access a part through emotion, image, body sensation, and inner voice. You know what it means for a part to be activated. You can work with a trailhead or with your current experience to access all the parts that are activated. You have learned how to allow a vague part to gradually become clear and how to choose a part to focus on. You have also learned how to notice a part when it is activated in real time. The next two chapters show how to access your Self so that you can work with a protector successfully.

Chapter 5

Becoming Centered

Unblending from a Protector

———— • ————

Sheila's husband was wrapped up in his work and not paying much attention to her. Then he forgot her birthday. That was the breaking point. She stood up and yelled, "You don't love me anymore! All you care about is your work. You spend all day in front of that *&?!*! computer and have no time for me. You are so selfish!" The Temper Tantrum Part of Sheila was activated. At that moment, she was so seized by it that she *became* the Temper Tantrum Part and lost access to her Self.

Sometimes we can stay in Self even though a part of us is angry. Sheila could have said, "I know he loves me, but he's not paying attention to me right now because he has a really important project with a tight deadline. He is a good man." The calmness and caring of her Self would have allowed her to relate to her husband in a reasonable way. She might even have reminded him about her birthday after asking him how his project was going.

Relating from Self

Sheila's husband is frantically working on a project, ignoring her birthday.

Sheila's Temper Tantrum Part is activated and enraged at her husband.

When Sheila's Self is in the seat of consciousness, she relates to her husband in a reasonable way.

The Seat of Consciousness

We can explain this in another way using the concept of the *seat of consciousness*. We each have a place in our psyche that determines our identity, choices, feelings, and perceptions. This seat can be occupied by Self or by a part. *Whoever resides in the seat of consciousness at any given moment is in charge of our psyche at that time.* Whether it is a part or the Self, the occupant of the seat determines how we feel, what our intentions are, how we perceive other people, how we relate to them, and what our choices and actions will be. This is a refinement of the idea from the last chapter that your activated parts determine your feelings and actions. At any given moment, all activated parts have some influence over you, but the occupant of the seat of consciousness has the overriding influence. It determines your dominant emotion and your actions.

We aren't necessarily aware of the occupant of our seat of consciousness at any given time. In fact, it tends to be invisible to us because it is the one who looks at other things. The occupant of the seat of consciousness is the one who is aware or conscious. We take it to be ourselves. It is the observer, or witness, and it wields the flashlight of consciousness. We are conscious of whichever part is illuminated by this flashlight, but it rarely gets pointed back toward the one who holds it. So we tend not to be aware of the witness. The witness sees but is not seen.

Ideally the Self is the occupant of the seat of consciousness. In Sheila's case, this would mean that the Self would be in charge of how she interacted with her husband. The occupant of the seat of consciousness determines how Sheila perceives her husband (as busy vs. uncaring), how she feels toward him (concerned vs. angry), how she acts toward him (reasonable vs. blaming), and what she is trying to accomplish in her interaction (connection vs. revenge). The seat of consciousness even determines your identity—that is, who you take yourself to be. For example, in this situation, if Sheila were in Self, she would take herself to be a connected partner to her husband, but if she were the Temper Tantrum Part, she would identify with being a victim who was being mistreated by him.

The Self is the natural occupant of the seat of consciousness because it is who we truly are. It is our essential nature, our spiritual center. This means that the Self occupies the seat of consciousness unless a part (such as Sheila's Temper Tantrum Part) takes over the seat and pushes the Self into the background. Then that part is in charge of your psyche for a while. This can happen in an instant and usually without our realizing it. However, as you will learn later, if you pay close attention, you can notice the shift and work with it. If the part steps aside, the Self will automatically occupy the seat of consciousness again.

At any given moment, you are identified with the occupant of the seat of consciousness. If the Self is in the seat, you are identified with Self. If a part has taken over the seat, you are identified with that part; that is who you take yourself to be in that moment. We don't usually notice these shifts in identity; we think we are always the same unitary personality. However, they happen all the time, and IFS will help you become aware of them.

Throughout the book, when I refer to "you," I am referring to the occupant of the seat of consciousness at that moment because that is who you think you are. Sometimes, this will be the Self; sometimes it will be a part.

In Sheila's situation, the Temper Tantrum Part took over the seat of consciousness almost completely, and the Self was pushed into the background behind the seat. Sheila became identified with the Temper Tantrum Part. In IFS terminology, this part *blended* with the Self, and the Self was no longer determining how Sheila related to her husband. She wasn't able to be separate from her anger, to understand her husband's behavior from his point of view, or to act in a reasonable way. She couldn't even talk about being angry. All she could do was act out the rage and denigrate him.

Relating from a Blended Part

Sheila's Self is pushed behind the Seat into the background.

Sheila's husband

Sheila's Temper Tantrum Part blends with Self (takes over the seat of consciousness) and yells at her husband.

Here is another way to understand blending. Think of the Self as a clear cup of water, calm and centered. If you put a teaspoon of instant coffee into the water, it immediately turns dark and smells strong. The coffee (part) has blended with the water (Self) and completely changed its appearance. The water is still there, but it is totally obscured by the coffee.

It is an hour later, and Sheila's feelings toward her husband have shifted. Now that she has calmed down, she is ashamed of how she reacted. "I hate it when I get that way. I know he loves me. He has just been really busy and distracted lately. I don't know what came over me. I wish that part of me that gets so enraged would go away." At this point, the Temper Tantrum Part is no longer blended with Sheila. That doesn't mean, however, that she is in Self, because now another part is blended with her. Sheila is judging her Temper Tantrum Part and wishing it would go away. This is coming from another part of her, not from Self. We know this because Self is open, curious, and compassionate toward each part as well as toward other people. It is never judgmental and never wants to abolish a part. Sheila has been taken over by a judgmental part.

This example shows the two most common ways we relate to our difficult parts—either we are blended with them or we judge them. However, neither attitude is helpful in getting to know a part and connecting with it. To do that successfully, you must be centered in Self so you can relate to the part with curiosity and compassion. In this chapter and the next, you will learn how to recognize these two attitudes and how to return to Self. This chapter explains how to recognize when the target part is blended with you and how to unblend and access Self. Chapter 6 shows how to recognize when you are blended with a part that is concerned about the target part and how to unblend from it.

Blending

A part is *blended* with you and has taken over your seat of consciousness when any of the following is true:

1. You are flooded with the part's emotions to such a degree that you aren't grounded. You are lost in those feelings. For example, if the part feels resentment, you are fully caught up in its anger without having any reflective distance.

2. You are caught up in the beliefs of the part so that you lose perspective on the situation. You see the world through the distorted perception of

the part. In addition, you aren't able to recognize that this is one of many perspectives—you simply see it as the truth. If the part believes that the world is dangerous, that is the way you see the world, without any thought that you might be projecting your own beliefs onto the world.

3. You don't feel enough of your Self. You don't have enough access to a place in you that is separate from the part from which to witness it and understand it. You have no center or ground.

Blending is a more extreme form of activation. Even when a part is activated to the degree that you feel its emotions and it influences you, you may still feel separate from it. You may be able to see that your emotional response is exaggerated or that your perspective is skewed. Imagine a scenario in which your boss tells you that you have to rewrite a report you submitted. You feel inadequate and a little depressed, but you still have enough perspective to recognize that this is a passing reaction. You have thought about the supervisor's criticism, and you understand what happened and can think through what to do in the future. Your inadequate part is activated, but you have some distance from it. It isn't completely blended with you. Your Self is still occupying the seat of consciousness, which allows you to see that you are basically competent. Even though you feel down, you know it will pass.

However, suppose you react to your supervisor differently. The criticism of your report stings, and you have barely walked out of the office before you are in a state of deep depression. You sit at your desk and throw the report into the wastebasket, certain that you are completely incompetent. You cannot see the feeling of inadequacy as something that will subside by tomorrow. You don't see the belief in your incompetence as just a belief. It is just the truth; you are incompetent. Your world looks bleak, and you feel terrible about yourself. Life seems hopeless, and you feel empty and listless. This indicates that the inadequate part is blended with you. It has taken over the seat of consciousness. Your Self is obscured.

Of course, blending is not a black-and-white affair. There are degrees of it. Like tea that has been steeped briefly, a part can be a little blended with you. You can have a great deal of Self available, a moderate amount of Self, or none at all. When there is partial blending, it means that the Self and the part are sharing the seat of consciousness; they both influence how you relate to others. If Sheila had experienced this, she would have been able to be somewhat kind and reasonable to her husband, though her attitude would have been tinged with anger.

Partial Blending

Sheila's husband

Sheila's Self and the Temper Tantrum Part are partially blended (share the seat of consciousness) and therefore both influence how she relates to her husband.

Requirements for Getting to Know a Protector

You must be able to deal with blending in order to successfully work with protectors. In Chapter 4, you learned how to access a protector (P1) and focus on it, which makes it the target part. In order to get to know it, you must be in Self with respect to that protector. Your Self must be in the seat of consciousness, and the part must be separate so the Self can shine the flashlight of consciousness on it and develop a relationship with it. This is an interesting experience of what is sometimes called "dual consciousness." You can feel both the part and the Self. Since you have accessed the part experientially, you can feel its emotions to some extent. However, at the same time your consciousness is primarily centered in Self. This combination provides extraordinary healing power.

Relating to a Part When Unblended

Sheila's Self is separate from the Temper Tantrum Part, so she can get to know it by shining the flashlight of consciousness on it.

However, if the part is blended with you, it has taken over the seat of consciousness and pushed the Self into the background. You have become the part, and you can't get to know it or interact with it because there aren't two entities. It takes two to have a relationship. If there is only the part, no relationship is possible.

Difficulty Relating to a Part When Blended with It

Sheila's Temper Tantrum Part has taken
over the seat of consciousness, so there is
no separate Self to relate to that part.

You don't need to be one-hundred percent in Self to work successfully with a part; you need to have a *critical mass* of Self available. You need just enough Self that you have a place to stand separate from the part. There must be more Self than part in the seat of consciousness. From this place, you can understand the part and help it. If you aren't in Self, you can't help the part because you buy its story too completely. To work with a part successfully, it is best if the part is activated but not too blended with you.

Step P2: Checking for Blending

The next step (P2) is to check inside to see if that part is blended with you. Here are some ways to do that:

How strongly are you feeling that part's emotions? If that part is angry at someone, how much do you feel that anger? For example, if you are in the middle of a fight with your spouse, are you screaming at her as Sheila was? Are you silently livid? Do you just *have* to tell her how horribly she is treating you? Or do you have some space from your anger so you can attempt to communicate in a way that is constructive?

How much do you buy into the part's perspective—its beliefs about you and other people? For example, if a part of you believes it is hopeless for you to ever find love in your life, how much do you accept that perspective? Have you given up on finding a satisfying relationship? Have you come to believe this is your lot in life? Or do you have some sense that this is just an irrational idea? In Sheila's case, how much did she buy into the Temper Tantrum Part's belief that her husband didn't love her?

How much are you centered in a place in you that is separate from the part, a place from which to witness the part's emotions and belief? Can you find an inner space that is larger than the hopes and fears of the part, a presence that is relatively calm and clear about what is happening? This is the Self occupying the seat of consciousness.

What you are feeling toward the part? Not what the part is feeling, but what you are feeling *toward* it, as if it were sitting in front of you. If you are focusing on a sad part and you feel sadness, that is the part's emotion. You need to know how you feel toward the sad part. Do you like it, appreciate it, judge it, hate it? Do you care about it? Are you curious to learn more about it? Or do you want to get rid of it? If you receive a clear answer to this question, the part probably isn't blended with you. If it is blended with you, it will be hard to answer the question. After all, if you *are* the part, it will be hard to feel something *toward* it. Sometimes just asking this question serves to help you unblend from the part because you must step into a separate place in order to answer it. This question is also crucial to step P3 in the IFS process in Chapter 6, so it serves a double function. We will revisit this question then.

Sometimes just inquiring into whether a part is blended with you creates enough separation that you can work with it, but at other times you must do more in order to unblend. If the target part is not blended with you, go on to Step P3 in the next chapter. If it is blended, continue with Step P2 by unblending from the part. There are a variety of approaches to doing this.

Asking the Part to Separate

Ask the part to separate from you so you can get to know it. It is important to understand what this means. You aren't asking the part to go away. In fact, you want to connect with the part and understand it. But in order to do that, you must be separate from it. It takes two to relate. You can't have a relationship with a part if there is only one of you. So you are asking the part to separate enough that you have a place to stand from which to connect with it. Parts generally understand this, and they are willing to separate once they see what they will get from this—someone to understand them. There are other ways to phrase this request, if you prefer. You can ask the part to contain its feelings or to not flood you with them. You can ask the part to move out of your body. You could ask the part to move over and allow space for you to be there, too.

Let the part know that you are asking the part to separate from you just for the next few minutes in this session, not for good. You aren't asking it to take the gigantic step of giving up its emotions or beliefs. You certainly aren't asking it to transform; that takes a whole session or series of sessions. You can explain to the part that it can blend with you again after the session is over, if that is what it wants. All you want right now is a little space from it so you can become acquainted with it.

This is a request. The part may say no. If there is no change in your inner state, that means that the part hasn't separated. In this case, ask it, "What are you afraid would happen if you separated from me?" Most likely the part is afraid that in creating the space, it will give you the opportunity to push it away or ignore it. Many of our parts feel alienated from us because we have never taken the time to get to know them. We *really have* pushed them away and tried to disown them. The only strategy they know for being seen and heard is to blend with us. Explain to the part that you want to get to know it. In fact, that is *why* you want some separation—so you can relate to it. This will reassure the part so that it is willing to separate.

Sometimes a part won't separate from you because it is afraid you will do something unwise if it does. It believes it is protecting you from taking a dangerous or foolish action. For example, recall the Food Controller part from Chapter 2. It might be afraid that if it unblended, you would go on a chocolate binge. Explain that you just want the separation for a few minutes during this session, and reassure it that you won't do anything foolish. You're not asking it to give up its protective role; you just want some space to get to know it.

This usually works. Just having this more extended conversation with a part helps to create separation.

Other Ways to Unblend

If the part won't separate from you, you can separate from it. You can take a more active role in creating the separation and accessing Self. There are a number of possibilities for doing this.

Moving into Self

You can create an experience of separation inside yourself so you feel your Self as different from the part. You might experience this as moving back from the part into a grounded place, or shifting into the stance of a witness, or moving deeper inside to a centered presence. Some people sense this as a stepping back away from the part *into* themselves. One way to look at this is that you are moving the seat of consciousness back from the part so that the Self can occupy the seat.

Visualizing the Part as Separate

Allow a visual image of the part to arise. This will give you the sense of it as a separate entity. This approach is even more effective if the part is clearly a certain distance away from you. The further away it is, the more separation this creates.

Another way to accomplish visual separation is to draw or paint an image of the part. Or you can choose an object from your home that represents the part for you or find an image of it in a magazine or on the Internet. Having a concrete token of the part helps to create separation.

Finding an Opposed Part

Look around inside for a part of you that is the opposite of the target part or a part that is in conflict with the target part. For example, Sheila might locate a part of her that wants harmony with her husband no matter what. She would access that part and hear what it has to say. This would help her to realize that there is more to her than the Temper Tantrum Part. She would then find a place inside her that is neither the Temper Tantrum Part nor the Harmony Part. This is likely to be Self.

Self Meditation

Let go of your focus on the target part for a moment and guide yourself in a meditation in which you become grounded and present in your body. If you are familiar with meditation, you can use whatever form works for you. If you aren't, you can use the following as a guide. This should be read slowly with many pauses. If you are working with a partner, you could ask her to read it to you.

Sit quietly with your spine relaxed but straight. Close your eyes and focus your attention on the sensations in your body. You might notice tension in your shoulder or pressure behind your closed eyes. There might be a sensation of warmth in your chest or fullness in your belly. Take your time and notice whatever body sensations come to your attention. These will probably change from moment to moment. As you notice each sensation, take some time to feel it and be present with it in that moment. If you notice your attention wandering away from your body, gently bring it back, without judgment. Don't worry at all if this happens more than once. Without judgment, bring your attention back to your body each time.

After a while, allow your attention to move down into your belly. Be aware of the sensations in your belly. Or even just sense the physical presence of your belly. Relax into this. Allow this to calm you and center you. Be with your belly for a while in a soft, open way. Allow your sense of yourself to deepen.

As time passes, become aware of the sensations in your chest, in your heart. Allow your heart to soften a little, to open as much as seems right at this time. Let your heart be open to all your parts, feeling compassion for them and their struggles and pain. Welcome each of your parts and extend a tendril of connection to them from your heart.

When you are located solidly enough in Self, end the meditation and return your attention to the target part. See if you now feel separate from it.

Feel free to vary this meditation according to your preferences and your experience with similar guided meditations. Use what works for you. A short Self meditation like this can also be used at the beginning of a session before you access any parts. Many people use a meditation like this in order to start every session in Self.

Once you are unblended from the target part, move on to Step P3 in the next chapter.

Transcript to Illustrate Unblending

This is a session with Ben, a student in one of my classes. He is a 45-year-old Canadian teacher who is the oldest in a large family. He has a history of drug addiction but has been sober for many years. He starts out talking about a conflict he had with his sister. One part of him sees her as being at fault because of being controlling and unable to see anyone else's perspective. I suggested that he begin the session by going inside and getting to know that part.

> **Jay:** Take a moment to focus on the part that believes your sister is at fault, and notice how you sense that part in your body.
>
> **Ben:** Okay. I have some sensations. I feel quite calm, clear … There's also a lot of distress in my shoulder from a part that says, "You've got it all wrong."
>
> *No sooner has Ben started to access the part that is critical of his sister, when a second part emerges with the opposite perspective. This is quite common.*
>
> **J:** I see. There's a part that says you've got it wrong about your sister.
>
> **B:** Yeah. "You probably need to try harder. You're kidding yourself." This is a familiar part that causes me to doubt myself.
>
> **J:** Would you like to stay with the part that is critical of your sister or focus on the self-doubting part?
>
> **B:** The Doubting Part seems much more important.
>
> **J:** Okay. Are you feeling separate from that part, or have you become that part?
>
> *I ask him to check for being blended with that part.*
>
> **B:** It's hard to say because I go back and forth between the two parts. It might be that the Doubting Part is a bit blended with me, because when I'm with my family, I'm often confused.
>
> *It is probably true that Ben is blended with the Doubting Part when he is with his family. However, that isn't what matters now. What is*

important here is whether he is blended with that part at the moment. So I ask about that.

J: But is that happening right now?

B: Yes. It is a little.

J: Okay. In order to keep checking about this issue of blending: When you are doubting yourself, do you sense enough Self that you could get to know the Doubting Part?

B: Well, actually I do.

J: Alright. So we'll go a little further. Check to see what you are feeling toward the Doubting Part now.

This is another check for blending, and it will also lead to Step P3 if he isn't blended.

B: I've had a pretty long struggle with self-doubt.

J: That is important to know about your history with self-doubt. But in this moment, how do you feel toward that part.

We want to know if he is in Self right now, so the question is about the here and now.

B: Well, I feel unsteady ... I just realized that I am doubting my ability to do this process, so I think I'm blended with that part. So I will ask the Doubting Part to separate.

This is a good recognition by Ben, to see that he is blended. And from what he has learned in class, he knows to ask a blended part to separate from him.

J: Yeah. Go ahead and do that. Ask that part to separate so you can get to know it.

B: Okay. I've got an image ...

J: Do you have a sense of it being willing to separate from you?

B: No. This part doesn't trust that I would be safe if it separated.

J: Ah.

B: If I stop self-doubting, it thinks I will get into some kind of trouble.

J: Let the part know that we aren't asking it to stop doubting you. We are just asking it to separate from you enough that you can get to know it.

The part has misunderstood what we are asking it. Giving up its doubting role would be quite premature. It just needs to be separate from Ben in the moment.

B: Okay. That is easier.

J: Is it willing to do that?

B: Yeah.

J: So check and see what you are feeling toward that part right now.

Now that he has some separation, I return to the other way of checking for Self.

B: Neutral. Somewhat curious. A little bit guarded.

It seems that he is now separate enough from the Doubting Part that we can move on to step P3.

This transcript shows how to recognize when you are blended with the target part and how to unblend.

Exercise: Unblending from the Target Part

Do a short IFS session with a part that is blended with you at the time. There are three ways to do this:

1. When you are starting the session, see if there is a part blended with you. Choose that as your target part.

2. If there is a part that is blended with you a lot and you know what external events tend to trigger it, arrange to do a session on a day when it is likely to be activated and blended with you.

3. Do a session on the spur of the moment when a part is blended with you. Practice unblending as discussed in this chapter. Then go ahead and get to know the part a little. Ask what it is feeling or what it is concerned about. Ask it what it wants you to know about itself.

If you are working with a partner, do this exercise with your partner. See Chapter 16 for advice on how to do this. You may also want to try it on your own.

Noticing When You Are Blended

Once you have unblended from a protector and started to get to know it, it may blend with you again later in the process. As the part is telling you its story, it may take you over, which means you become the part without being aware that this is happening. It is good to notice this as soon as possible so you can return to Self.

How can you become aware of blending as the process goes on? Watch for the same kind of experiences as when you initially checked for it. Are you starting to become emotionally heated? Have you bought into the part's beliefs and worldview?

There are two additional clues to recognizing that a part is blending as it is telling its story.

1. You start speaking *as* the part rather than reporting, in the third person, what the part is telling you. Instead of saying, "The part feels upset with my sister," you say, "My sister is a bitch." You have become the part rather than looking at it.

2. You start telling a detailed story about a person or event from the part's perspective. You go off on a riff and get lost in the details of events; you have lost any sense that you are hearing from a part or even exploring yourself. You are just explaining what happened or how someone has treated you. You have gotten emotionally pulled into the story and can't view it objectively.

Here is an example of how this might have happened in the session with Ben. He is getting to know the part of him that is critical of his sister.

Ben: This part is upset and judgmental of my sister for the way she communicates with me.

Jay: Okay. Ask that part to tell you more about what it feels.

B: It is angry at her for being so controlling. She always has to have everything her own way. The part is scared that she will take me over. The other day she wanted to move our mother into assisted living, but I didn't agree with that. She couldn't hear me at all. She felt that I was dictating to her, when all I was doing was expressing my opinion. (*Now his voice changes and he grows increasingly annoyed.*) That really upset me. I just wanted to offer my perspective on the best way to deal with Mother and she acted as if I was trying to dominate her. That is so typical.

Notice that Ben has switched from reporting on the part's feelings to expressing them as his own. He is saying "I" rather than "it."

B: She has always been this way. Whenever I have an opinion, she thinks I'm trying to control her. And what ends up happening is that she does exactly what she accuses me of: *she* controls *me*. That really annoys me, but I don't want to fight, so I just shut up and agree with her. Two weeks ago ...

The part of Ben that feels critical of his sister has taken over and is complaining about her. He's not listening to the part or exploring himself; he's just complaining. Self is nowhere in sight.

As soon as you notice that a part is blended with you, stop and reflect. Use one of the methods in this chapter to unblend. Then return to asking the part to tell you about itself while you listen for its answers.

Exercise: Daily Parts Check-In

For the next week, take a little time each day to check in with your parts. Notice which parts are activated at that moment as you learned to do in Chapter 4. By doing this regularly, you will get used to paying attention to your inner family. Plan a certain time each day to do this exercise. Some people prefer to do it first thing in the morning, others at night before they go to bed. Make a list of each part that is activated at that time. For each one, fill in the following answers, if you know them:

Name of part _____

What it feels _____

What it looks like _____

Where it is located in your body _____

What it says _____

How it makes you behave _____

Don't be concerned if you don't know all this information about the part. Just fill in what you can.

Summary

In this chapter, you have learned what it means for a part to be blended with you by taking over the seat of consciousness and how this will interfere with the rest of the IFS process. You now know how to determine if you are blended and how to unblend from the part and access Self. You can ask the part to separate from you and, if needed, you can reassure it that the separation will allow you to get to know it. You can also move directly into Self in a variety of ways. This is Step P2. You have also learned how to recognize if you become blended later in the process.

Please note that I am teaching IFS as a step-by-step procedure in this book. This is a good way to learn the method, but don't feel bound by it. When you have finished the book and have practiced enough that you really understand the model, you can let go of the steps and work intuitively, if you prefer.

Chapter 6

Being Open and Curious

Unblending from a Concerned Part

———————— • ————————

Suppose you were approached by someone and she invited you to open up and reveal yourself to her. If you sensed that she was angry at you or judging you, would you open up? Of course not. What attitude would you need in a person you were going to confide in? I would want her to be genuinely curious about me, interested in knowing who I am from my perspective, without any agenda. I would want her to care about me and my emotions, certainly not be bored or indifferent.

The same goes for your parts. They need you to be openly curious and caring about them. That means being in Self. They can usually tell if you feel negatively toward them, and frequently they won't show you much about themselves if you do.

In the last chapter, we met two parts of Sheila. Her Temper Tantrum Part was enraged at her husband when he forgot her birthday, and a different part of her judged her for getting angry. The last chapter dealt with how to unblend from parts like the Temper Tantrum Part. This chapter deals with how to unblend from parts like Sheila's judging part. This is a second form of unblending—where you separate from parts that feel negatively toward your target part.

Step P3: Checking to See if You Are in Self

Let's assume that you have accessed a part to focus on, and you are separate enough that you aren't blended with it. Now ask yourself how you feel toward this target part right now. Not what you *think* of the part or how you feel *about* the part. This is likely to bring up an evaluation process—is it helpful or harmful, familiar or unfamiliar? This is not what we are looking for. Instead, check to see how you *feel toward* the part, how you are relating to it, what your attitude is toward it. Do you like the part or hate it? Do you appreciate it or judge it? Do you want to banish it? Are you afraid of it? Are you curious about it? Are you feeling removed from it?

Don't concern yourself with how you feel toward the part in general or at those times when it is activated. The question is how you feel toward it *right now*. It is important to understand that you are not checking to see what that part feels; you are checking to see how you feel *toward* it. It can sometimes be tricky to distinguish between a part's emotion and your feeling toward it. For example, when you check to see how you feel toward a sad part, you find that you feel sad for it. There are two possibilities: It could be that you are experiencing the part's sadness. Or it could be that you are feeling pity or compassion for the part. For this step in the IFS process, we want to know about the pity or compassion, or whatever else you are feeling toward the part.

The purpose of this inquiry is to discover whether you are in Self with respect to this part. A key principle in IFS is that all parts are welcome. This means we need to be genuinely open to getting to know each part from a curious and compassionate place, which will encourage it to reveal itself. This stance is not always easy to come by. If a part has been causing you problems, it would be natural for you to be angry with it. It would be understandable that you might judge it and want to be rid of it. If the part has actually done things that were dangerous, it wouldn't be surprising for you to be afraid of it.

However, approaching a part with these attitudes won't lead to healing and reconciliation. The part probably isn't likely to trust you or open up. Therefore, in IFS you don't try to get to know a part unless you are in Self, which means that you feel open to the part and want to understand it from its own point of view. From Self, you are interested in what makes it tick, how it sees the world, and what it is *trying* to do for you. You can sympathize with the part's need to avoid pain and protect you from harm.

93

This is profoundly different from the way we usually approach our parts. It derives from the spirituality implicit in the IFS model. We approach all our parts with love and a desire to understand them. The Self reflects the deep interconnectedness of spiritual reality. It knows that, despite appearances, our parts care for us, and it cares for them.

When you ask yourself what you are feeling toward the target part, if you notice curiosity, openness, compassion, acceptance, or something similar, you are in Self, and you can proceed to the next step, P4. If you notice anger, judgment, fear, or anything negative, you aren't in Self. But don't worry—you aren't doing anything wrong. It just means there is another part that is blended with you which is feeling the anger, judgment, or fear. I will call this the *concerned part* because it has concerns about the target part. It is fearful or worried about what kinds of problems that part will cause.

When you are blended with a concerned part, it's like this. You are trying to get to know a new friend, and a third person keeps jumping in between you, taking over the conversation, and judging your friend. For example, remember that after an hour, Sheila judged her Temper Tantrum Part and wanted it to go away. This judgment was coming from a concerned part of Sheila, not her Self. When she explored inside, it looked like a Judge in a courtroom.

Concerned Part Blended with Self

Sheila's Judge has blended with her (taken over the seat of consciousness) and is relating judgmentally to the Temper Tantrum Part.

Concerned Parts

A concerned part is a part that has a negative feeling toward the target part, or any feeling other than those of the Self (curiosity, compassion, and so on). Concerned parts are aware of the ways that the target part is causing trouble in your life. They may be concerned that it alienates you from people, for example, or makes you feel worthless or cuts off your emotions. Naturally, they don't like the part that is doing this. However, if a concerned part is blended with you, it means *you* feel this way, and it prevents you from approaching the target part from an open and compassionate place—from Self.

In general, a target part can be either a protector or an exile. In this chapter, we are working with protectors, so the target part will be a protector. A concerned part is also a protector. It is worried that the target part will do something to cause you pain, and it wants to protect you from that. So in this situation, we are working with two protectors, the target part and the concerned part. The target part wants to protect you from pain in its way, and the concerned part wants to protect you from the pain caused by the target part's extreme behavior.

For example, Sheila's Temper Tantrum Part (target part) is trying to protect her from feeling hurt by her husband. It wants to confront her husband in an attempt to make him remember her birthday in the future, so she won't be hurt again. The tantrum also serves to distract Sheila from her hurt. Her Judge (concerned part) wants to protect her from the pain of the marital fights caused by the Temper Tantrum Part. If only this part would quiet down and stop causing confrontations, everything would be all right. This is a common occurrence—two parts are protecting you from two different things and are at odds with each other.

I have now presented two classifications of parts—protector and exile, target part and concerned part. Let me clarify. Parts are intrinsically either protectors or exiles, depending on whether they are in pain or protecting against pain. Either one of these can also be a target part. That simply means you have chosen to focus on it. And any protector can also be a concerned part if it has concerns about your target part.

In some cases, you may have a mix of attitudes toward the target part. For example, you may feel open and curious, and you may also feel distant and guarded. This just means that some of your attitudes (open and curious) are coming from Self, and some (distant and guarded) are coming from a concerned part. In this case, the concerned part is *partially* blended with Self. The Self qualities are showing through, but the part is also there. You still need to unblend from such a concerned part until there is enough Self to proceed to the next step in the IFS process.

If you aren't sure whether you are in Self, ask yourself if it is all right for the target part to show up any way it needs to. Do you have a fixed view of the part? If you do, it means you aren't openly curious about it. This tips you off that a concerned part has taken over that has an agenda for the target part; it needs to see the target part in a certain way. For example, suppose you are getting to know a protector that gets enraged at certain people, and you are visualizing the part as a monster. You check to see if it would be all right with you for the part to see itself in some other way that is perhaps more benign, such as a powerful sword fighter. You realize that you would object to this, which helps you realize that you are invested in seeing it as a monster. This is a clue that you are blended with a concerned part that has judgments about the enraged part.

Don't just try to force yourself to have the "right" attitude toward the target part. Now that you know the Self attitudes you are looking for, it can be tempting to just adopt that stance, to *try* to be curious and compassionate. However, this may simply mask what you are really feeling. Take the time to really check inside to see what your *actual* attitude is toward the part. Then, if necessary, you can unblend in order to access Self. This is a sure way to get there.

Step P3: Unblending from a Concerned Part

When you ask how you are feeling toward the target part, if you have a non-Self attitude, you need to return to Self before you can effectively get to know the target part. Otherwise, the non-Self attitude will undermine your relationship with it. The part probably won't reveal much of itself to you, or it won't give you permission to work with the exile it is protecting. If it doesn't trust you, it won't cooperate with you.

However, remember that all parts are welcome in IFS. This includes any concerned parts. You don't want to push them away either. It is best to hear from a concerned part briefly—get to know what it's worried about—and then help it to unblend from you, so that your Self is available. The concerned part doesn't have to go away or change what it feels. It just needs to unblend from you enough that you can be open and curious about the target part. This is a continuation of Step P3.

Here's how to begin this process. Access the concerned part, and ask what its worries are. Listen respectfully to what it has to say. Find out about its negative attitudes toward the target part, and be open to understanding why it holds them. Make sure to let it know that you have sympathy for its concerns. It is more likely to let go if it feels heard—if it believes that you understand why it doesn't like the target part.

Then ask if it would be willing to step aside so you can get to know the target part from an open place. You can reassure it that you're not banishing it, just asking it to give you a little room. Alternatively, you can ask it to relax, step back, stand down, separate from you, go into a waiting room, or any other phrasing that seems right. Or you could ask it to allow you to get to know the target part from a curious, open place. For example, Sheila asks the Judge why it feels judgmental and ashamed of her Temper Tantrum Part. It says that the Temper Tantrum Part causes trouble in her marriage with its attacks and intense emotions. She says, "I completely understand why you feel that way, but could you step aside and allow me to get to know the Temper Tantrum Part from an open place?"

Keep in mind that you are *asking* the concerned part to step aside, not *pushing* it aside or *making* it step aside. This means that it may say no, and you must be open to that. IFS makes this easy to do because there is always a way to continue working with a part that says no. This is covered in the next section below.

If the concerned part stands down, check again to see how you are feeling toward the target part now. You may notice that you are feeling open or accepting or one of the other Self qualities. For example, if Sheila's Judge agrees to step aside, she may now feel openly curious about what drives the Temper Tantrum part.

Concerned Part Stepped Aside

Sheila's Judge has stepped aside...

allowing Sheila to relate to the Temper Tantrum Part from Self.

However, in some cases you may notice another non-Self feeling, another negative attitude toward the target part. This indicates that there is a second concerned part that is blended with you. In this case, repeat the procedure with this part. Find out its concerns, and ask it to step aside. Continue until all concerned parts have stepped back and you are in Self.

If you aren't sure whether a concerned part has stepped aside in response to your question, check to see if your feeling toward the target part has changed. If you feel less judgmental and more open to it, or if you notice a shift in your body (more openness or relaxation) this means the concerned part has stepped back. If your negative attitude toward the target part is unchanged, that means the concerned part hasn't stepped back.

What to Do if the Concerned Part Won't Step Aside

It is important that you *ask* the concerned part to step aside rather than *making* the part step aside. IFS is a cooperative venture. We never make parts do anything. We never battle with them. We don't have to. Since they have our best interests at heart, we can easily become acquainted with them and learn how to cooperate with them. Since you are making a request, not a demand, it is fine for the part to refuse. It may say no to you directly, or there may be no change in your feelings toward the target part. This is not a problem. You can take further steps toward unblending, which can be summarized as follows:

1. Explain to the concerned part the value of stepping aside. Parts have their own intelligence and are open to reasoning.
2. If it still won't, ask it what it is afraid would happen if it did, and reassure it that you can handle whatever it fears.
3. If it still won't, make the concerned part the target part and work with it.

Let's look at these steps in more detail.

1. Explaining the Value of Stepping Aside
Explain to the concerned part why it would be helpful for it to relax. It is concerned about the target part causing you trouble, so explain that when it steps back and allows you to get to know that part, you will be able to

heal it so that it won't be a problem anymore, which is exactly what the concerned parts wants. This helps the concerned part to realize that by stepping aside and allowing you to proceed along this healing track, it is fulfilling its own agenda. For example, if Sheila's Judge won't step back, she could explain that if it allows her to get to know the Temper Tantrum Part from an open place, she can heal that part so it won't keep picking fights with her husband. Once a concerned part understands this, it is usually willing to step back. If it does, remember to check to see how you are feeling toward the target part after it does. This is to make sure you are in Self and to notice any other concerned parts that are around.

You may not be ready to say that you can heal the target part because you are just learning IFS, and you don't yet know how healing works. Here is what you can do. Explain to the concerned part that IFS has a method for healing parts, and even though you haven't learned the whole method yet, you are planning to heal the target part when you do know how.

2. Reassuring the Concerned Part

If the concerned part is still not willing to step aside, there is more you can do. Ask the concerned part what it is afraid would happen if it did. Take some time to fully understand its fears and empathize with them. Concerned parts are usually afraid that if they give the target part an inch, it will take you over and be stupid, destructive, or dysfunctional. For example, Sheila's Judge might be unwilling to step aside because it is afraid that the Temper Tantrum Part will overpower her and start a nasty fight with her husband (see Illustration 5.2). Once you have really heard the part's fears, let it know that you understand.

Consider this: Suppose you were concerned that someone you love was going to do something dangerous or destructive, and you were preventing this by your protective presence. You wouldn't be willing to step aside unless you felt that he really understood your concerns. Otherwise, how could you trust the outcome? If you relaxed, all hell would break loose. Instead, you would want him to guarantee that those destructive actions wouldn't happen. Our concerned parts feel the same way. In IFS, we respect the reasons parts have for what they are and aren't willing to do. That's why we don't try to coerce them. We want to help them trust us and work with us. We know they want the best for us, and they will cooperate once they understand what we intend to do and why, and we reassure them about their fears.

Therefore, once you understand the concerned part's fears, reassure it that you will handle the situation safely. Explain that you won't allow the target part to take over—that you will be in Self and in charge during the session. Sheila's Judge was afraid that her Temper Tantrum Part would take over and start a fight with her husband. She could explain that she won't let that happen. She will stay in Self (Illustration 5.1), where she has the maturity to know not to talk to her husband about her birthday when she is angry at him.

Furthermore, explain to the concerned part that if the target part does blend with you, you have ways of returning to Self (which you learned in the last chapter). Assure the concerned part that you are only asking it to step back for this session. After that, it can blend with you again if it believes it must do so to keep you safe. For example, Sheila's Judge can take over after the session if it is still concerned that she will pick a fight with her husband. If the concerned part really wants to be heard, then reassure it as follows: "After you step aside so I can get to know the target part, I will spend some time getting to know you as well."

If the concerned part has other fears, reassure it about them, too. No matter what concerns it has, you can always reassure it about them because it wants the best for you and because the IFS process is safe and will lead to a healing outcome.

If the concerned part is leery about leaving, ask if it would be willing to let you experiment with getting to know the target part from an open place, and see what happens. It is welcome to stand nearby and watch from the sidelines so it can jump in and protect you if this seems necessary. This is often reassuring because the part doesn't have to give up its protective role completely. It just needs to give you room to relate to the target part with an open heart, but it can still stand guard.

3. Changing Target Parts

If the concerned part still won't step aside, it clearly needs some concentrated attention to assuage its fears. Therefore make *it* the target part. Change your focus from the original target part to the concerned part and get to know it fully. For example, if Sheila's Judge really won't stand down, she can make it the target part. She puts all her attention on it and finds out about its role in her psyche. Being concerned about the Temper Tantrum Part is only one aspect of the Judge's story. What is its larger role? Maybe it generally protects her from getting into fights. Maybe it is a champion of doing what is right. She might discover what exile it is protecting.

Changing Target Part

Sheila turns her attention toward the Judge to get to know it. She will get back to the Temper Tantrum Part later.

It is probably a good idea to start by checking how you feel toward this new target part to make sure you are in Self with respect to it. As you proceed in this vein, you may end up doing a complete session on this part. That is fine. It will be just as valuable to work with this part as with the original target part because it probably plays a significant role in your life. You can always return to working with the original target part in a future session. Alternatively, once you have gotten to know the concerned part more fully and it has begun to trust you, it may step back and allow you to return to working with the original target part, but now from Self.

Transcript

The following is a transcript that illustrates many points about how to unblend from a concerned part. Lisa is a 56-year-old graphic designer from the Northeast who is the older of two sisters. There is a big gap in age between the two sisters, and Lisa ended up mothering her baby sister in many ways. Lisa has explored herself extensively over the years, especially through art therapy. She starts out by identifying a target part that she would like to work with. She mentions that other parts of her are ashamed of this part.

Lisa: It's a part that hates my little sister. Every once in a while it comes up with outright hatred. It wants to wring her neck. Intensely negative.

Jay: Take a moment and sense that part in your body.

L: Yeah. It lives in my stomach, like a little black demon, covered with chimney soot. It says "Grrrr."

Lisa has accessed the part (P1).

J: Okay. Do you feel separate from that part?

L: Not completely. It's part of why I'm interested in it. When I feel it, I'm not completely separate from it.

J: You don't have to be *completely* separate from it. You just have to be separate enough that there's a Self there that can get to know it. Is that the case?

Lisa may be mixing up activation of a part with being blended with a part. That's why I ask this additional question.

L: Somewhat, yeah.

J: Okay. That sounds like enough unblending to go on, and if it turns out that it's not enough, we can always return to this step.

It looks as though she is not too blended with the part (P2).

J: Check right now to see how you're feeling toward this Sooty Part that hates your sister.

L: Somewhat frightened.

J: Okay. Then there's a part that is frightened of that Sooty Part.

This is a concerned part.

J: Ask the part that is frightened if it would be willing to step aside for now so that you can get to know this Sooty Part from an open place.

L: That part is willing to step back half an inch. It's right over my shoulder, very close because it is absolutely sure it will have to leap out any moment now and protect me from this Demon. It's like these two go together.

This concerned part has stepped aside a little bit, but not enough for us to proceed in getting to know the Sooty Demon.

J: OK. This part is on guard to protect you from the Demon.

L: Yes.

J: What would this part like to be called?

L: The Watcher. This part is fixated on that little Demon. Its sole purpose is to keep a bead on the Demon. The Watcher doesn't know me very well at all.

J: Yeah, it doesn't trust that you can handle things.

L: It can't even turn to look at me. It has to keep fixing its gaze on that little Demon or it thinks all hell is going to break loose. The Watcher hardly even sees me. It's just muttering to me out of the side of its mouth. It's quite sure that its job is very, very important.

Notice that part of the reason why the concerned part won't step aside is that it doesn't know the Self. The Watcher is partially blended with Self, so they are sharing the seat of consciousness, but it isn't really aware of Self. We need more unblending for the work to proceed.

J: Let the Watcher know that if it allows you to get to know this Demon, you can heal that part so it won't be so dangerous.

L: I need to take a minute here ... Well, that certainly got the Watcher's attention. It turned and looked at me for the first time. It has an incredulous look on its face, like: "Are you serious?" And it plops itself in a chair, saying Okay. It hasn't completely gone away, but it's amazed that I would even think of getting to know that Demon. It's quite intrigued.

J: Is it willing to allow you to try that out and see how it goes?

L: Yeah, definitely. Because once it swung its gaze on me, it realizes that it's quite tired of its job.

Sooty Demon

allowing Lisa to take the seat of consciousness.

The Watcher steps aside and relaxes...

Now that the Watcher is aware of Self, it can relax its guardedness, and that allows it to realize that it is tired of its role. This is a crucial shift for protectors.

J: With the Watcher stepped aside, check and see how you're feeling toward the Sooty Demon now.

One concerned part has stepped aside, so we check again.

L: I feel even more frightened. Now that the Watcher has stepped aside, the fright has elevated, actually.

J: It sounds like there is another part there that's frightened of this Sooty Demon. That part was somewhat kept safe because of the Watcher, but now that the Watcher has stepped back, this new part is really frightened. Is that right?

L: It's exactly what I'm noticing. It is a wide-eyed, very good little girl in a pretty little dress who is scared that the world is going to come apart.

Here is a second concerned part.

J: Ask that Little Girl if she would also be willing to step aside so that you can get to know the Sooty Demon.

L: Yes. She is willing. She's a bit wide-eyed, but she steps back right away.

J: Good. Check and see how you're feeling toward the Sooty Demon now.

L: I have some apprehension in my tummy, but I'm quite intrigued now. Quite interested and open. My tummy is beginning to feel like a little bit of excitement as well.

J: Does that seem like enough Self, or do we need to ask the apprehension to step aside.

L: Let's see ... That's interesting. The apprehension comes from another part. It feels like a tried, harried, overwhelmed mother who has fallen short. She is overwhelmed and incapable. I took care of my little sister when we were kids. I tried to be a mother to her. That Mothering Part is very tearful, very sad.

This isn't a concerned part, since it doesn't have negative feelings toward the Sooty Demon, but it is another part that has feelings toward her sister. It would be useful to work with this part at some point, but right now we are focused on the Sooty Demon, so we ask it to step aside so we don't get sidetracked.

J: Mm hmm. Ask that Mothering Part if she's willing to step aside so you can get to know the Sooty Demon from an open place.

L: That part is very willing, and I can tell that at another time she would very much like my attention.

J: Good.

L: I'm touched. I feel a lot of compassion toward her, a strong response.

J: Good. You can let her know that you'll work with her another time.

L: Yeah. That seems important.

J: Check and see now how you are feeling toward the Sooty Demon.

L: (Laughs) Funny thing to say. I like it.

J: It sounds like you are understanding and maybe even appreciating what the Sooty Demon is trying to do for you.

L: Yes. That's what has changed here. I still feel the intensity of the dynamic, but I admire that little Tasmanian devil rather than seeing it as something that's going to make a big mess. Wow! It's a buzz saw that's incredibly effective. It has a mission.

Now that Lisa is seeing the Sooty Demon through the eyes of Self, it looks like a Tasmanian devil, which is a little animal rather than a demon. When she was seeing it through the eyes of the Watcher, from a place of fear and judgment, it looked quite evil. Now, through the eyes of the Self, from a place of compassion and curiosity, she can see the part for what it really is. It is fairly common for images to morph like this.

Tasmanian devil

Lisa sees the part through the eyes of Self,
allowing it to assume a more benign form.

Lisa has now completed step P3 and can move on to P4, which you will see in Chapter 7.

107

Other Types of Concerned Parts

Concerned parts usually feel judgmental or angry toward the target part. However, they can have other attitudes as well. In this section, we discuss how to work with these concerned parts.

Sometimes positive feelings can interfere with your being in Self. If you admire the target part to such an extent that you lose sight of how it is causing you problems, you are not in Self. For example, suppose you have a part that is really angry at your boss and is creating a lot of drama at work. You start to explore it, and when you check to see how you feel toward it, you realize that you love how it stands up to your boss. You have lost sight of the fact that it could cost you your job, and this means you aren't in Self. Ask this admiring part to step back.

Sometimes a concerned part is frightened of the target part. If it can't step aside, as Lisa's did, there are a couple of ways to make this easier. You could ask the scared part to move into a safe, comfortable room while you get to know the target part. This may reassure it enough for it to leave. You can also visualize the intimidating target part in a room where you are seeing it through a window, which provides containment. It lessens the fear that the target part might spontaneously attack.

Exercise: Unblending from a Concerned Part

Choose a protector that you don't like or have concerned feelings about. For example, you might judge it or be angry at it or want to get rid of it. You also might feel distant from it or scared of it. These attitudes come from a concerned part of you. First access the protector (P1), and then unblend from it, if necessary (P2). Then practice unblending from the concerned part (P3), as you have learned to do in this chapter. Then go ahead and get to know the protector at least a little (P4). Even though we haven't covered this step yet, you probably have some idea about how to do this. Ask the part some questions to learn about it and its role in your life. Use the Help Sheet below to guide your steps. Refer to the sheet after each step to help you know what to do next.

If you are working with a partner, I recommend that you do this exercise with her. (See Chapter 16 for tips on how to do this.) This recommendation holds for each chapter from now on. Most people find the work easier to do with a partner. In addition, when you commit yourself to a session time with your partner, you are more likely to follow through.

The next page contains a Help Sheet which is a summary of the steps for getting to know a protector. It is meant to guide your steps while you are working on yourself or partnering with someone. I recommend you use it in doing the exercises in each chapter from now on.

Help Sheet 1: Getting to Know a Protector

P1. Accessing a Part

If the part is not activated, imagine yourself in a recent situation when the part *was* activated. Sense the part in your body or evoke an image of the part.

P2. Unblending Target Part

Check to see if you are charged up with the part's emotions or caught up in its beliefs right now. If so, you are blended. Check to see how you feel toward the target part right now. If you can't tell, you may be blended. If you are blended with the target part, here are some options for unblending.

- Ask the part to separate from you so you can get to know it.
- Move back internally to separate from the part.
- See an image of the part at a distance from you or draw the part.
- Visualize the part in a room to provide a container for it.
- Do a short centering/grounding meditation.

If the part doesn't separate, ask what it is afraid would happen if it did.

Explain to it the value of separating and reassure it about its fears.

P3. Unblending Concerned Part

Check to see how you feel toward the target part right now. If you feel compassionate, curious, and so on, you are in Self, so you can move on to P4. If you don't, then unblend the concerned part:

- Ask the concerned part if it would be willing to step aside (or relax) just for now so you can get to know the target part from an open place.
- If it does, check again to see how you feel toward the target part, and repeat.
- If it isn't willing to step aside, explain to it the value of stepping aside.
- If it still won't, ask what it is afraid would happen if it did, and reassure it about its fears.
- If it still won't, make the concerned part the target part and work with it.

P4. Discovering a Protector's Role

Invite the part to tell you about itself. The part may answer in words, images, body sensations, emotions, or direct knowing. Here are questions you can ask the part:

- What do you feel?
- What are you concerned about?
- What is your role? What do you do to perform this role?
- What do you hope to accomplish by playing this role?
- What are you afraid would happen if you didn't do this?

P5. Developing a Trusting Relationship with a Protector

You can foster trust by saying the following to the protector (if true):

- I understand why you (do your role).
- I appreciate your efforts on my behalf.
- I know you've been working very hard.

Exercise: Keeping Track of Your Parts

Look at the list of parts you made in Chapter 4. Add to this list all the new parts you have discovered since then, with descriptive paragraphs for each. Add information to the descriptions of the old parts, reflecting anything new you have learned about them since then. For each part, include the following information (if you know it):

Name of protector _____

What it feels _____

What it looks like _____

Where it is located in your body _____

What it says _____

How it makes you behave _____

What it wants _____

What situations activate it _____

What concerned parts react to it _____

Other information _____

Each time you do a session or exercise, add to your list and descriptions.

Summary

In this chapter, you have learned to check how you are feeling toward the target part to determine if you are in Self. If you have a non-Self attitude, it means a concerned part is blended with you. You have learned to unblend by asking the concerned part to step aside, which is Step P3. If it is reluctant, you know how to reassure it so it will. You have a Help Sheet to use in keeping track of the steps during exercises. Now you are solidly in Self and can get to know the target protector in the next chapter.

Chapter 7

Knowing Yourself

Discovering a Protector's Role

———————— • ————————

No matter how much pain or dysfunction you have to deal with in your life, every part of your psyche is doing its best to help you. This may sound strange. If you are depressed or lonely, if you have outbursts of anger that distance you from others, if you always pick the wrong person to fall in love with—how it could possibly be that all your parts are doing their best for you? If they're all trying to help, why are you having such problems?

That's what you will discover in this chapter. Each of your protectors has a role to play. You will find out what each one is trying to do for you from its own perspective. (Of course, it might be misguided, but that doesn't mean it isn't doing its best for you.) Protectors believe they must perform their roles to prevent you from being harmed, even if this inadvertently gets you in serious trouble. Knowing this will help you to understand and have compassion for them—and ultimately to transform them. When that happens, their positive qualities will shine through and they can take on a new role that is *truly* in your best interest, working in harmony with the rest of your inner system.

In your progression through the steps of an IFS session, you have now accessed a protector and unblended so that you are in Self. You are now in a position to become acquainted with this protector successfully.

Working with a Part the IFS Way

In most forms of therapy, when you want to work with a part (or a psychological issue or reaction), you either analyze it intellectually or dive into it emotionally. Let's look at each of these possibilities in turn. (I will discuss this in terms of parts, even though many systems of therapy don't recognize parts explicitly.)

In some forms of therapy, you figure out your reactions or emotions by relating them to what you know about your psychological makeup. For example, if you have a part that feels angry whenever you are evaluated by people, you might remember that your father was very judgmental and assume that this part's emotions come from that history. Or you might know that you are insecure about your self-worth and assume that this insecurity gets triggered when you are being evaluated.

This intellectual approach is a good first step, and it can provide important information, but since it is based on guesswork and theory, it can't give you a full, nuanced understanding of a part. And even if your guesses are right, it will be difficult to heal the part since you aren't in direct contact with it. Full transformation requires direct experience of a part and a trusting relationship with it, something we will see clearly as the book unfolds.

Other forms of therapy take the opposite approach. They ask you to *become* the part so you can work from inside it. In IFS, this is called blending, which we discussed in Chapter 5. You fully embody the part and feel all of its emotions. If it were a lake, it's like diving right into the water. Let's look at that previous example, where a part grows angry when you are evaluated. Using this approach, you would inhabit that part experientially, sensing it in your body and maybe even expressing the anger that it feels. The idea is that you can learn most about a part by allowing your insights to flow from your experience.

This can be quite effective, but there is a downside. You run the danger of getting lost in the part (being blended with it) and buying into its beliefs. Not only do you dive into the lake, but you are pulled under by strong currents. For example, you might end up believing that the person who evaluated you really *was* being judgmental and that anyone would react the way you did, ignoring the fact that you overreacted. A second difficulty with this immersion approach is that when you dive into a part, it is easy to lose direct contact with the healing, compassionate presence of Self which is so important in the therapy process.

In IFS, we do something different from either of these approaches. First we inhabit the Self and then get to know a part by asking it questions and listening to its responses. We don't dive into the lake; we sit at the edge of the lake with our feet in the water, looking into its depths. We also don't just spin intellectual ideas about the part, which would be like taking photographs of the lake from an airplane. Instead, we are right there and truly listening to what it has to tell us without falling into its deep waters and getting lost. We are learning about its feelings experientially, but from the vantage point of the Self.

It is best to have your eyes closed and be free of distractions for this work and, in fact, for the entire IFS session. This allows you to feel your body, see images, and hear internal dialogue more clearly. As the session proceeds, you will naturally go deeper inside yourself into a state of consciousness where you are removed from everyday concerns and thoughts, and able to contact your parts more easily and fully. This permits you to access unconscious parts that you normally aren't aware of.

Step P4: Discovering a Protector's Role

In this step in the IFS process, you find out about the protector's emotions, concerns, and beliefs, and the role it plays in your life. And you are open to whatever else the protector wants you to know about itself. If you happen to have a protector that is fully accessed and eager to talk to you, you can just invite it to tell you whatever it wants. However, you need to prompt most parts with specific questions, especially at first. I often start out by asking a protector to tell me about its feelings or concerns. Or if I already know something about the part, my first question may be based on that. For example, if I know that a part feels insecure, I might start out asking it what makes it feel insecure or what it feels insecure about.

Here are the most basic and useful questions to ask a protector with examples of the protector's answers in *italics*.

- What do you feel?
  I feel suspicious and judgmental.

- What are you concerned about?
  I am concerned about people turning on you.
- What is your role? What do you do to perform this role?
  I check people out carefully to see who can be trusted and who can't.
- What do you hope to accomplish by playing this role?
  I want to make sure you only open up to people who are safe.
- What are you afraid would happen if you didn't do this?
  I'm afraid you would be betrayed.

There are many others helpful questions you can ask. Here are some examples:
- What makes you so angry? (Or sad, depressed, and so on?)
  I am angry about people abandoning you.
- How do you relate to people?
  I tell them when they aren't treating you well.
- How do you interact with other parts?
  I fight against the part of you that tries to please people.
- How do you feel about getting sad? (Or any other emotion?)
  I think it is childish and stupid.
- How do you feel about reaching out to people? (Or any other external event or action?)
  I am frightened of it and want to avoid it.
- What do you want?
  I want to be safe from criticism.
- What emotions are you afraid would come up if you didn't play your role?
  I'm afraid of overwhelming grief.
- How long have you been performing your role?
  Since age 7.
- What caused you to take on this role, and when?
  I took it on when I sat on the stairs and realized that I would never get what I wanted from my parents.
- How do you feel about your role?
  I'm very tired of it because it doesn't really seem to work half the time, but it has to be done.
- What do you want from me?
  I want you to appreciate how hard I work for you.

Don't feel obliged to ask all of these questions. Often you only need to ask three or four to find out about the part and its positive intent. When the protector gives an answer that piques your curiosity, follow it up. For example, if the part says, "I want to keep you safe," you might ask, "What do you want to keep me safe from?" However, don't come off like an interrogator. Instead of pushing it, allow time for its answers to unfold naturally and just insert questions when needed to facilitate the process. Permit the part to reveal itself to you in its own way. Sometimes parts need questions to help them do this, and at other times they will do it without assistance.

So far I have discussed becoming acquainted with a part using the internal voice channel. However, this is not the only way. You can also use body sensations, emotions, or images.

Body and Emotion

You can use body sensations or emotions to get to know a part. You can sense the part in your body or tune in to its emotions. A part might feel like buzzing excitement in your solar plexus, in which case you can ask what it is excited about. A protector part might feel like a tense holding in your mid-back, giving you a sense that it is protecting you from attack or holding back anger. You might sense that a part feels wistful sadness, and the meaning of this will gradually unfold as you focus on it.

When sensing the part in your body, you might want to notice the details of the felt experience, such as its size or shape. Is it a small tube or a large ball? What are its boundaries like? Is it amorphous or well defined? You might notice what it seems to be made of—rubber, iron, fluffy cotton candy, ice, fire. There many other qualities you can notice. Is it warm or cool, dense or spacious, bubbling or stuck? Each of these qualities will give you more information about the part. For example, if your head feels like fluffy cotton candy, this might indicate that the part is causing you to space out so you can't see clearly. If your heart feels frozen like ice, it might mean that the part is closing off the heart so you won't be hurt. If your belly is shaky, it might indicate a part that feels insecure.

Image

You can also learn about a part visually by allowing an image of it to arise in your mind. For example, you see the part as a gigantic ogre with a scowl on his face, which tells you how powerful and menacing it appears to you. You might see an image of the ogre attacking people who threaten you. This is a visual representation of an angry protector.

Look for specific details in the image. What clothes is it wearing? What expression is on its face? What is its body posture? How far away is it from you? Is it facing you or someone else? What is the part doing? What color is it? You may see the part interacting with other people or other parts, or taking certain actions in the world. You can invite it to show itself to you by acting upon an inner stage, which gives you a detailed understanding of its role in your life.

As you become more fully acquainted with the part, its image may go through permutations. It may change its facial expression, or its activity, or how it is relating to you. Its size, color, or age may shift. For example, a part may start out as a little girl who is dressed in gray, who is frowning and curled up in a ball. As she realizes you are there in Self and she begins to connect with you, she may suddenly be wearing bright colors. She might sit up, look at you, and smile. In some cases, a part may transform into a completely different image. For example, after this part has been healed, she might appear as an older girl in a sparkling jumpsuit who is happily running around.

Direct Knowing

Sometimes you understand a part without explicitly using any of these sense channels. You just know something about it, not through your ideas about the part, but through direct knowing. For example, you focus on a part, and right away you know that it feels mistrustful. It doesn't tell you this in words, and you don't feel it emotionally, you just know.

Multiple Channels

Many people interact with their parts using more than one channel. They may see an image of a part that is accompanied by body sensations and emotions, and the part may also tell them about itself in words. For example, with the little girl dressed in grey, in addition to the image of her, you may feel her sadness and sense her resignation in your body, and she may tell you how unhappy she is. In some cases, you may ask a part questions in words, and it will respond in images or body sensation. Be open to receiving communication from the part through whatever channels it uses.

When a Part Is Vague

Sometimes a part is not clear at first. It starts out as a vague image or felt sense—for example, "folded over on itself." You get to know a part like this by staying with your experience in a patient and curious way. Don't push for clarity prematurely. If you are open and interested, the part will know that it is welcome, and the nature of it will become clearer in the course of a few minutes. For example, "folded over on itself" might gradually reveal itself as a part that is curled up to protect itself from attack.

You might feel a vague emotion, such as a sense of poignancy, or you might sense a narrowing in your chest or an empty place in your body. When the sensation or image isn't entirely clear at first, it simply means that your access to the part is still in the process of forming. Some of the most interesting parts start out this way. The practice of Focusing[1] is an excellent method for allowing parts to gradually come into view.

This process of clarification can happen slowly in stages. Take your time and the part will gradually emerge, like the development of a photographic image in a darkroom. For example, what started out as an empty place might begin to include an experience of feeling unsatisfied. Then you might sense that it is in your belly. Over time it might show itself as an empty sack needing to be filled. Finally, it might reveal itself as a child who needs nurturing because she feels empty inside.

---

[1] Ann Weiser Cornell, *The Power of Focusing*.

Names for Parts

It can be useful to have names for your parts. Since your goal is to develop a relationship with each part, giving it a name enables you to keep track of it over time. The name can be a descriptive phrase, such as the Controlling Part or the Sooty Demon. It could be a person's name, such as Walter. It could be the name of a character, such as the Tin Man; a famous person, such as the Buddha; or a mythical being, such as Athena.

Instead of imposing a name on a part, let it name itself. That way, the name will reflect how the part sees itself rather than how you see it. For example, you might see a part as the Monster, while it might see itself as the Warrior. If you keep referring to it as the Monster, it may feel judged and close down its communication with you. It is best to get to know a part as *it* understands itself because your view of it may be biased by your judgment of it, and therefore you won't learn what the part is trying to do for you. You goal is to understand the part from its perspective.

Sometimes the name of a part will change over time as you get to know it better, just like the image. Allow this to happen. Let the name change anytime that feels right so the name reflects your new understanding of the part or how the part has transformed. For example, suppose the sad little girl in gray started out being called the Resigned Part. After she transforms to the older girl in the sparkling jumpsuit, she might be called Jazzy Girl.

A Protector's Positive Intent

As you get to know a protector through this process, it is crucial to find out its positive intent. What is trying to do for you? How is it trying to protect you? This may come out naturally in the process of revealing itself to you, but sometimes you need to ask specific questions to discover its intent. One such question is: "What are you trying to accomplish by performing this role?"

The most potent question is: "What are you afraid would happen if you didn't perform your role?" This is powerful because the protector believes it must protect you from a dire event or the eruption of some kind of pain. That is why it feels it must perform its role no matter what. The answer to this question tells you what the part is protecting you from or what it is protecting an exile from. Don't ask what the part *thinks* would happen if it didn't do its role. Don't ask what *would* happen. Either question is likely to prompt an intellectual answer about consequences, not about the part's motivation. For example, suppose you have a part that becomes enraged when someone tells you what to do. If you ask what *would* happen if you didn't express rage, you might hear, "You wouldn't have so many fights." That is undoubtedly true, but this answer is probably coming from a rational part of you, not from the enraged protector. The key question is: What is it *afraid* would happen? Suppose you ask the enraged part what it is *afraid* would happen if it didn't become enraged when you are given orders. It might say, "I'm afraid that you will be controlled by other people and become just a puppet on a string." That's why it believes it must protect you with its rage. That is its positive intent—the answer you are looking for.

Notice that this answer points toward the particular exile that is being protected by the enraged part, probably one that already feels that it is being controlled like a puppet. Most likely it was treated that way in childhood, and the feeling of victimization has persisted—hence the need for protection. So this particular question will provide information about the exile as well as the protector that is its guardian.

Two Kinds of Protection

As you explore the positive intent of protectors, you will discover that they protect in one of two ways.

1. External Protection. Some protectors try to keep an exile from being harmed by other people, like the enraged protector mentioned above that wants to prevent the exile from being controlled. These protectors see the exile as vulnerable and unable to protect itself. Consequently, they will take whatever actions they think are necessary to keep people from harming it.

2. Internal Protection. Some protectors try to protect *you* from feeling the emotion an exile carries, such as an intellectualizer that keeps you in your head to numb emotional pain. These protectors close you down or distract you to block out the pain or trauma that the exile feels. Or they may try to provide you with comfort or pleasure or self-esteem, to override the exile's suffering.

Both types are protecting exiles, but they have two very different relationships with the exile. Protectors of the first type care about the exile and want the best for it, so they try to protect it from the world. Protectors of the second type think that the exile is dangerous because it might flood you with pain, so they judge it and push it away.

Understanding Our Enemies

Because some protectors cause us serious problems, we often see them as "bad"—as enemies to be expunged from the psyche. For example, an inner critic part reproaches you for every little thing you do and makes you feel inadequate and worthless. It might criticize your social skills, intelligence, appearance, or competence. All it ever seems to do is attack you and make you feel bad about yourself. When you see what this part is doing, you may want to get rid of it. A second example is a protector that you view as downright evil, such as one that lashes out in harsh ways or explodes in rage. This can get you fired or create a huge rift in your family.

However, once you get to know any protector, no matter how destructive it is, you discover that it isn't your enemy after all. It is trying its best to protect you from harm or pain, and when you realize this, you soften towards it. You understand that the protector is simply misguided and doesn't know any other way to protect you from what it sees as horrendous suffering. This helps you to understand it and have compassion for it. We will see this in the next segment of transcript of Lisa and the Sooty Demon.

Imagine what it would be like to see other people in this way too—as well meaning at heart but sometimes misguided. We would understand that even our worst enemies are driven by parts of theirs that are just trying to protect them from shame, fear, and other difficult feelings. We could soften towards them despite how onerous their behavior has been. We could feel compassion for difficult and destructive people in our lives. Furthermore, imagine what the world would be like if we could all feel this way toward our international enemies, the people in the world who threaten us, and those politicians we judge most harshly. Perhaps if we began to genuinely see their good intent and relate to them with understanding, they could trust us enough to respond in kind.

Lisa and the Sooty Demon

Let's see some examples of step P4. We will continue the session with Lisa from the last chapter as she gets to know the Sooty Demon Part, which hates her little sister. We pick up at the point where Lisa is clearly in Self with respect to this part.

Jay: Invite that part to tell you about itself, and especially how it feels toward your little sister.

Lisa: It seems like a little Tasmanian devil, and when I allow it to show itself, it starts whirling, like a little attack thing. It says "Grrr" and latches onto my sister's leg tenaciously.

J: You might ask the Sooty Demon what it does to your sister.

L: It would like to judge her and attack her, but I don't let it do anything outwardly. It just makes me feel really angry at her, but I don't express this to her.

J: Okay. You might ask the Sooty Demon what it is trying to accomplish by attacking your sister.

L: It seems like it does this to protect my heart. It's a protective action. It fearlessly throws itself into the fray. Specifically with my sister, it does this because my heart has no defense against her. It can't close itself off to her because I love her.

This tells us something about the part's role, which is to attack her sister. The Sooty Demon believes that its anger acts as a barrier to keep Lisa's heart from being wounded by her sister's judgments. It is interesting that she says she has no defense against her sister. To me, that means there is no protector that can shut down her love for her sister, which means that some exile is very open to her sister and vulnerable to being hurt. She is calling this exile her heart. Since this Heart Part is so vulnerable and no other protectors arise, the Sooty Demon comes forward to protect it.

J: Yes. You might ask the part what makes it want to attack your sister.

L: If my sister turns toward me with a sharpness or a hardness, it calls up this little attack Demon.

J: To protect your heart?

L: Specifically to protect my heart. Yes.

She's actually referring to her Heart Part here.

J: Ask the part what it is afraid would happen if it didn't attack your sister.

L: My heart would be really wounded by her.

J: Yes. Your heart would feel deeply wounded.

The Sooty Demon tries to protect Lisa's Heart Part from being broken by her sister's sharp remarks.

Lisa now has a good understanding of the Sooty Demon. At first it looked like a really nasty part, but now she sees that all along it has been looking out for her welfare. We will continue this session in the next chapter.

Ben and the Self-Doubt Part

Let's continue Ben's session with his Self-Doubt Part which questioned his perception about his sister and doubted his ability to do the work. We pick up at the point where Ben is clearly in Self with respect to that part.

Jay: Invite the Self-Doubt Part to tell you what its concerns are and what its feelings are.

Ben: Well, Self-Doubt says my instincts aren't good, so it has to question any impulse or thought I might have.

Now that we know what the Self-Doubt Part does—drives a wedge between Ben and his instincts—I move on to finding out about its motivation for this.

J: Okay. You might ask what it is trying to accomplish by questioning your thoughts and impulses.

B: To stop me from acting on my own impetus. So I will always check out external information before I act. It says whatever it is I'm thinking is probably wrong.

J: Ask that part what it's afraid would happen if it allowed you to just act on your impulses.

This question aims to uncover the threat that the part is trying to protect him from.

B: I'm getting a different answer than the last time I had a conversation with Self-Doubt, actually. Less worried. It doesn't think things will be as catastrophic as it did before I started this kind of work. I guess what I'm sensing is, "Yeah. You will screw up for sure, but you won't lose everybody in the process." The part is saying it's not the end of the world.

It is nice to know that the part has relaxed somewhat as a result of the work he has already done.

J: The fear has to do with losing everybody. Is that right?

B: I think that might be at the bottom of it.

This answer seems to be coming from an intellectual part of Ben, not from the Self-Doubt Part, so I have him check with the part directly.

J: Ask the part. See what it is most afraid of.

B: Yeah. It's afraid of my doing really stupid and destructive things and alienating people. "You'll get out of touch with what is sensible and safe."

J: You'll do dangerous things?

B: Yeah. I was doing a lot of drugs about twenty years ago, and I did some really impulsive things. I got myself into trouble. I hurt some people I was close to.

J: You might ask the part if that's what it is afraid of.

B: Yeah. The part thinks that it could happen again at any time. It wants to make sure that it doesn't—ever.

J: Okay. This part wants to protect you from that.

B: Yeah. From being seen as out of control and harmful.

J: Yeah. And it believes you are on the edge of that, just as you were twenty years ago.

B: It says, "It's happened once, so you always have to be careful. You're a bad risk now." So it won't ever trust me again.

This part's fears are fairly typical of a protector. It is stuck in the past and doesn't realize that Ben has matured a great deal and has been drug free for a long time. Because of its distorted perception of him as immature, it believes it must go right on protecting him.

B: So in Self, I feel some compassion now. This part has been awfully worried, has been working very hard to spare me the trauma of getting impulsive and crazy again.

This is good news. Now that Ben understands what the part is trying to do for him, he feels caring for it.

Christine and the Confuser

This is a section of the transcript of Christine's session with the Confuser from Chapter 3 that you have already seen. The Confuser makes Christine feel fuzzy, confused, and distracted. We pick up at the point when Christine has gotten into Self.

Jay: Invite that part to tell you or show you more about what it feels.

Christine: It says that it feels sleepy and dull. I can sense that it goes blank.

J: It feels dull and blank.

C: Yes. It says, "I want to go to sleep. I don't want to be awake or conscious." Sometimes it can't answer people's questions.

J: Mm hmm. Ask the part what its name is or what it would like to be called.

C: I get the word *Confuser*.

J: Okay. We'll call it the Confuser. Ask it what it is trying to accomplish by being sleepy and confused.

I pose this question to discover the Confuser's positive intent for Christine.

C: It says, "I don't want to see something. I don't want to know something." This part has to conjure up unclarity and confusion, blandness. It wants to make sure that I don't know what is going on.

J: It creates confusion to protect you from whatever is going on ... You might ask the part *how* it creates confusion and not knowing.

C: Various ways. It internally changes the subject; it takes my attention away; it looks or acts very agitated, so there is no settling or landing in one place. It draws attention to itself and therefore away from whatever else is there. All those ways. Now the part looks like a person who is making magic signs in the air to create confusion and distraction.

J: OK. Ask the Confuser what it is afraid would happen if it stepped aside and allowed you to see things.

C: What it says is: "What would happen is just unthinkable, unspeakable." It is so frightened, we can't even go there.

J: I see, so it is very frightened about this.

C: At a survival level.

J: Yeah. You might ask the Confuser how long it has been doing this job.

C: It feels like forever.

J: How does it feel about its job?

C: It's a completely impossible job, overwhelming. Yet it is unable to stop.

Christine has now gotten to know the Confuser and understood something about what it is trying to protect her from. All this time, it has been trying to safeguard her from something that it finds absolutely terrifying. Christine doesn't know what it is (I know, however, that it is an exile), and the Confuser doesn't want her to know. It uses confusion to keep her from being able to clearly seek the truth. If she did, she might actually find this exile, and the Confuser believes she can't handle the trauma. We will continue this session in Chapter 8.

Exercise: Getting to Know a Protector

Choose a protector to get to know. Do a session in which you follow all four steps you have learned so far, P1-P4. Use the Help Sheet from Chapter 6 to keep track of the steps. If you are working with a partner, the partner should also follow along on the Help Sheet. When you are finished, write down what you learned about the part:

Name _____

What it feels _____

What it looks like _____

Where it is located in your body _____

What it says _____

How it makes you behave _____

What situations activate it _____

What concerned parts react to it _____

What its positive intent is _____

What it is protecting you from _____

Other information _____

Ending an IFS Session

Whenever you are ending a session, it is a good idea to take a moment to connect respectfully with the parts you have worked with and bring closure to the work. It's like saying good-bye to a friend at the end of a visit. This allows you to separate without leaving any parts hanging. You also find out if there are any loose ends or unresolved feelings that you must deal with in future sessions. And it strengthens your relationship with the part. Here are some suggestions.

Thank the target part for making itself known to you. If the work was only partly finished, let it know that you will come back to work with it more. This will reassure the part that you won't forget about it. Ask if it wants anything from you over the next week or so, and remember to provide whatever it asks for. For example, it may ask you to stay in relationship with it. If you have completed the work, let it know that you will check in with it later to see how it is doing.

Thank any concerned parts for stepping aside and allowing you to do the work, and, if appropriate, see how they feel about what has happened. This helps confirm that you aren't just going to ignore parts that you ask to step aside.

See if any parts need to say anything before you stop. You don't want them to feel cut off when the session ends. This also gives you a chance to discover what might be unfinished. For example, a part might say that it is frightened about something that happened and needs attention soon. That way, you know to work with it in the next session.

See if you want to say anything to any of your parts. This is an opportunity for you to acknowledge and strengthen your relationship with a part. For example, you might want to tell the target part that you admire its courage.

If you have worked with a protector and it has given you permission to work with an exile (this is covered in Part II), thank the protector and see how it feels about the work you have done with the exile. This lets the protector know that you are still connected to it, and it gives you an idea of whether the protector approves of the work you are doing.

Working Through Avoidance of the Exercises

Some people decide that they want to do the exercises as they read the book but don't follow through. If you are stuck in this way, it would be helpful to explore what is going on inside you. Why might you want to do something and then not carry through? Often this happens because a hidden protector doesn't really want to do the exercises. In other words, even though a part of you has decided the exercises would be beneficial, another part of you is balking. This might be a protector that is afraid that if you follow through with an exercise, you will encounter strong emotions that you can't handle. Or it might be a protector that doesn't think you will benefit from this work and so doesn't want to bother. This avoidant protector is clearly in control (since you aren't doing the exercises), even though it may be unconscious.

The best way to handle this situation is to commit to doing a session in which you work with this avoidant protector. In this session, check inside for a felt sense of not wanting to do the exercises. You may even feel resistant to the session you are engaged in right now. You might want to get up and leave, or tell yourself that you don't have time, or generally feel uncomfortable. Tune in to that feeling of resistance. It might feel like stubbornness or annoyance or defiance. You might sense apathy or anxiety. Whatever it is, this feeling will give you access to the avoidant part. Then continue through the IFS steps to get to know this part. See what you can discover about why this part doesn't want you to do the work and what it is afraid would happen if it allowed you to.

Then see if you can reassure this protector that its fears won't come true, just like you might reassure a concerned part. For example, you might explain that you aren't going to dive into overwhelmingly painful emotions, and you won't allow any dangerous parts to take over. Assure it that you will stay in Self while you become acquainted with your parts.

For this reassurance to be effective, you may need to develop a trusting relationship with the avoidant protector, which is covered in the next chapter. However, even one short session with an avoidant protector can make a big difference in your willingness to do the exercises. If you do such a session but your avoidance doesn't change, it is possible that there is more than one avoidant protector. Do another session in which you check for others and work with them.

Since you are avoiding doing sessions, it may be difficult to do even this session on the avoidant protector. You might keep making excuses instead of doing it. One way to make this session happen is to schedule it with a partner. If someone else is counting on you to be there, it makes it harder to avoid. Or you could do this session with an IFS therapist, who might help you get at deeper issues behind your avoidance.

Finding Out about Protectors in Real Time

If you are doing a session at a time when a protector isn't activated, it may not be very accessible, making it hard to find out much about it. For example, if you decide to work with an angry part at a time when you aren't feeling angry, it may be difficult to get in touch with it. Often this problem can be solved by imagining yourself in the kind of situation that activates that protector, as we discussed in Chapter 4. For example, to work with that angry part, you could imagine being with someone who irks you.

However, if this doesn't work, there is another way to learn about this protector. You can wait until it really *is* activated in real time. Set an intention for yourself to notice when this part is triggered in the course of your life. (See Noticing a Part in Real Time in Chapter 4.) When this happens, take some time *right then* to become acquainted with this part. If you are in the middle of an activity or you're in an environment that doesn't allow this, then take that time as soon as you can. You might do this when a conversation has ended, or at your next work break, or that night. If you don't wait too long, you will find that the part is still within reach.

The same thing applies to trailheads. Sometimes you are aware of a trailhead that you want to work on—an issue you are concerned about in your life—but you aren't sure what parts are involved. It all seems a little vague. It can be useful to learn about these parts in real time, as they are activated in your life. This is when their feelings will be most obvious. Set an intention to notice when this trailhead is activated in your life. When you realize that it is, take some time to notice all the parts that are activated at that moment, and access them briefly. (See Accessing Parts from a Trailhead in Chapter 4.) If you are too busy at that exact time, use the next available free moment. After you access each part, take a little time to get to know it. Later, follow up with sessions in which you become acquainted with these parts more fully.

Exercise: Working with a Trailhead in Real Time

Choose a trailhead that you are curious about. _____

_____

The exercise is to notice, over the next week, when this trailhead is activated and then access the parts involved. It will help to know what cues will tip you off that it is activated. What kinds of situations or people tend to activate this trailhead? _____

When are these trigger situations likely to occur during the next week?

_____

Set an intention to be especially aware, during those times, of whether this part becomes activated. _____

There are also other ways to notice a trailhead. What body sensations, thoughts, or emotions will let you know it is up? _____

_____

What behavior will cue you? _____

Each time you notice the trailhead, access each part briefly and make a list of them. If you can't stop at the moment to make the list, do it at your next break, or as soon as you can. To help you keep on track with this exercise, take a little time each night before you go to bed to think about whether this trailhead came up that day.

If so, did you access the parts involved? _____

If you didn't, what kept you from doing this? _____

Did you fail to notice that it was activated? _____

Did you notice but not do the exercise? _____

If you did the exercise, what did you learn from it? _____

Take notes and try to answer the above five questions each night. This daily review will also help you to keep the exercise in mind the next day. Don't expect yourself to catch all the times this trailhead is activated or to access the parts each time. This is very difficult to do. If you are driving or in the midst of a conversation, for example, it's hard to pull your attention away and tune into the workings of your mind. Just do the best you can.

Summary

In this chapter, you have learned how to get to know a protector, using internal dialogue, body sensation, emotion, image, and direct knowing. This is step P4. You know what questions to ask the protector, especially the ones that will lead to an understanding of its positive intent and what it is protecting you from. You have seen how to name parts. You have learned how to end a session respectfully, how to deal with resistance to doing the exercises, and how to learn about a protector or a trailhead in real time. Now that you understand the protector and its positive intent for you, the next chapter shows how to develop a trusting relationship with it.

Chapter 8

Befriending Yourself

Developing a Trusting Relationship with a Protector

You have probably heard how important it is to love yourself, to be your own best friend. These maxims are important but hard to put into practice. What does it mean to love yourself? How do you go about that? How can you be your own best friend? IFS makes these ideas concrete and specific. It shows you exactly what they mean and how to accomplish them. Loving yourself really means loving each of your parts. Befriending yourself means developing a relationship with each of your parts and having them trust you. The IFS method accomplishes this—not as a side effect but as a central aspect of the therapy. This chapter demonstrates how to develop a trusting connection with a protector. Later we will see how to do this with an exile.

So far you have learned how to access a protector and find out about it. It isn't enough to just gain information and insight; you must develop a real relationship with a protector. A crucial part of your success in IFS depends on the degree to which you are connected with each protector so that it trusts you.

As discussed in the last chapter, protectors act out extreme roles in reaction to situations that threaten to cause you pain, shame, fear, or grief. They want to protect you from feeling such emotions, and they think this entire burden falls on their shoulders. They don't know about the Self, and they don't trust you to be able to handle a threatening situation. They believe that if they don't do something, no one else will, and a disaster will ensue. They think they are still back in childhood where they had to deal with life's trials and tribulations all by themselves.

In reality, most protectors are child parts that developed their protective strategy when you were young and didn't have the capacity to act in skillful and mature ways. So their actions are simplistic and often extreme like a child's, and their strategies carry over into adulthood. When a protector is faced with a situation that it perceives as threatening, it will act the only way it knows how, using the tactic it learned in childhood, which is usually dysfunctional in your adult life.

For example, Jim has a protector whose strategy is to avoid conflicts at all costs. Whenever Jim and his girlfriend have a disagreement over something, Jim either withdraws or gives in right away. This comes from a protector that Jim calls the Conflict Avoider. It is afraid that if Jim were to allow himself to get into an argument, he would quickly become enraged and start yelling and throwing things. This protector is also afraid that if Jim got hurt by her, he might dissolve in a puddle of tears. His girlfriend has grown frustrated because she can't reach him. She doesn't know that Jim's fears are rooted in the past. When he was a child and got upset with his parents, he sometimes erupted in temper tantrums and bouts of crying that got out of control. His parents punished him harshly for this, and the Conflict Avoider learned to stay away from any disagreements with his parents to protect Jim from harm. This strategy of avoidance was actually functional at that time. It kept him from reeling out of control emotionally and therefore being punished. As a strategy, it was really the best that Jim's protector could manage under the circumstances, given his immaturity and his parents' intense reaction.

Now in adult life, the Conflict Avoider continues to withdraw at any hint of conflict. It doesn't know that Jim has a Self who can handle confrontations from a centered place. So it believes that it must always be in charge and not let Jim's emotions "slip out." You can imagine why it feels such a sense of urgency about this. If you believed that any anger would get you severely punished, you would be cautious, too. All of this goes on outside of Jim's awareness. All he knows is that he hates any conflict. This avoidance strategy, which genuinely helped him stay out of trouble in his childhood home, is now dysfunctional. Jim's not a child anymore, and he is capable of a healthier response to conflict; in addition, his parents aren't around to punish him. So extreme avoidance is no longer called for. However, the Conflict Avoider doesn't realize this. This is a common dynamic. A protective strategy that worked well and was appropriate in childhood is carried over into adult situations, where it is completely outmoded.

The Conflict Avoider is operating in the dark without any awareness of Jim's maturity and current capacities. If it could learn to trust Jim's Self to negotiate an argument with his girlfriend without getting overly emotional, it could relax. When Jim and his girlfriend have a conflict, it could allow him to engage with her and trust that things would work out.

Trusting the Self

A major goal in IFS is for protectors to learn to trust the Self. Then they can relax and allow the Self to take the lead when they hit rough spots. A protector needs to know that Self is there, with strength, compassion, and other qualities that are needed in dealing with problematic life situations and underlying pain. The protector needs to learn that you (from Self) care about it, understand its role, and appreciate the work it has been doing for you all these years. This allows the protector to relax, begin to trust you, and permit you access to the exile (or exiles) it is protecting. If you were a scared kid but you knew there was a big brother around that you could trust, you would no longer feel so scared. You would have someone to lean on.

If you don't connect with a protector so that it knows it can count on you, it will continue to believe that it must handle these scary life situations by itself. As a result, it will continue acting in a dysfunctional manner, such as avoiding all conflict. And it probably won't give you permission to work with the exile it is protecting. Therefore, it is important to develop a trusting connection with each of your protectors. The issue of trust will become important again later in the IFS process, after the exile has been unburdened, when it is time for the protector to let go of its protective role. This can only happen if it trusts you.

This relationship of trust will not develop if you aren't in Self. When you're in Self, you are truly interested in connecting with the protector, not just using it to gain access to the exile. People who have experience working on themselves often have the goal of getting to their childhood wounds as quickly as possible. They think that healing their exiles is "where the gold is." In IFS, healing exiles *is* a central aspect of the work, but it is important not to rush it. Don't say, "Oh, here's a protector. Just move aside please, and let me access the important part, the exile." Take the time to develop a relationship with each of your protectors.

The bigger perspective here is that all parts of us are important—none of them are just in the way. Each part is there for a reason, and it must be honored and respected. So don't just give lip service to the fact that this protector has a positive intent for you. Be truly interested in learning what it has been trying to do for you and why it thinks its protective role is so important. Honor the part for trying to help you.

Appreciating Your Protectors

Most protectors have been working hard and tirelessly for your benefit for many years. At least they *think* their job is for your benefit, whether that's actually true or not. In fact, they think their role is crucial—that you would be in serious trouble without them. Often they don't even like their role, but they believe that someone has to do it. Imagine doing a tough, unpleasant job for years at a time that no one thanks you for. And when you finally get noticed, all you hear is, "I wish you weren't ruining my life like this. Step aside so we can get to the important player, the exile." Protectors frequently feel misunderstood and judged for performing their role. And this is because we frequently do judge them. Once Jim became aware of the problems caused by his avoidance of conflict, he judged the Conflict Avoider by calling it a wimp. These protectors need our appreciation for their attempts to protect us.

Even a protector that is proud of its role can grow tired of it as the years go by. It would love to take a rest, but it believes this is impossible. Like the little Dutch boy with his finger in the dike, it is afraid if it let up for even a moment, you would be flooded by pain or left defenseless in a dangerous situation.

Protectors long for someone to understand why they are performing their roles and appreciate their efforts. As you find out about a protector and understand its motivations, it is very helpful if you appreciate what the protector has been trying to do for you and express this, as will be described below. Remember, even if the protector is causing problems in your life, its heart is in the right place. If you can't appreciate it for anything else, you can appreciate it for that.

Many of the world's spiritual traditions tell us that at our core we are made of love and that reality is essentially benign and loving. IFS reflects this idea in its recognition that all of our parts want the best for us. And the Self manifests this love in its capacity to care deeply about all our parts and connect with them.

Some protectors have mixed roles. They do a job that works well for you at times, but when they go overboard, they can make trouble. For example, I have a protector, called the Accomplisher, that works hard to do tasks in my life in an efficient, organized way. It really does help me to be functionally competent and successful in my career. However, the Accomplisher doesn't believe that I can have any pleasure or aliveness while I am getting tasks done. It believes that this work is just drudgery and I must do it as quickly as possible so I can enjoy myself afterward. The problem is that "afterward" practically never comes because I always find more tasks on the pile. I used to spend a lot of my life accomplishing tasks in a boring, mechanical way, which took much of the aliveness and enjoyment out of my life. Though this protector has relaxed because of the IFS work I have done, it is still a problem at times.

In a healthy internal system, some protectors will continue to play a role because they have an important job to do that really does improve your life. However, they will do their job in a healthy way. Protectors become extreme or dysfunctional because they are trying to protect against the pain of an exile. For example, my Accomplisher is trying to make me successful in life so I can feel good about myself and feel valuable. This is an attempt to protect against the pain of an exile that feels unlovable. When you are working with a protector that sometimes performs a healthy role, it is very important to appreciate the part for this.

My Story

I remember a time when the importance of connecting with protectors was forcefully brought home to me in my own work on the Accomplisher. I had worked with this part many times and gotten to know it. I had worked on the exiles that it protects and healed them to some extent. I worked on letting go of extreme Accomplisher behavior, such as devoting all my time to finishing a project quickly or speeding in traffic just to get to work quickly. I aimed at taking it easy while working, being more present, and enjoying myself more, all of which was happening to some degree. However, one day I realized that I hadn't really formed a cooperative, trusting relationship with this part. I had just been trying to sidestep it.

So I took some time to reconnect with it and appreciate not only what it was *trying* to protect me from but also the many ways this part *has* contributed to my life. Because of the Accomplisher, I am able to get a lot done, which really does make my life easier and helps me to write books and create classes and workshops. For the first time, instead of trying to abolish the Accomplisher, I gave it appreciation. I understood that my goal wasn't to let go of the Accomplisher but rather to work with it in a cooperative way so that it could still do its job while allowing me more freedom and aliveness in the process. As a result of this shift in my attitude, I began to experience an unusual sense of well-being, which came from having more inner harmony among my parts.

I did this work one morning. By late that afternoon, I noticed that I was feeling very sad. I couldn't imagine why, so I took so time to explore myself. I discovered that the Accomplisher was feeling sad about all the times in the past that I had devalued it and tried to get rid of it. These feelings came up that afternoon because I had stopped treating it with disdain and respected it enough to want to connect with it. It was actually grateful for the way I had changed my relationship with it, which freed it to feel its pain about the way I had treated it before. This was a real eye opener for me. I realized that my parts really do have feelings about the way I treat them and that my relationship with them is crucial.

Step P5: Developing a Trusting Relationship with a Protector

This is the last step in getting to know a protector. Check to see if you understand and appreciate the protector's *efforts* on your behalf, even if its *actions* cause problems. If you don't feel appreciation, this might stem from your not understanding the protector's positive intent. In this case, go back to Chapter 7 to help you with this. If you do understand its intent but don't appreciate it, this might be due to your not being in Self. In this case, go back to Chapter 6 to unblend from any concerned parts so you can be.

Once you understand and appreciate the protector, you can enhance your relationship with it by letting it know that you understand and appreciate it. This will help the part to feel connected with you and trust you. It will also deepen your sense of connection with the part.

You can say any of the following statements to it, if they truly reflect how you feel.

I understand why you perform your role.

I understand why you think that is important.

It makes sense to me.

I know how hard you have had to work.

I understand the responsibility you carry.

I understand what you have sacrificed.

I appreciate your efforts on my behalf.

I appreciate what you did for me when I was a child.

I appreciate what you have been trying to do for me throughout my life.

I appreciate what you are trying to do for me.

I appreciate what you do for me.

I see how you contribute to my life.

After saying one of these statements to the protector, check to see how it is responding to you. You will often notice a shift in the part's feelings, a sense of gratitude or deeper connection, or some relaxation of its rigid stance.

Helping the Part to Be Aware of You

If you don't notice any response after thanking the part, check to see if it is aware of you. You've been talking to it all this time, thinking you're having a good conversation. How can it *not* be aware of you? But even though this may be surprising, sometimes the part doesn't know you're there. Sometimes a part is only aware of the past, not of you talking to it in the present. It may not have the kind of perspective on the situation that you do. It may not be aware that you are an adult or that you have a Self. All it knows is the danger it sees. For example, a protector might think, "I see someone coming towards me who looks like my father when he was in a rage. I have to stop him from hurting me, and there's no one to help."

Sometimes protectors aren't even aware of the exile they are protecting; they just have a sense of danger or pain that must be avoided. The reason for their restricted vision is that many parts are much more narrow and one dimensional than a whole person is. They have a limited understanding of both the external situation confronting them and your internal system. When triggered, they tend to respond in stereotypical ways, and they're not particularly sophisticated or intelligent. Not all parts are like this, however. Some can be quite clever and subtle, but most of them are pretty shortsighted. By engaging with them the way we do in IFS, we are helping them broaden their horizons and increase their awareness. This is helpful in itself.

Even if the part has been responding to your questions and giving you information about itself, it may not be fully aware of you as a separate entity (as Self). The conversation so far may have been one-sided. You need to turn this into a full-blown relationship. The best place to begin is to find out if it is aware of you. And if it isn't, ask it to notice that you are there. Here are some ways to do this, depending on which channel you use to communicate with this part.

(a) If you have an image of the part, see if it is looking at you and responding to your presence. If it isn't, ask it to look at you.

(b) If you know the part by feeling its emotions or feeling it in your body, switch places and temporarily identify with it. Up till now, you have been identifying with Self (because it *is* your natural identity), but now choose, consciously, to identify with the part—to become the part. Feel the part emotionally or in your body, and then enter that feeling deliberately. If you've been feeling the part as a sadness in your belly, enter that sadness. From that place, look back to sense the presence of the Self.

(c) If you communicate with the part through internal dialogue, ask the part if it is aware of you. If it says it isn't, ask it to notice you.

When you ask the part to become aware of *you*, this is the beginning of a crucial internal shift because before, there was no real relationship. Now you are truly starting one. Many parts aren't used to this. They've existed all this time without knowing that there was a Self. It is confusing to them; they don't know what to make of it at first. And if it is the first time you have done this with one of your parts, it may not just be confusing for the part; it may be confusing for you, too. You may not know at first how to be aware of both sides of the relationship. Take your time and feel into it. Once your inner world is reorganized so that your parts are aware of you, it often feels comforting and brings a sense of inner harmony and well-being. Your parts don't feel alone anymore. They realize that a larger benevolent presence is available.

For example, Janet had a Little Girl Part that felt unseen and unappreciated by her parents when she was a child. This part was completely caught up in wanting acknowledgement from them and doing her best to please them. When Janet, from Self, told the Little Girl that she understood what the girl was feeling, the part didn't respond to her at all. When Janet checked, she saw that the Little Girl was looking away from her, at the parents instead. The Little Girl believed that she was still back in childhood, where she needed her parents' approval.

but she is completely focused on her memory of her parents, hoping for approval from them.

Janet's Self reaches out to the Little Girl...

They are distracted and aren't seeing or appreciating her.

Janet asked the Little Girl to notice that she (Janet in Self) was there. At first, the Little Girl didn't know what to do with this. She had been focused on the past and her parents for so long that she didn't know how

140

to relate to anyone else. However, as Janet kept gently making her presence known, the Little Girl slowly got it. She turned her head and looked at Janet. She began to realize that someone else was there who was paying attention to her. Suddenly she realized that she wasn't alone. Janet told her that she really understood how painful it was for her to be ignored and dismissed by her parents. Now the Little Girl could take in this attention and understanding from Janet. She began to brighten up and feel a sense of well-being. Janet had succeeded in establishing a connection with her. This prompted a major shift in Janet's internal sense of connectedness.

Janet's Self stays present with the Little Girl...

and she eventually takes in the caring from Self, allows the connection, and feels happy.

Once the part is aware of you, say the statement of understanding or appreciation again, and check to see how the part is responding to you. You will probably sense a clear and strong response now because the part can take in your appreciation and feel it.

Exercise: Developing a Trusting Relationship with a Protector

Do a session in which you get to know a protector, using steps P1-P5 that you have now learned. Pay particular attention to step P5 from this chapter. Follow the Help Sheet to keep track of the steps. When you are finished, write down what you have learned about the part:

Name _____

What it feels _____

What it looks like _____

Where it is located in your body _____

What it says _____

How it makes you behave _____

What situations activate it _____

What concerned parts react to it _____

What its positive intent is _____

What it is protecting you from _____

What you understand or appreciate about the part _____
_____

How the part responded to your saying that _____
_____

Christine and the Confuser

This is another section of the transcript of Christine's session with the Confuser. This is the part that makes Christine feel fuzzy, confused, and distracted; it is terrified of something unspeakable happening. I have added some new comments to bring out this chapter's ideas. We pick up at the point after Christine has gotten to know the Confuser but hasn't yet moved on to the exile it's protecting.

Jay: How does it feel about its job?

Christine: It's a completely impossible job, overwhelmed. Yet it is unable to stop.

Notice how the part is tired of its job but doesn't feel it's safe to stop.

J: Yeah. See if there is anything else the part wants you to know about itself.

C: I feel clearly that it does want my love, respect, and gratitude for suffering on my behalf.

Here is the where Christine's relationship with the Confuser comes to the fore (Step P5). Asking for appreciation is a sign that a real relationship is forming. It isn't unusual for parts to want appreciation, but they don't usually waltz right out and ask for it.

J: And what's your response to that?

C: I do feel a lot of appreciation.

J: So really let the Confuser know that.

C: I feel I can't even express in words how much I appreciate the degree of dedication and desperation this part has shown in doing this job. (Christine is really moved.)

J: So you really get it. And how is the part responding to you?

C: It's softening. And as it softens, I see one very clear thing. When I said earlier that it didn't know how to stop, that was because it had no connection with Self. There was nothing for it to release into, relax into. But now the Confuser is softening because it does sense that I'm here.

This is very moving to me. Christine has really connected with the Confuser, and it is beginning to trust her and relax. This is an important step.

C: I don't know why it is that all the experiences I've had of Self never touched this particular part.

Christine has done a lot of psychological and spiritual work on herself and has had many experiences of what IFS calls Self. However, this past work didn't involve Christine relating to the Confuser from Self, so the part hadn't had an opportunity to know about Christine's Self and connect with her.

C: One other thing. This part has been hugely mistrustful of love in my life. I knew this, but now that I see how the Confuser wasn't connected with a bigger Self, it makes sense in a new way.

In order for this part to trust love, first it had to trust Christine's love for it, which began to happen in this session.

Lisa and the Sooty Demon

This is a continuation of the transcript of Lisa's session with the Sooty Demon, which wants to attack her sister in order to protect Lisa's heart. We take up after she has gotten to know this protector.

Jay: It sounds like you are understanding and maybe even appreciating what the Sooty Demon is trying to do for you.

Lisa: Yes. That's what has changed here. I still feel its intensity, but I admire that little Tasmanian devil rather than seeing it as something that's going to make a big mess. Wow! It's a buzz saw that's incredibly effective. It has a mission.

J: Yeah.

L: It's very dedicated to that mission, and I feel respectful and admiring. I'm very interested to know it more.

J: Good. Let that part know about your respect and admiration for it. You can do this silently, or out loud, or through your heart.

L: (Laughs) It stops for a moment and says, "Oh gosh." As if it is embarrassed, shuffling its feet. And then it wants to show off. It wants to show me what else it can do. (laughing) "I can really attack. Watch this." A kind of joy starts to arise. This is amazing. I am an appreciative, slightly amazed witness.

The Sooty Demon has really taken in Lisa's appreciation and is feeling connected to her. This allows it to shift into a different mode of being.

L: What's also interesting is that the Sooty Demon no longer seems paired with my sister. It's like a part in itself. She seems quite different to me at this moment, too.

J: So the Sooty Demon is there anyway, and it just happens to get triggered by your sister.

L: Yeah. And as I admire it and become interested in it, it seems like my sister is coming in through a different door, with a freshness to her. As if I didn't know my sister at all.

It looks as if Lisa's work has freed her up to have a new relationship with her sister.

J: Interesting. Are there other parts that want to say anything before we stop?

L: The Watcher is snoring, exhausted. The little Demon Part is racing around going "Yippee," having a grand time. I'm admiring and amazed by the whole thing. It's funny: As the little Demon has more room to buzz around and be hyper-energized, it makes the

Little Girl part giggle. And the Mothering Part feels like her load is a bit lifted too. There's something in the little Demon getting freed up that seems to affect the whole system. Not a resolution, but an energetic lift. Thank you. I initially felt very frightened to step into that territory.

There has been a shift in Lisa's whole inner system as a result of her new relationship with the Sooty Demon. Her other parts are more relaxed; the system has more of a playful atmosphere and is less harsh. In addition, Lisa has a different attitude toward her sister. This whole shift illustrates the value of having a good relationship with each of your parts; it can change your entire relationship with yourself and others. It also shows the importance of seeing your parts as a system. When you change your relationship with one, it can shift how you feel about others as well.

When a Part Doesn't Relate to You

So far in this chapter, we have been discussing how to enhance your connection and trust with a protector that is already somewhat open to you. However, sometimes a part is so actively mistrustful of you that more work is needed. In fact, some protectors mistrust you so much that they won't even talk to you or show themselves to you.

Consider the following situation: You know about a protector you would like to work with, and you can sense how it manifests in your body. When you check for blending, it seems that you are in Self. You ask this protector what it feels or what its concerns are, and you receive no answer. Then you try focusing on getting an image of the protector, but nothing comes up. You can't seem to get an answer. This is unusual. You are used to getting responses from your parts. What is going on?

This lack of response may manifest in other ways. Instead of silence, the target protector may simply tell you it doesn't want to talk to you. You may see an image of the part with its back turned and its arms crossed, signifying that it is blocking you out. You might even be in the process of getting to know a protector when suddenly its image disappears or it stops talking to you. The whole process grinds to a halt.

This lack of communication might be happening because a concerned part is blocking your access to the target protector. It thinks that protector is too dangerous to connect with. It is like a censor that tries to keep subversive ideas from spreading. You can check for this possibility by calling forward any part that doesn't want you to talk to the target protector. Or you can check inside to see if there is a part like this. When you find it, work with it the way you would with any concerned part (see Chapter 6). Explain that you will stay in Self and won't let the target protector take over, and ask it to step aside.

When a Part Doesn't Trust You

If this technique doesn't work, you look for other reasons that the protector isn't relating to you. The most likely reason is that it doesn't trust you. First, ask the protector whether or not it trusts you. Even if it won't respond to any of your other questions, it is likely to respond to this one. If it doesn't trust you, it will probably say so. There are two reasons why a part might not trust you.

Blending with a Concerned Part

One possibility is that you aren't coming purely from Self, even though you believe you are, because you are blended with a concerned part. Our parts are often very sensitive to our attitudes toward them. They can tell if you are coming from a pure place or if you have been taken over by a concerned part that doesn't like them and judges them. Any sort of judgment will make them feel that it is not safe to talk to you. In some cases, they will talk, but they won't reveal much of themselves to you. After all, you wouldn't reveal anything vulnerable about yourself to someone who was judging you or angry at you. Our parts feel the same way.

Ask yourself what you are feeling toward this protector. Look for any subtle angry or judgmental parts. If you discover one, ask it to step aside, and if this isn't enough, work with it in the way you have learned to work with concerned parts in Chapter 6. Once it has stepped aside, the protector will very likely reveal itself to you easily. If the concerned part steps aside and the protector is still not trusting you, check to see if there is another concerned part. Or investigate the second possibility below.

History of Betrayal

Another possibility is that the target protector has suffered hurt, abandonment, or betrayal in the past, and now it doesn't trust anyone, including you. In fact, the part may not really be aware that there is a Self. When it trusted people in the past, it got hurt. So it decided that people aren't trustworthy, and it will never allow itself to trust anyone again, including you. Your job is to work with this part sensitively and respectfully until it begins to trust you.

In some cases, a part won't trust you enough to tell you anything other than the fact that it doesn't trust you. Then you need to just be with it without prodding it. Let go of any expectations you have that the part should open up to you quickly. Just offer it your attention without hoping for anything in return. Don't be in a hurry to get on with the process. Suppose you came upon a wild animal, such as a deer, that was wary of humans, and you wanted it to trust you enough to allow you to approach. What would you do? You would just sit quietly with it until it got used to your presence. This is the way you need to relate to a mistrustful part. Be patient with it as you would with a frightened animal; it will gradually come around.

Once the part is willing to talk, ask it what it doesn't trust about you. Trust is a very broad notion. When a part doesn't trust you, there is usually something specific that it is afraid of. It may not trust that you care about it. It may not trust that you are strong enough or intelligent enough to handle the situations it is concerned about. It may expect you to abandon or attack it if it opens up to you. It may be afraid you will dismiss it. A crucial first step is to find out exactly what it doesn't trust in you.

Once the part lets you in on what's bothering it, it is usually a good idea to invite the part to tell you what happened to it to make it feel mistrustful. Even if you think you know (because this obviously comes from your history), ask the part to tell you in its own words. You may be surprised at what you hear. For example, it may show you that it really felt close to your mother as an infant, and then as it got older she became angry and distant. It didn't know why she changed, but it could no longer trust her. Take time to empathize with the part's feelings about what happened, as you would with a friend, and be understanding about why this would cause mistrust. An important aspect of gaining its trust is for it to feel heard by you. When this has happened, you can reassure the part that you won't treat it the way it was hurt in the past.

Throughout this dialogue, don't expect the part to drop its guard and instantly trust you. It doesn't usually work that way. It may resist by saying, "You weren't there for me back then when I needed someone, so why should I trust you now?" Apologize to it, and explain that you were young, too, and didn't have the resources or understanding that you have now. Let it know that now you are older and wiser, and are there for it.

Don't pressure the part to trust you too quickly. Trust comes with its own time frame and can't be pushed. Be patient and let the part take as much time as it needs to trust you. It could take a number of sessions or even longer. Furthermore, remember that the reason you want the part to trust you is so it will tell you about itself. If you have gotten this far in your dialogue, you have already achieved that goal. The part is explaining why it mistrusts you and other people. This is probably the most important thing it could possibly tell you about itself. There is no need to get the part to say that it now trusts you because it has already been doing that in a gradual way, just by revealing its issues around trust. Just continue this kind of respectful, non-coercive interaction and gradually move toward asking whatever additional questions might be needed. This dialogue will eventually build enough trust that the protector will allow you to work with and heal the exile it is protecting. Once that has happened, it will probably be able to trust you completely.

Transcript

Here is a transcript that illustrates how to work with a mistrustful part. Carl is a 40-year-old client of mine who has a high-pressure management job. He gets irrationally angry at people every once in a while, especially at work. This has created some difficult reactions in others.

> **Carl:** I want to work on the part that gets so riled up at people at work.
> **Jay:** Okay. Sense that part in your body.
> **C:** I'm gritting my teeth and clenching my fists.
> **J:** Good. Check to see how you are feeling toward that part.
> **C:** I am fairly curious about this Angry Part, like why does it flip out like that?

J: Okay. Ask the part to tell you what makes it so angry.

C: (pause) I'm not getting any response.

J: Do you have a visual image of the part?

C: Well, let's see. Yeah, it's a guy who is glaring at me ferociously, and now he's turning his back on me.

Carl wants to engage the Angry
Part, and he thinks he is in Self.

The Angry Part
doesn't trust him.

J: Maybe he doesn't trust you. Check again to see if you are really in Self. In other words, check to see if curiosity is all you feel toward the part, or if there are other attitudes as well.

Since this looks like a trust issue, I want to check if the part is mistrusting Carl because he is judging the part or because some other negative feeling is coming up.

C: Well, now that you ask, I am aware of feeling some judgment and annoyance, like I wish this part would stop causing me so much trouble.

J: Well, that may be why the Angry Part isn't cooperating with you. Ask that Judgmental/Annoyed Part if it would be willing to step aside so you can get to know the Angry Part from an open place.

C: Okay. It sees the value in that, so it is willing to step back.

J: Good. Check to see how you are feeling toward the Angry Part now.

C: Now I am more open to him.

J: See if he is willing to talk to you now.

C: How do I do that?

J: Ask him to tell you what makes him so angry.

C: He still has his back to me, and I can sort of sense resentment coming from him. And he's not answering the question.

J: Okay. Ask him if he trusts you.

C: Well, that got a response. He said, "Hell, no!"

J: Good. Ask him what he doesn't trust about you.

C: (pause) I'm still not getting a response. I think his back is still turned to me, though that isn't entirely clear.

J: Just let him know that you'd like to get to know him whenever he's ready to allow that. And just hang out with him now for a bit.

C: I'm not sure what you mean by that.

J: Focus your attention on him—the image or the sense of him in your body. Do this from an open place where you are just receptive to him and you aren't in a hurry for him to open up to you.

C: That's not easy to do. Just sit here? For how long?

J: It sounds like there may be an impatient part of you here now. Check to see if there is a part that is impatient with the idea of just being with this part.

C: Yes, there is. It wants to move ahead with the therapy.

J: That is really understandable because you want to get somewhere in this session, but that isn't going to work with this Angry Part. So ask that Impatient Part if it would be willing to relax and allow you to quietly be with the Angry Part.

Asking Carl to be patient with this part requires a degree of Self, of patience, that is greater than has been needed so far in this session. When I asked him to be patient, this revealed that there was a concerned part there, an impatient part.

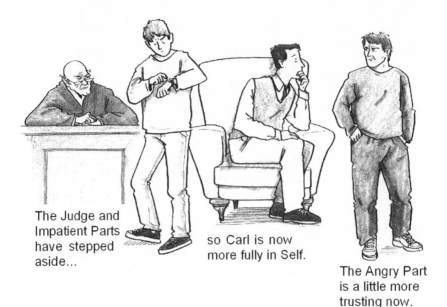

The Judge and Impatient Parts have stepped aside...

so Carl is now more fully in Self.

The Angry Part is a little more trusting now.

C: Well, it's willing to give that a try ... Okay. So I'm just here with the Angry Part.

J: Good. Let him know that you would like to get to know him but only when he's ready.

C: Okay. I said that. (pause) Well, now I can see the image more clearly though he still has his back to me.

J: Let him know you appreciate his coming in clearer to you.

Parts have the capacity to allow us to see them clearly or not. I am assuming that the clearer image was allowed by the part, which is an indication that some trust is entering the picture.

C: Okay. (pause) Now he's slowly turning around and looking at me. It seems that he is starting to get interested in who I am.

J: Good. See if he is willing to let you know what he doesn't trust about you.

C: He says that he doesn't trust me to mean what I say.

J: Mm hmm. Ask him to say more.

C: He says I may seem like a safe guy, but then I'll turn on him.

J: Thank him for letting you know that. (pause) You might ask him if that has happened to him in the past, where people who seemed safe turned on him.

C: Oh yes, plenty of times.

Carl later revealed that his father was an alcoholic who was good to Carl when he was sober and became an abusive drunk at other times.

J: No wonder he doesn't trust you.

The past experiences with the father taught this part that no one was to be trusted.

C: He says, "Yeah, and you weren't there when I needed you. Why should I believe you'll be there now?"

J: I can understand why he would feel that way. Can you?

C: Yeah, I suppose I can.

J: What is your response to him?

C: (speaking to part) I'm sorry I wasn't there for you then. Back then, I wasn't aware of what was going on, and I was just a kid. I will be there for you now. (pause) He doesn't trust me about that.

J: That is totally understandable. But don't worry, we don't need him to trust you yet. Let him know there is no hurry, and thank him for being so willing to talk to you and tell you what he feels.

*In fact, the part **does** trust Carl to a certain extent. Otherwise, it wouldn't be telling him so much about its experience. More trust is not required at the point to go on with the process. Carl just needs to appreciate what he has. The very act of appreciating and not prodding goes a long way toward creating trust.*

C: OK, I did. He appreciates that. It seems like he is softening a little. His stance is more relaxed and his face isn't scowling any more.

The part is trusting Carl a little more because he gave it space to be itself. It can see that Carl is letting it set the terms and not forcing it to go farther than it wants to. This means the part can feel that it is in control and therefore not in danger, which allows it to relax.

This session illustrates a number of aspects of working with a mistrustful part—making sure you are in Self, being patient with the part, and exploring why the part doesn't trust you. If you apply this approach with any part that isn't talking to you, it will come around in time and open up to you. This comes out of its positive intent. Once it can see that you're approaching it from a cooperative place, it won't sit in its corner and hold back. It will be a team player.

Exercise: Gaining a Part's Trust

Choose a protector that you have tried to work with that hasn't been responsive to you.

In what ways has it not responded to you? _____

_____

First make sure that you are in Self with respect to this part and not blended with any concerned parts. If you discover any concerned parts, ask them to step aside so you are truly in Self.

Concerned parts _____

Check to see if this protector will now talk to you. If it still won't, work with it as discussed in this chapter and see if you can gain its trust. Answer the following questions about this work:

What does the part not trust about you? _____

_____

What happened in the past to make it mistrustful? _____

_____

This may take more than one session.

Helping a Protector to Relax in Real Time

Once you have gotten to know a part and developed a trusting relationship with it, you have a good chance of being able to work with it whenever it arises in real time in your life. Here is a way to do this that may help it to relax and allow you to lead from Self.

When you notice that a part is activated at some point during your day, access it briefly and see if you are blended with it. Often, you are. The part is blended with you because some situation in your life has come up that frightens the part and makes it believe that it must take over.

For example, you are at a party with a lot of strangers and are afraid of being rejected. A Shy Part takes over and makes you slink back into a corner and not talk to people. To work with this situation, ask the Shy Part to separate from you so that you can be in Self. Remind it that you are there, so it doesn't have to deal with this situation all on its own. Because you are an adult and you are in Self, you have much more capacity than the part thinks you have. (I mention this because the part is stuck in the past and may think that you only have the capacity of a child.) Ask the Shy Part what it is afraid of. It says it is afraid of rejection or ridicule if you reach out or talk to someone. Ask the part what its role is. It says its role is to withdraw to protect you from being rebuffed.

When it feels right, ask the part to relax and allow you to lead from Self. In this case, you would ask the Shy Part to not withdraw but rather to allow you to reach out and make conversation with people, even though this feels like a risk. It probably can't completely let go of its fear until you have healed the exile underneath, but it may be able to relax to some extent because of its connection with you and may allow you to interact with people from Self.

Ask the part if there is anything it needs from you so it can do this. The Shy Part says it wants to know that you won't be awkward and tongue-tied when you talk to people. You can reassure it that you will be able to make intelligent conversation. (If you aren't sure about this, do some work on this issue before you ask the Shy Part to step aside. You may want to practice conversational skills or do some healing work with the underlying exile.) When you are ready, at the next party, ask the Shy Part to allow you to lead. If you end up having a better time at the party because Self was in the lead, the Shy Part is more likely to trust you in the future.

Exercise: Helping a Protector to Relax in Real Time

Think of a situation in which a protector gets triggered that causes you to behave in a problematic way. _____

_____

Do a session in which you get to know the protector that is causing the difficulty. Form a trusting relationship with this protector.
Name of protector _____
Describe how it behaves _____
If you were able to act from Self, how would you like to behave? _____

_____

Ask the protector if it will let you lead the next time you are in such a situation. (Make sure you have the life skills to pull off the positive behavior you are aiming for.) If it says no, ask why, and then work with that protector to get to the point where it will agree. Think about when this situation

is likely to occur over the next few weeks. _____
_____

Set an intention to be aware of whether this protector takes over at those times. When it does, work with it as described above to help it relax and let you lead. If this works, take notes on what happened as soon as you can. What did your behavior look like when you were leading from Self? _____

What were the results?_____
_____

Continue to track this kind of situation over the next few weeks, doing this exercise each time the part is activated. Each evening before you go to bed, review the day to see if the situation arose, and take notes (or expand your notes) on what happened when you did this exercise. If the protector allowed you to lead and things turned out well, check to see if it now trusts you more. If you didn't notice the situation at the time or you didn't do the exercise, explore what got in the way. If this is a situation that doesn't come up very often, it wouldn't make sense to do this review every night. You might decide to review once a week. Choose a time frame that is appropriate. _____
_____

Summary

In this chapter, you have learned why protectors are often alienated from Self. You understand the importance of developing a compassionate and respectful relationship with each protector and what this feels like, which is step P5. You have learned how to foster trust in your relationship with a protector. You have seen how to work with a part that distrusts you so you can gain its trust. You have also learned how to help a protector relax in the midst of daily life so you can take action from Self.

Now that you have a trusting relationship with the protector, you can move on to working with the exile it is protecting. This is covered in Part II which begins with Chapter 10. But first, in Chapter 9, we will explore how to keep sessions on track when the unexpected happens.

Chapter 9

Keeping Sessions on Track

Detecting Parts that Arise

————————— • —————————

This book presents the IFS process in a way that looks fairly neat and straightforward. You choose a protector to work with, get into Self, and proceed through the steps almost like following a recipe in a cookbook. In reality, the psyche is messier than this. While you are focusing on one part, another might creep in unexpectedly and take you out of Self without your realizing it. Or a new feeling may burst into consciousness that is more intense than the part you are focused on. You might be flooded with a variety of intense feelings at once. It is as if you were following a recipe for a dish you are preparing, but the ingredients jump into the cooking pot at unexpected moments. Nevertheless, this chapter shows that IFS has ways of handling all these contingencies.

Our goal during a session is to stay on track while still being open to any parts that arise. IFS has a masterful way of finding a flowing place that is neither chaotic nor rigid. This allows you to be clear and focused during a session while also being open to whatever surfaces. IFS also has ways of detecting subtle parts that can take over and undermine the therapy process. This chapter teaches you methods for "parts detection" so you can recognize when this occurs and return to Self.

Here are some situations that this chapter will help you avoid.

- Believing that you are in Self when in fact another part has taken you over.
- Having your process blocked by a subtle protector.
- Thinking you are talking to one part when in fact another one is answering.
- Following each new part that arises and losing track of the thread of your exploration.
- Becoming overwhelmed when many parts are activated at once.
- Holding rigidly to your target part by pushing aside or ignoring other parts.
- Getting blocked by concerns about performance or doubts about the process.

We will examine each of these situations in turn and explain how to handle them.

The most insidious problem is that while you are working with one part, another will blend with you without your realizing it. You might suddenly space out and lose focus, you might become distracted, your feelings might go numb, or you might become confused. You might begin to doubt what you are doing, the process might seem abstract and distant, or the part might not talk to you. Whenever your process is blocked, it is usually because a protector has taken over that wants to stop you. You simply need to recognize that this is happening and engage with that protector to find out why it wants to derail your work.

Sometimes protectors erupt for other reasons as well—for example, being in a hurry, feeling inadequate, or judging the target part. This chapter will teach you to become adept at "parts detection" so you catch these problems when they occur. There are six common types of protectors that can derail your work—judgmental parts, avoiders, intellectualizers, impatient parts, inadequate parts, and skeptics.

Detecting Judgmental Parts

In Chapter 6, we discussed concerned parts, which have negative feelings toward the target part. You learned to check for being blended with a concerned part by noticing how you feel toward the target part. If you feel judgmental, angry, or frightened, for example, you are blended with a concerned part, and you ask it to step aside so you can work with the target part from Self. However, even if you start working with a protector from Self, a little later in the session a concerned part might blend with you without your realizing it. As a result, your attempts to connect with the target part will be sabotaged by the concerned part's anger, judgment, or guardedness.

Judgmental parts are the most common kind of concerned part. As you are getting to know the target part, you might begin to feel subtly angry or critical of it, or you might want it to go away. Maybe you start out in Self, being open and nonjudgmental, but as you learn more about the problems the target part is causing in your life, you start to feel annoyed with it.

For example, suppose you are getting to know an Arrogant Part that feels superior to people. As you recognize all the situations in your life where this Arrogant Part operates, you realize that it is a major factor in your unhappiness because it has kept your heart closed for a long time. This Arrogant Part looks down on the women you are involved with romantically, causing you to break off relationships that had real potential. It is condescending to your coworkers, causing them to be angry at you. It acts arrogantly toward your friends when they don't come through for you, which has ended some friendships. By now, you see all the damage this part has caused and you want to get rid of it. You can't help feeling resentment towards it for blocking your connections with people. These negative feelings don't come from Self but from a Judgmental Part that has crept in and blended with you. Though it is completely understandable that a part of you would be upset with the Arrogant Part for all the trouble it has caused, that critical attitude will undermine your attempt to get to know it.

Here is another example of judgment creeping in. Suppose you have a part that is self-effacing and quiet, and keeps you from speaking up or asserting yourself. At first, you feel quite open to connecting with it, and you're curious about why it needs to behave this way. However, as you begin to get to know it, a part of you surfaces that sees the part as a wimp and feels disdainful toward it. It is such a loser! You feel ashamed of it. A Disdainful Part has blended with you, and you are no longer asking the

Self-effacing Part questions from an open place. The questions begin to sound more like attacks. "What makes you act like this?" really means "What's wrong with you!" After a while, the image of the Self-effacing Part disappears and you lose contact with it. This is because this part is reacting to your disdain and no longer wants to talk to you.

Once you realize that you are blended with a Judgmental Part, ask it to step aside so you can get to know the target part from an open place. You may also want to acknowledge that you understand why the part might feel judgmental, but explain why that attitude isn't effective. If it won't step aside, follow the procedure you learned in Chapter 6 for working with concerned parts. It isn't unusual for a part to be hesitant to step aside. You already know how to deal with this. The important issue here is to detect it so you can apply that knowledge.

Detecting Avoiders

Here is another common occurrence. You begin to feel impatient with your IFS session; without warning, you want to stop and attend to other things in your life. "I've done enough in this session. I'm bored. I'll get back to this work later." Something else in your life feels pressing and must be taken care of. This is a clue that something is going on. An Avoidant part has blended with you that wants to avoid dealing with the target part or the exile underneath, probably because an emotion is starting to surface that the Avoider is afraid of. For example, the Avoidant Part can sense that underneath the protector you are working with is an exile that holds a lot of fear. The Avoider wants to keep you away from the fear, so it suggests you end the session.

There are other ways an Avoider might operate. You might space out or start daydreaming. You might begin to think about a project at work or your dinner plans that night, or anything other than the work you are engaged in. You might get distracted by a noise in the next room or your dog looking up at you. Normally these thoughts or stimuli wouldn't grab your

attention, but the Avoidant Part latches onto them as a way of preventing you from going through with the work. This part is using distraction as a means of avoidance.

Some Avoiders use a third strategy. You feel confused and lost. You can't follow the thread of your work. You can't remember what the part was telling you just now. You don't remember where you were in the IFS procedure. If a new emotion comes up, you get lost in it rather than asking it to step aside. This type of confusion is often created by an Avoidant Part so it can stay away from pain.

Another occurrence that can block your work is losing touch with the target part. If you are working visually, you lose the image of the part. If you are working with emotions or body sensations, your feelings go dead. This is usually the work of an Avoidant Part that is threatened by the direction the work is going.

Once you detect the operation of an Avoider, ask it to come forward so you can get to know it. Then treat it like any other concerned part. Ask it what it is afraid would happen if it allowed you to continue your work. Then validate its feelings, if that is appropriate, and explain how you will handle its concerns. This usually means that you will stay in Self. (See Chapter 6 for more on how to do this.) Then ask it to step aside.

Keep in mind that it really isn't possible to do the IFS process badly. It may seem to you that these interferences shouldn't be happening. "If I were good at this process, I would sail right through without any distractions." Not true. Avoidant reactions like those mentioned above are very common. Even if your process is completely blocked, it doesn't mean you are doing anything wrong. It just means that a protector is stopping things for some reason. All you have to do is access that protector and find out why it is blocking your process. Then you can usually connect with it, and it will allow you to go on.

There is another way that an Avoider can derail the therapy process. It can cause you to procrastinate about doing IFS sessions. You keep putting them off. You forget about them. You tell yourself that you have to do other things first. This procrastination is probably being caused by an Avoider that is afraid of what may come up in the session. The best way to handle this is to schedule a session in which you make this Avoider the target part. Work with it and find out what it is afraid would happen if it didn't procrastinate and simply allowed you to do your IFS work. Make a connection with it and explain how you will handle the situation it is afraid of. This should help to reduce the procrastination.

You may ask: But what if I avoid doing even this session with the Avoider? In this case, I recommend that you schedule the session with a partner. Making a commitment to someone else will help you to follow through and actually do the session.

Detecting Intellectualizers

When you are getting to know a protector, it is common to think you are in Self when in fact an Intellectualizer Part has taken over. One sign of this is that you analyze the target part rather than asking questions and listening for its responses. Ideally, you should allow the *target part* to tell you about itself. When you are truly in Self, you aren't an intellectual observer who is figuring the part out. You are a curious listener who is open to learning things from the target part, and what you hear is often a surprise. If you aren't open in this way, you are probably blended with an Intellectualizer or a part that needs to be in control and have everything figured out all the time.

For example, suppose you are getting to know a part that withdraws in social settings. You remember that, in the past, you have withdrawn because were afraid of people's rejection and judgment. This is useful information, but it isn't coming from the Withdrawn Part; it is coming from an Intellectualizer who is psychologizing about the Withdrawn Part. You aren't asking the part questions and being open to its answers; instead an Analyzing Part has taken over.

Once you realize you are blended with an Intellectualizer, focus on it. Validate the usefulness of intellectual insight, but explain that it derails the process if it happens when you are trying to get to know a part. Ask it to step aside so you can truly be in Self, and let it know that it can come back in at the end of the session to correlate what you learned with previous insights and develop a fuller intellectual understanding of your psyche. Intellectual Parts *are* valuable, but at the right time and place. When a part feels valued like this, it is more likely to cooperate with you.

Once the Intellectualizer has stepped aside, here's how to relate to the Withdrawn Part (or any part) from Self: You ask it what it is afraid of that makes it withdraw, and you wait for its answer with an open mind. The answer should come from some other part of your psyche, not from your head.

Detecting Impatient Parts

The following is a common situation that can be tricky to detect. You have been doing a session for a while and you find that you are in a hurry to get results. You naturally want your parts to heal so you will feel better, but there is an extra push to get on with the work. You can't just trust the process to unfold in its own time. For example, you may push ahead to access an exile before you have really connected with its protector. Or if a concerned part is getting in your way, you might become impatient with it and want to get rid of it. You label parts as "resistant" when they won't let you in fast enough, and you want to barrel past them. You have an agenda for what is supposed to happen in the session, and you aren't open to things progressing in a different way. If you hold any of these attitudes, it means that you are blended with an Impatient Part.

Paradoxically, being in a hurry to heal your parts actually slows things down because it tends to trigger protectors that block your path. And your target part may not trust that you really want to get to know it, and therefore it won't open up to you. It may sense that you just want to get past it to an exile, so it will refuse to cooperate. Parts will resist you if they don't trust that you really want to know them. Therefore, in IFS, the fastest way to resolve an issue is to work slowly, patiently, and respectfully with all parts involved.

When you realize you are blended with an Impatient Part, focus on it. Validate its desire to get on with the work and heal, but remind it that the fastest way to do this is by respecting all parts and following the flow of the work. Ask it to step aside so you can do that from Self.

Self doesn't push. When you are in Self, you know you are headed toward healing, but you aren't in a hurry. You are respectful of all your parts and the fears they have that may temporarily block your progress. You are interested in getting to know all the parts involved in the issue you're working on, and you want to hear whatever they need to say, however long that takes. You hold a space for all the parts to be known without losing sight of your goal of healing.

In Self, we recognize that it may be just as important to know a part that seems to be "getting in the way" as the exile you are trying to access. We don't label any parts as "resistant." A resistant part is just a protector that isn't yet ready to let you proceed with the work. It has played this protective role for a long time. Its protection was probably needed very badly when it took on this role in your childhood. We respect the part rather than being impatient with it.

Detecting Inadequate Parts

Therapy sometimes doesn't go smoothly. The psyche is inherently messy and full of defenses, protectors, and pain. We focus on those areas where there is much pain and dysfunction because that is where healing is needed. Naturally, these places are well defended. Therefore, when we work on ourselves, there will be many difficulties along the way. For example, an exile that holds a lot of pain can be protected by a large number of fierce protectors.

Many people who run into difficulties in their IFS process worry that they are inadequate IFS practitioners. They become concerned that they can't stay in Self, or that they have too many conflicting parts, or that they can't keep track of what is happening. They become afraid that they are so inherently flawed that they can't be healed. This is never true; it is just a belief held by one of your parts. It is true that, for some people, difficulties with the IFS process may indicate that you need more outside help and should consider working with an IFS therapist. However, most of the time, feeling incompetent about your IFS work simply means you are blended with a part that worries about your adequacy. You aren't inadequate; the part isn't inadequate. It just *feels* inadequate. A part has taken over that probably feels inadequate in many other areas of your life as well. Now it feels that way about your IFS work. This may be fueled by judgments from an Inner Critic Part that judges you as inadequate.

When you realize that you are blended with an Inadequate Part, you can reassure it and then ask it to step aside. Here are some helpful things to say.

"There is nothing wrong with me or my competence with the method. It is just a protector that is derailing the process because it is afraid to go further."

"It isn't possible to do IFS wrong or badly. There are just protectors in the way."

"I am just learning the IFS process, so naturally, I won't be very good at it at first. However, with practice I will get better."

Then tune into the Inadequate Part that is blocking your way and work with it in the ways you have been learning. When you have reassured it, ask it to step aside and allow you to continue the work with the confidence of Self. It usually will. Once you are in Self, call forward any protectors that have been blocking you, one at a time, and find out about them. Connect with them and reassure them. Then they will allow you to continue your IFS work in a more effective manner.

If the Inadequate Part doesn't step aside, ask what it is afraid would happen if it allowed you to go on with the work. It might be afraid that you will be judged or labeled a failure. In some cases, you may need to make it the target part and do some healing with it before you can continue with confidence.

Detecting Skeptics

Here is another situation that can cause trouble in an IFS session. You are in the middle of working with a part and a voice pops up and says, "How do you know that vague feeling (or image or sentence) you got from that part is really accurate? You're just making it up." Or a voice says, "I can't imagine that you really think this IFS work is going to make a difference. You can't heal longstanding problems like this." These are the voices of Skeptical Parts. Another one might say, "I don't think this is working. You don't really know what you're doing." When you hear a message like this, turn your attention to the Skeptic and get to know it. Remember that all parts are trying to help.

There are two possibilities here. One is that the Skeptic has a real concern about the efficacy of IFS or what is happening in your process at the moment. The other is that the part has hidden fears about where the work will lead and is using skepticism as an excuse to derail the work. In either case, it is best to start by focusing on the Skeptical Part and asking what it is trying to accomplish by doubting you. Or you could ask what it is afraid would happen if it stopped doubting and allowed you to continue with the IFS process. In other words, try to understand the Skeptic's positive intent and its underlying motivation.

If the part *is* really concerned about how well IFS works because it doesn't want to delve into pain for no reason, tell it that IFS has a long track record of success in helping people heal psychological problems. If the Skeptic is concerned about the validity of certain memories or feelings that are arising, explain that the only way to really tell is to follow them and see what happens. Ask it to allow you to continue as an experiment to see if these memories or feelings lead in a useful direction. Skepticism will undermine your therapy process if it occurs in the middle of experiential work. However, it can be useful after a session (or a series of sessions) in evaluating whether or not the work was really helpful. Ask it to apply its skepticism after the session. Skepticism can be very useful if it is applied at the right time. At the wrong time, it will derail the process.

If you discover that the Skeptic is mainly concerned about painful emotions that are about to come up or a dangerous angry part that might get triggered, validate its concerns and explain how you will handle this. For example, you might reassure the Skeptic that you will stay in Self and not let those parts take over. Then ask it to step aside.

If you have a Skeptical Part that tends to undermine almost everything you try to do in life, spend a few sessions working directly with that part. For some people, the Skeptic holds a lot of power, and if they don't address it, no further work is possible. It may need some healing in order to allow you to proceed confidently with the flow of the work.

Exercise: Parts Detection

Do an IFS session starting with a protector. Before you start, write on a piece of paper the following words: Judgmental, Avoider, Intellectualizer, Impatient, Inadequate, Skeptic. Set an intention to notice whether any of these parts get activated while you are doing the session. If so, work with them as described in this chapter. If you have a partner, ask her to be on the lookout for these parts as well.

Detecting Exiles

Another frequent occurrence that can sidetrack your work is when the part you are talking to changes without your realizing it. You are asking a part questions and receiving its answers, but at some point the answers start to come from a different part. It is important to detect this when it happens. The usual way this happens is that you are working with a protector and you start hearing from the exile that is being protected. However, you don't realize that this has happened; you think you are still talking to the protector. Since the protector and exile are closely linked, this is not surprising. However, you must learn to recognize when this occurs because we work with protectors in a different way than with exiles in IFS. You will recognize an exile because it has a vulnerable emotion such as shame, fear, sadness, or hurt. It is important to have the protector's permission *before* exploring the exile, so if an exile pops up, ask it to wait until you have finished with the protector.

Here is an example from Christine's session in Chapter 3. The following is a segment of the transcript from that chapter, plus an extra section that was omitted earlier for the sake of brevity. This demonstrates a protector switching to an exile without the person realizing it. Christine has identified a protector that doesn't want to see or know certain things. She is getting to know it. Let's take up the session at that point.

Jay: Invite that part to tell you or show you more about what it feels.

Christine: It says that it feels sleepy and dull. I can sense that it goes blank.

J: It feels dull and blank.

C: Yes. It says, "I want to go to sleep. I don't want to be awake or conscious." Sometimes it can't answer people's questions.

J: Mm hmm. Ask the part what its name is or what it would like to be called.

C: I get the word Confuser.

J: Okay. We'll call it the Confuser. Ask it what it is trying to accomplish by being sleepy and confused.

C: It says, "I don't want to see something. I don't want to know something." This part has to just make unclarity and confusion, blandness. It wants to make sure that I don't know what is going on.

J: It creates confusion to protect you from whatever is going on ... What else does this part want you to know about itself?

C: (pause) Well, it's showing me a demonstration of its panic state, which has something to do with being alone. For this part, any other way of life is unthinkable.

J: Any way of life other than what?

C: Other than extreme terror.

Here is where the switch happens. Christine is now hearing from the exile. The Confuser produces confusion and not-knowing, while the exile is terrified. So I ask about this in order to clarify what has happened.

J: I'm a little confused. I thought this was the part that didn't want to see anything.

C: It's two sides of the same coin. The one that doesn't want to see, doesn't want to see because it's terrified.

This is true, but the part that actually feels the terror is the exile, so I focus her back on the protector, whose job is to avoid the terror.

J: I suspect that the one who is terrified is actually a different part. Ask the terrified part if it would be willing to wait a bit, and let's focus on the part whose job is not to see, if that's Okay.

C: Yeah. Now the part is showing me how it does this. It internally changes the subject, takes my attention away. Looks or acts very agitated, so there is no settling or landing in one place. Draws attention to itself and therefore away from whatever else is there. All those ways.

Now Christine's work is focused back on the protector, the Confuser. We get to the terrified exile later in the session.

Why was it important to turn our attention back to the Confuser? You may remember from Chapter 8 that when Christine gave the Confuser appreciation, it felt connected to her. The Confuser never knew there was a Self with qualities of calmness and strength that it could rely on, and once it realized this, it relaxed quite a bit. If Christine had stayed with the terrified exile when it came up, she would never have made this connection with the Confuser.

This switch from protector to exile often happens because the exile desperately wants to be heard. It senses that you are approaching and wants out of exile, so it rushes the gate. When you detect that this has happened, ask the exile to wait until you have gotten to know the protector and received its permission to proceed. So the exile doesn't feel ignored, let it know that you want to get to know it, but ask it to wait while you continue with the protector.

Dissociation and Addictive Behavior

When you are working with an exile or moving in that direction, a protector might get triggered that is very frightened about the pain of the exile. We have already discussed a variety of such protectors, but there are a couple of serious protector reactions that need to be understood.

One possibility is that you can become dissociated. If you get sleepy, spaced out, or fuzzy, or if you feel far removed from your body and feelings, this is known as dissociation. It comes from a protector that is taking powerful measures to prevent you from feeling an exile's pain.

Another possibility is that you might feel an urge to go on a drinking binge or overeat. Or you might feel a compulsive desire to shop, watch porn, gamble, or engage in some other potentially addictive activity. This comes from a different type of protector, which is trying to distract you from the exile's suffering, numb you, or soothe you in the face of intense exile pain.

If either of these things happens to you, ask the dissociative or addictive protector to come forward, and take some time to get to know it. Make it your target part, and start the IFS process over at the beginning to understand it. Once you have learned about it and developed a trusting relationship with it, it may allow you to access the exile.

If you can't make contact with this protector or you have a difficult time working with it, it might not be a good idea to continue trying to do exile work on your own. These extreme protectors are probably coming up because there is intense exile pain or trauma underneath. It will be necessary to do this exile work with an IFS therapist. It would be dangerous to keep going on your own or even with a friend. The Center for Self-Leadership has a listing of trained IFS therapists organized by geographic location at www.selfleadership.org.

Keeping Track of Your Thread

The human psyche is a complicated weave of many colored threads of material. It is easy to get pushed and pulled from one thread to another as they are activated. For example, suppose your lover threatens to leave you, and you have a strong reaction of insecurity. You begin to explore your reaction, and you discover a defensive part that wants to prove to your lover that it's not your fault that he wants to leave. You switch to that part, but before you have gotten very far in getting to know it, you become aware of a feeling of terror coming from a different part. You begin to explore this terrified part and discover that it is frightened about being alone if your lover leaves. Before long, a loud inner voice starts telling you that it is all your fault that this is happening. This is a self-judging part that insists on being heard, so you switch your attention to it and begin to listen to what it has to say. It starts telling you all the things you have done wrong in the relationship, so no wonder your partner is fed up with you. You get curious about why the self-judging part feels a need to berate you so strongly. In the middle of this exploration, you notice an intense feeling of shame coming from a part that is being impacted by this self-judgment. The self-criticism is making this part feel worthless and unlovable.

Through all this, your attention is constantly being pulled to the part that has the strongest feeling at any moment. You haven't been able to stick with any one part long enough to understand it or connect with it. Your attention is a soccer ball on a field being booted around by a team of players. And by the time all these parts have come up, it is easy to forget the part you originally wanted to work with.

It can be useful to access all parts as they arise, because this gives them a chance to be heard, but in the scenario I outlined above, the parts jumped in on each other so fast that none of them really got much attention. And you couldn't progress toward healing because you kept getting derailed. IFS provides a way to follow one thread at a time through the tapestry of your psyche until you have unraveled it and healed the part it represents. *Plan to stay with the target part you have chosen unless you have a good reason to switch to a different target part.* Ask the other parts to step aside. Let them know that they will have a turn to be heard, and ask them to let you proceed with the one you picked. You might want to take notes so you can keep track of all the parts that have come up.

For example, suppose you decide to focus on the defensive part and then the self-judging part comes up. Let the self-judging part know that you will take time to listen to it later, but you need to get to know the defensive part now. Ask the self-judging part to wait. If it can't wait, encourage it to tell you about its judgments, and take some time to hear what it has to say with curiosity and compassion. Once the self-judging part feels heard, ask it to allow you to proceed with the defensive part. It is likely to do that now, which allows you to stay on track. Notice that you are *asking* the self-judging part to let you go on—you aren't *making* it step aside. In IFS you always ask; you never order or coerce. This is because you want to develop a cooperative relationship with your parts. You may want to review techniques for asking parts to step aside, which were discussed in detail in Chapter 6.

If any other parts jump in while you are listening to the self-judging part, ask them to step aside, too. And let them know that you will get to know them in the future. Keep track of all the parts that come up and need to be heard so you can keep your promise to listen to them later. This procedure allows you to stay on track with your work without ignoring or dismissing any parts. If they feel dismissed, they might resent you and resist you later. Continue with your target part through the steps of the IFS procedure until you have healed that part or the session is over. Then take notes on what you have done, and continue your work with this part at your next session.

Changing Target Parts

There are times when it is appropriate to change target parts, but do this only for a good reason. For example, if the self-judging part was not willing to step back even after you explored its fears, you would *have to* make it the target part because it is blocking your way. You might also switch to the self-judging part if you decided that it was more important to work with it because self-criticism is such a crucial issue in your life. Another reason for changing target parts is when a part insists on being heard right now. A fourth reason is when a part comes up that is usually hard to access but feels really alive and juicy in the moment. Seize this opportunity to work with this part since it is available. If you switch target parts for any reason, remember the original target part and come back to it at another time.

Be judicious in your choice to change target parts. Be careful that you don't switch parts in order to avoid something painful or frightening. If you notice that you are changing target parts frequently, this may be a sign that a protector is attempting to keep you away from an experience it thinks is dangerous.

How to Tell One Part from Another

Suppose you are focusing on one part, and a new emotion comes up. A natural question is whether this emotion comes from the target part or from a new part. In a situation like this, how do you tell one part from another? There is no cut-and-dried way because a part isn't simply defined by a certain emotion. For example, if you have a sad part, that part isn't defined by sadness; it might also be angry or scared. And you might have another part that is also sad. A part is also not limited by a certain quality or role, or by any concept you may hold about it.

So how do you tell one part from another? There is a felt sense of identity. Let's suppose you have accessed a part that is sad, and then you notice that you are feeling hurt. You want to know whether the hurt comes from the sad part or from a different part. There is no way for an outside person to know this. There is no intellectual way to distinguish one part from another. It's simply intuitive. The way you tell if the hurt is a different part from the sadness is to feel into it with that question in mind. You will get a felt sense of whether they are two different parts or just one part. Or you could ask the parts and they will probably tell you. If you check inside and don't get an answer to this question, it simply means that you don't yet have full access to the part or parts. Keep working with them, and in a while you will know.

Dealing with Overwhelm

Your inner world can be a garden of riches, but at any moment it can also erupt in a chaotic confusion of intense feelings. Sometimes when a loaded issue gets triggered, instead of parts appearing one at a time, which would

172

be more workable, they all become triggered at once, vying for control and attention, and fighting with each other. Suppose that, in the example above, as soon as you hear your lover threatening to leave, many parts come up at the same time. You feel terrified, defensive, self-judging, angry, ashamed, and abandoned, all in one intense moment. At first, you may not be able to distinguish these individual feelings; you may just experience inner confusion, conflict, or chaos. You might feel overwhelmed and flooded with emotion.

In IFS, we want to welcome all our parts, but we don't want to be overwhelmed by them. A good way to handle this is to slow down, take a deep breath, and feel your belly and legs. This will help to ground you. Then take your time and pay attention to one emotion (and therefore one part) at a time. Even if you are feeling them all at once, focus on just one emotion or experience at a time, just enough to recognize the part and access it, as you learned in Chapter 4. For example, you single out the defensive feeling and hear that part say it wants to defend you against your partner's accusations. Then you access the part that is terrified of being alone. Then you hear from the self-judging part, and so on. Give each one the microphone and let it speak. You don't have to spend much time with each part—just enough to access it and get a sense of what it feels. Once you have accessed all the parts, you will have an overall perspective on what is happening, and it will feel less chaotic.

At this point, you can choose one target part and proceed to get to know it. If the other parts keep jumping in, listen to them but then ask them to step aside as we discussed above. This way you can avoid being overwhelmed and stay focused on a productive track of discovery and healing.

Acknowledging All Parts

The opposite can happen. You might be so focused on getting somewhere in the session that you are determined to stay with your original target part, so you push aside or ignore other parts that arise. Suppose you are pursuing work with a part called the Judge, and you single-mindedly ignore everything else that is happening in your psyche. If sadness arises, you ignore it because it doesn't fit your agenda with the Judge. If there is a part doesn't like the Judge or is frightened of it, you try to *make* it step aside rather than *asking* it. This closed-minded attitude is not coming from Self but rather from a rigid, driven protector.

There are two difficulties with this tunnel-vision approach.

1. You may miss something that is actually relevant to your work with the Judge. Maybe a part comes up that is polarized with the Judge, or perhaps a part arises that is being hurt by the Judge. These parts are crucial to your work with the Judge. They are members of a cluster of parts that interact with the Judge, and if you don't deal with them, you will never complete your work with this protector. Therefore, it is important to acknowledge them and understand who they are and how they are related to the Judge before you continue on your original track.

2. This driven approach can foster internal alienation and conflict. If you ignore a part, it won't trust that you care about it and want to know it. Then later when you need to work with it, it may be hurt and therefore less likely to show itself to you. It will be hard for it to relax its extreme position because it doesn't believe that you are there to help with its concerns. It is very important to create an atmosphere of curiosity and compassion in which your parts know you care about them. Your parts want to feel that they are part of the internal family and that you, Self, are interested in them personally, that you value them and feel that they have a valuable contribution to make. If you ignore them or push them aside, you will have to repair the damage later. Even if you don't want them interfering at the moment, be interested in them and respectful of them. Remember the IFS principle, "All parts are welcome."

Continuing Work in a Subsequent Session

Frequently, you will end an IFS session before you have completed the piece of work you started—in other words, before you have fully unburdened your target part and any exiles it is protecting. When you begin your next session, it is often useful to pick up the work where you left off in the previous session. This isn't always necessary. Sometimes you may want to begin a new session with a different part because something urgent has come up in your life. However, don't wait too long to pick up the thread of previous work so you don't leave your parts hanging or lose track of the exploration you have already begun.

Here's how to continue from where you left off in a previous session. First re-access the part you were working on. Review your notes from that session to jumpstart your memory, reminding yourself of what you learned about the target part, your relationship with it, and where you were in the IFS process. Remember to be aware of any concerned parts or protectors that didn't fully step aside. You may need to begin with one of them. If there was more than one part in the previous session, sense which one seems most important to begin with.

When you have chosen a part to re-access, remember how you knew the part in that session through a visual image, body sensation, emotion, and/or internal voice. Re-access the part using that modality. For example, if you had an image of the Caretaker as a mother with an apron, use that image to re-access the part. Ask the part what it is feeling now and if it is ready to continue interacting with you. Then continue where you left off at the end of the previous session. For example, if you were getting to know the caretaker but hadn't yet understood its positive intent for you, ask questions that will uncover that. Sometimes you may need to get to know the part over again to renew your connection with it experientially.

Don't assume that the part will be exactly the same as before. Be prepared for it to feel different now than it did in the last session or have different things to say to you. For example, maybe the caretaker was very concerned about your husband in the last session, but now it is worried about your child.

Summary

In this chapter, you have learned how to detect parts that can take over while you are getting to know a protector—judgmental, avoidant, intellectual, impatient, inadequate, skeptical, and exiled parts—and how to handle each of them. You know how to stay on track with your IFS work and how to keep yourself from being overwhelmed if many parts arise at once. You have seen how to acknowledge all parts that arise in your consciousness while at the same time staying with your thread. You have also learned how to continue previous work with a part at the beginning of a new session.

All this allows you to see and acknowledge all the parts that may arise, while preventing them from derailing you. In this way, you can keep your session on track.

Part II: Exiles and Unburdening

Once you have gotten to know a protector and developed a trusting relationship with it, you have made important progress toward helping it to relax and let go of its protective role. Until then, the protector will be worried that the exile will be harmed or that you will feel the exile's pain. Think of it this way. If you felt protective of a younger sister who was in danger from bullies at school, you wouldn't be able to relax your guard until you were certain the bullies were neutralized and your sister could take care of herself. It is the same with a protector. It may relax some, but it can't fully let go until the exile it shields is healed. It might actually be destructive to try and push past the protector or to convince it to drop its role entirely. This could set up an adversarial relationship with the protector in which it feels that it must resist you instead of cooperating with you.

Therefore, we don't waste time trying to induce the protector to change. We simply ask permission to work with the exile it is guarding and then move on to healing that child part. Once this has been accomplished, we come back to the protector. At that point, it is more likely to release its protective role because the exile is no longer fragile and in need of protection. Thus there is a trajectory to this process; we move from protector to exile and back again. This is in contrast to many therapies that just try to get past protectors to heal exiles. They don't respect and connect with protectors, so the protector's healing is often incomplete. And protectors are the parts that run our lives.

Part II describes in detail the series of steps involved in healing an exile of the pain and burden it carries. This is the heart of the depth work with exiles in IFS. We don't just explore our underlying pain—we transform it. After obtaining permission from the protector to work with the exile, you listen to the exile's pain from a compassionate place. Then you witness the childhood origins of that pain, reparent the exile in the way it needed back then, take it out of that oppressive situation, and help it to release the pain or negative belief it has been carrying. This allows the exile to transform and begin manifesting those positive qualities that are natural to it. Once this has happened, you return to the protector, which recognizes that its "ward" is now safe, and you help it to let go of its protective role and choose a new job, if it wants to.

The seven steps for working with an exile are presented in Chapters 10-15. This covers all of what is needed for complete psychological healing, thus paving the way for profound personality change.

Be Careful

A lot of painful and debilitating feelings can come up when working with exiles. Since these parts hold childhood pain and trauma, this work may trigger intense emotions which can sometimes be overwhelming. Most people find it necessary to work with a partner in doing exile work. It is very hard to do this successfully alone, especially if you are dealing with significant childhood pain.

Furthermore some people have so much pain and trauma in their background that it isn't safe to work on their exiles without an IFS therapist. If you are one of these people and you attempt to work with your exiles on your own, you could become terrified or seriously depressed or feel confused or dissociated. You also could be triggered to start drinking, overeating, or engaging in some other addictive activity. If you sense that working with exiles might be dangerous for you, find an IFS therapist to work with. The Center for Self-Leadership has a listing of trained IFS therapists organized by geographic location at www.selfleadership.org.

Steps in Healing an Exile

In Part I, you learned the five steps in getting to know a protector. These same five steps also apply to getting to know an exile, although they are handled somewhat differently. The getting-to-know-a-protector steps are labeled P1-P5 and the getting-to-know-an-exile steps E1-E5.

Here is the entire sequence of steps for the IFS process. They generally happen in sequence, but there are times when they naturally need to occur in a somewhat different order.

1. Getting to know a protector
    - P1: Accessing a part
    - P2: Unblending from the target part
    - P3: Unblending from a concerned part
    - P4: Discovering a protector's positive intent
    - P5: Developing a trusting relationship with a protector
2. Getting permission to work with an exile
3. Getting to know an exile
    - E1: Accessing an exile
    - E2: Unblending from an exile
    - E3: Unblending from a concerned part
    - E4: Learning about an exile
    - E5: Developing a trusting relationship with an exile
4. Accessing and witnessing childhood memories
5. Reparenting an exile
6. Retrieving an exile
7. Unburdening an exile
8. Transforming a protector

Chapter 10

Being Allowed In

Getting Permission to Work with an Exile

The only reason a protector is active is that an exile is in pain; that is, protectors take on extreme roles in order to protect us from the pain of exiles. They are often reluctant for us to contact exiles because they fear that we will be overwhelmed by this pain. A central principle in IFS is: *We don't work with an exile until we have permission from any protectors that might object.* If you violate this principle, protectors are likely to interrupt your work with the exile. Their job is to make sure that you don't ever have to be in touch with the pain that the exile is holding. Consequently, if you try to dive in, you can antagonize these lions guarding the gate, and they will assail you with defenses like sleepiness, intellectualizing, distractions, dissociation, or anger, which will derail your work with the exile. This chapter explains how to get permission to enter the land of the exiles. It reveals what to do if a protector refuses to let you pass and how to reassure it so it will open the gate and let you enter.

How to Discover the Exile Being Protected

Let's assume that you are working with a protector and you have gotten to know it, discovered its positive intent, and developed a trusting relationship with it. This is Step 1 in the IFS process (P1-P5). Your next step will be to get the protector's permission to work with the exile it is protecting. But first you must recognize which exile the protector is guarding. There are a number of ways to do this.

Sometimes the emotions of the exile come up while you are working with the protector. For example, you are talking with a protector that feels it must always be right. As you are getting to know it, you begin to feel a hurt feeling in your chest. This is probably coming from the exile that is being protected.

Sometimes you hear the voice of the exile. For example, while you are talking with a protector, you hear a voice that says, "I feel so alone and left out." That doesn't sound like the protector, so it is probably the exile.

Sometimes you get an image of the exile behind or below the image of the protector, or you see their relationship in some other way. For example, suppose you have a protector that keeps you overly busy so you don't feel the pain of an exile who is a lost little girl in the dark. You might visualize the little girl partially hidden behind the busy protector.

You can ask the protector what it is afraid would happen if it didn't perform its role. This answer frequently points toward the exile because the reason the protector is there is to guard the exile. For example, if the protector says it is afraid you will feel hurt or scared or lonely, it is probably protecting an exile that feels one of those emotions. If the protector says it is afraid that you will be judged or humiliated, it is probably protecting an exile that was judged or humiliated in the past.

You can ask the protector to show you the exile it is protecting. If you have built enough mutual trust, it will usually do that.

So far, I have talked as if there were a one-on-one correlation between protector and exile, but in fact the psyche can be much more complex. Sometimes one protector looks out for several exiles, or several protectors all guard a single exile. Therefore, when you are looking to discover the exile being protected, be prepared to find two or three, or even more. If you do find multiple exiles, you must still work with them one at a time, so choose one to start with and remember the others for later sessions.

Step 2: Asking Permission

Once you are aware of the exile being protected, ask permission from the protector to get to know this child part. You may receive an explicit yes or no. Or you may just sense that your way to the exile is clear or that it is blocked. Or the exile may suddenly emerge into consciousness, indicating that you have permission. Once you get permission, it may be a good idea to check if there are any other protectors that object to your contacting this exile so you can get their permission, too. If you don't get permission, see "Addressing the Protector's Fears" below.

This step highlights a major advantage of using IFS—its cooperative approach. Let's consider a situation where your heart is contracted to keep you from feeling the pain of being rejected by a lover. In many forms of therapy, you would focus on the contraction and try to get your heart to open so you could feel the underlying hurt and thereby heal it. But this means fighting against the part of yourself that is contracted, which is a protector. This part believes that it must keep contracted so you don't feel this intense pain. Turning it into an adversary usually backfires. The more you try to get past the contraction, the more it fights you. And if you do manage to break through this protector, you may accomplish a dramatic, cathartic healing, but the contracted protector is likely to reconstitute itself soon afterward because you didn't respect it and get its buy-in.

There is a powerful advantage to understanding that there are two parts involved. Though the protector is keeping you from the pain, it may not realize that there is an exile that is *already* feeling the pain. It may think it is actually preventing the pain from existing at all rather than preventing you from feeling what the exile is already experiencing. Using IFS, you don't try to break through the protection; you don't even ask the contraction to let go. Instead, you make it clear to the protector that the exile is already in pain, and you just ask permission to work with the exile so you can relieve it of the pain that exists. This way the protector feels you are trying to help rather than to cause pain, so it is much more likely to agree.

181

Addressing the Protector's Fears

If the protector doesn't want to give permission, it can be useful to reassure it that you won't try to barge through without its approval. Tell the protector that it is completely in charge of whether or not you have access to the exile. You won't try to ignore it. This often relieves protectors that are skittish and helps them to trust you. Then ask the protector what its concerns are about the exile or what it is afraid would happen if it allowed you to contact the exile. Protectors will usually tell you quite clearly what they are afraid of. Here are the eight most common fears of protectors and how to address them so the protector will allow you to access the exile.

1. The Exile's Pain Is Too Much

The protector says the exile has too much pain and you wouldn't be able to handle it. Or it says it doesn't want to deal with the exile's pain at all. It might also say that the exile is a black hole of chaos that you could get sucked into. Some protectors say that you will be flooded or overwhelmed by the exile's pain.

Whatever the exact concern about the exile's pain, acknowledge to the protector that it is valid. Many people do get overwhelmed by the pain their exiles carry, and working on it can be harmful if not done in a conscious, careful way. Explain to the protector that you don't want too much pain either. You will ensure that the exile doesn't get overwhelmed by staying in Self while you work with it instead of diving into its pain. You will stay in a grounded place where you are separate from the exile and its pain, so you won't get pulled in or flooded. (See Chapter 11 for how to do this.)

Normally, we flip back and forth between two extremes. Either we are caught in an exile's pain or we are closed off behind a protector's defenses. This is usually all the protector has experienced, so it is not surprising that it doesn't want to give permission at first. If it opens the gates, it expects that you will be flooded by the exile again. IFS does something quite different from either of these options. It helps you to work with the exile from the safe vantage point of Self. Explain this to the protector so it understands this novel way of proceeding. Then it will be more likely to relent.

You can also explain to the protector that if you do get blended with the exile, IFS has ways of helping you to unblend and return to Self. We already learned how to unblend from a protector in Chapter 5. In Chapter 11, you will learn how to unblend from an exile that is flooding you so you can return to Self. If you have a protector that is hard to reassure, it might be useful to read Chapter 11 before continuing. This will give you the confidence to reassure the protector.

You can also invite the protector to help you with the unblending process. Since it is concerned about overwhelm, it can watch carefully while you work with the exile, and as soon as it notices that the exile is starting to flood you with too much emotion, it can signal you to instigate unblending procedures. This invitation will reassure the protector even more because it can play an active role.

2. There Is No Point

The protector says there isn't any point in opening up the exile's pain. It simply doesn't believe that the exile can be healed. The past is the past and can't be changed. You just have to keep it buried and go on with your life.

Acknowledge that you understand why the protector might feel this way. The exile has been carrying this pain for a long time. Maybe you have tried some avenues of healing that haven't worked, so it isn't surprising that the protector would thinks it is futile. Explain that, by using IFS, you *can* heal the exile. IFS has a long track record of healing people's exiles successfully. Remember the transcript in Chapter 3 where this happened. This assurance is usually enough so the protector will give permission.

If this doesn't work, ask the protector if it will allow you to try using IFS with the exile for a while so the protector can see if this procedure indeed leads to healing. Once it has seen positive results, it is more likely to relent. And the more experience you have with successful IFS work, the more confident you will be, and the more your protectors will trust you and let you in. Therefore it might be a good idea to begin your work by choosing exiles that don't carry too much pain. This way you can gain access to them and heal them. Then your protectors will see that the method works and will grant you access to the more intense exiles.

If this still doesn't work, it might be a good idea to do a few sessions with an IFS therapist, who has the experience and expertise to help you heal your exiles. Or take one of my classes so you can see other people working successfully on their material and you can develop your skills further. Then your protectors will be more likely to trust that the IFS process works and that you can do it successfully.

3. The Protector Doesn't Want to Be Eliminated

The protector says that if it allows you to heal the exile, it will no longer have a role to play in your psyche and therefore will lose power or disappear. This seems like death, and it doesn't want this to happen. Parts tend to resist being eliminated; they don't want to die.

You can explain to the protector that if it lets you heal the exile and its current role becomes unnecessary, it doesn't have to go away. It can choose a new role in your psyche. A part isn't defined by its role or job. It took on a certain role many years ago and keeps at it doggedly, but this is not who it *really* is. If the exile is healed and the protector realizes that its job is no longer needed, it is welcome to choose any new role that it would like. Ask the protector what it would like to do if it didn't need to play its usual role. For example, an Intellectualizer whose job has been to avoid emotions might choose to be a philosopher who contemplates the meaning of life. Once the protector realizes that its existence is not at stake, it is more likely to give you permission to proceed.

4. The Exile Will Be Harmed

The protector says it is afraid that if the exile shows itself, it will be seen as wimpy, ugly, worthless, or bad, and therefore it will be judged or rejected. The protector may even be afraid that the exile will be harmed in a more direct way, such as being yelled at or attacked. There are three possibilities: It may fear the harm will come from you, from your partner (if you are working with one), or from other people. Let's examine these one at a time.

(a) If the protector fears that you will harm the exile, this may indicate that there is a part of you that is angry at the exile, and the protector can sense this. For example, if the exile is small and weak, there may be a part of you that hates weakness and wants to punish the exile for that. Check for this by asking yourself how you feel toward the exile. If you discover that there is indeed such a part blended with you, ask it to step aside so you can approach the exile from an open, compassionate place. If it won't, you may need to work with the punishing part first.

If you are clearly in Self, reassure the protector that you genuinely care about the exile and only want the best for it, so it is safe from you. You may need to forge a deeper connection with the protector before it will believe you. Once it does, it will allow you to contact the exile.

(b) If the protector doesn't trust your partner, ask what it doesn't trust about her. She needs to make sure she is in Self and then reassure the protector that she cares about the exile and won't harm it.

(c) The protector might be afraid of other people in your life harming the exile. If the exile comes out in a session, it may also show itself in daily life. For example, maybe the protector is afraid that the exile will act needy with your boyfriend and he will reject you for that. Sometimes this fear is justified and sometimes not. We will look at both possibilities.

If your boyfriend wouldn't really reject you for being needy, then the protector's fear probably comes from your childhood—for example, it wasn't safe to show needs when you were a child. In this case, sympathize with the protector's fear since it was realistic in the past. Then reassure the protector that you are now in a life situation that is safe for this exile; you won't be rejected for your needs. This should reassure it enough to give you permission to work with the exile.

If your boyfriend might really reject you for showing needs, explain to the protector that you are only asking permission to work with the exile in this session. Afterwards, the protector can come back and hide the exile if it seems necessary. If this isn't enough to reassure the protector, it may indicate that your life situation really isn't safe enough for deep therapy work because there really are people in your life who would react badly if they saw your exiles or if you made substantial therapeutic changes. If so, you may have to do something about your relationship or family situation before it is safe to access your exiles and transform them. You might need to work with an IFS therapist who can also do couples therapy or family therapy to help improve your life situation.

5. The Protector Doesn't Trust Your Competence

The protector says it doesn't trust you to work well with a vulnerable exile. You can ask the protector what it doesn't trust about you. It might be afraid that you won't stay on track, for example, or you don't know what to do, or you won't care for the exile.

Explain to the protector that you are just learning the IFS process, and you will become more skilled as you practice. You will be very careful with the vulnerable exile, and ask the protector to allow you to proceed so you can develop your capacities. Assure it that you won't take on an exile whose pain is too intense until you are more experienced. If you are working with a partner, explain that your partner can help with the process.

Sometimes the protector's fears are justified because there is a part of you that might handle the work poorly. For example, maybe a part of you would space out or dive into pain too quickly. Explain that if these parts are triggered, you will work with them and ask them to step aside. You might even want to work with them first to clear the way for safer and more effective work with your exile. This will be very effective in reassuring the protector so it will give permission.

6. A Secret Will Be Revealed

The protector says it is afraid that the exile will reveal a secret that should be kept hidden. This is usually something that was covered up in childhood that you don't consciously know about. It would have been dangerous for this secret to come out in your family of origin, so the child part that holds it was exiled. The protector thinks you are still a child caught in that family situation where the secret would have been dangerous to expose. It doesn't realize that you are now an independent adult and your family no longer has power over you. Validate the protector's fear as something of real concern when you were little. Then bring the protector up to date. Show it that time has passed, and give it an idea of your current life and capacities. This way, it will be able to see that the secret can't cause you trouble now.

Sometimes the exile holds a secret that the protector thinks would be too disturbing for you. Explain that you will stay in Self, where you can handle anything because you are grounded and centered. Let the protector know that if any parts are triggered by the information, you will be there to nurture and soothe them.

7. A Dangerous Protector Will Be Triggered

The protector says that bringing up the exile's pain will trigger a different protector, one that is dangerous or destructive. For example, it is afraid of activating a protector that would fly into a rage or go on a drinking binge. It might not be wrong; this is sometimes a real possibility. There are extreme protectors, and in IFS they are called *firefighters*. They jump in impulsively to douse the fire of an exile's pain when it is starting to come up. They have no concern for the possible destructive consequences of their actions. They just want to stop the pain at any cost. They are the last resort in trying to avoid or distract from pain. If the ordinary protectors fail to guard against anguish, firefighters will do anything to prevent it from overwhelming you. Therefore, if you bypass a relatively mild protector, such as an intellectualizer or caretaker, a firefighter could be triggered, which would act rashly and destructively in order to stop the exile's pain. Often this happens after a session. For example, a firefighter might cause you to have an affair or a traffic accident to distract you from the exile's suffering. The mild protector may be aware of the more dangerous one and warn you not to open up the exile.

First, check to see if you have such a firefighter, and, if you do, validate the protector's concern. Then work with the firefighter; connect with it and get to know it just as you would any other protector. Find out its positive intent and forge a trusting relationship with it. Then obtain its permission to engage with the exile. This makes it safe to go ahead. Then check back with the original protector; it will probably give you permission now that the firefighter is not going to erupt.

8. The Exile Will Re-experience the Wound.
The protector says that it doesn't want the exile to re-experience its wound or to be wounded again. This is based on a false understanding that the protector holds. It believes that it is protecting the exile from being wounded again, the way it was in childhood. If that were true, then it would be questionable whether it would be a good idea to make the exile feel that pain again. However, the truth is that the exile is stuck in that childhood situation of wounding. It is *already* experiencing the wound. The protector is just keeping you from feeling this. If you explain this to the protector, and it will probably give you permission to access the exile.

We have now explored the eight most common fears that prevent protectors from giving permission and what to do about each one. However, you don't have to memorize all these options and responses. The principles are what is important. Find out what the protector is afraid of and reassure it that you will handle the process safely.

Working with a Stubborn Protector
What do you do if you've tried everything and the protector is so stubborn that it still won't budge? Sometimes you have a protector that is strongly resistant to allowing you to access the exile because it doesn't trust that you will be careful or it doesn't feel respected by you. It is afraid that you will try to push past it or sneak around it to get to the exile. It believes that its protective role is essential and must not be violated. With a protector like this, it can be helpful to reassure it that *it* is in charge of whether or not you work with the exile. Let it know that you respect its need to protect, and you won't do anything without its permission. This is actually true. The way IFS operates is that we never work with an exile without getting

187

permission from *all* protectors that might object, no matter how long this takes. We only work in a cooperative manner. Let the part know that you won't try to take away its power. You will only move ahead if it agrees to do so. (Of course, you have to mean it.) If you make this very clear to the protector, this will help it to trust you. It is likely to listen to you because it realizes that you want to cooperate with it, not fight it. And once it is willing to listen, you will be able to reassure it about its fears and gain its permission.

The Promise of a New Role
Here is an additional approach to gaining permission that can be effective. Offer the protector hope. Protectors are often tired of their jobs, even though they hold tightly to them because they believe they are necessary. A protector's role often requires it to do distasteful things like being shut down or judgmental. Furthermore, this role often doesn't work very well— the exile gets hurt anyway. It's been a long, hard road, and the protector gets little or no appreciation; in fact, other parts often judge the protector for doing its job. If you ask a protector how it feels about its role, many will tell you that they are very tired of it and would love to give it up, but they don't think that is possible.

Here is a scenario that demonstrates how to give a protector hope in order to obtain its permission. You must have already identified the exile that is being protected.

> **You:** If we healed the exile you are protecting so that it was no longer vulnerable and in pain, would you still need to do your job?
> Protector: I don't believe you can do that.
> **You:** Okay, but what if we could? Would you still need to do your job?
> **Protector:** No, I guess I wouldn't. And that would be a great relief.
> **You:** What job would you like to do instead?
> Protector: I would like to be a supporter to the exile (or perform some other positive role).
> *Secretly, this is what all protectors really want.*
> **You:** Will you give me permission to work with the exile so I have a chance to show you that it can be healed? Then you can give up this burdensome job and be a supporter instead.
> **Protector:** Okay. You can give it a try.

This approach offers the protector the hope of giving up a job that is onerous, unrewarding, and thankless, and instead taking on a role that feels much better for the protector as well as for you.

After You Have Obtained Permission

Now that you have obtained permission from the target protector, are you free to work with the exile? That depends on whether there are other protectors that feel this exile is dangerous. Often you can simply move on to working with the exile, but it would be wise to deal with any additional resistance now. Otherwise, these protectors will repeatedly interrupt your work with the exile. Therefore, if it seems called for, ask if there are any other protectors that don't want you to access the exile. Usually they will step forward, and you can ask about their fears and reassure them, just as you did with the primary protector. This will usually clear the way for uninterrupted work with the exile.

However, sometimes protectors pop up later. While you are working with the exile, if a protector feels threatened by the pain that is coming up from the exile, it may reactivate to block that pain. You may get sleepy or distracted. You may go into your head or get angry. Use your parts-detecting ability (from Chapter 9) to recognize when such a protector has been triggered. If it is the same protector that has already given you permission, ask what happened in your work with the exile to make it change its mind. Usually it's because the pain of the exile started to emerge in an intense way. Find out what it is afraid of now and reassure it about that fear. If it is a new protector that you haven't gotten permission from or haven't worked with before, you may need to spend some time with this protector, getting to know it and its positive intent, perhaps even going through Steps P1-P5 with this part. Then ask its permission to go on with your work with the exile.

Sometimes, if an exile's pain is threatening to overwhelm you, a protector will keep jumping in to stop this from happening, and no amount of reassurance will work. Then you must negotiate with the exile about unblending even before you ask the protector for permission. This is covered in Chapter 11. Once the protector sees that the exile has agreed not to flood you, it will probably give the go-ahead.

If you are unable to get permission from the protector despite following the directions in this chapter, or if it keeps jumping back in to disrupt your work, this may be an indication that it isn't safe for you to be working with this exile (or perhaps any of your exiles) on your own. You may need to work with an IFS therapist, who can provide additional support and expertise.

Getting Permission from Christine's Confuser

Let's look at an example of the process of getting permission. This involves a segment of the transcript of Christine's work with her Confuser Part from Chapter 3. This part creates blankness and confusion so Christine won't be able to see certain things (which hadn't been named at this point in the session). First, we will see how Christine finds out who the exile is.

Jay: Ask the Confuser what it is afraid would happen if it stepped aside and allowed you to see what it has been hiding.

This question tends to lead the inquiry toward the exile that is being protected.

Christine: What it says is: "What would happen is just unthinkable, unspeakable." It is so frightened, we can't even go there.

J: I see; it is very frightened about this.

C: At a survival level.

J: Ask the Confuser if it would be willing to show you a part that it is protecting with its confusion.

C: Oh! Now I'm getting a glimpse of a panic state behind the Confuser.

J: Check to see if the Confuser will give you permission to get to know this panicked part.

C: … Okay. It isn't sure about this. It's very nervous.

J: You might ask it what it's worried about. What is it afraid will happen?

C: The Confuser is afraid that the exile will come rushing up and swamp me.

J: You might invite it to signal us in some way if it feels that the exile is beginning to swamp you, because we can keep that from happening. This protector can actually help us by letting us know if that starts to happen, and then you can return to Self.

This is the first fear in our list—that the exile's pain will be overwhelming, so I have Christine reassure the part that she will stay in Self and invite the part to aid in that process.

C: All right. It seems Okay with that ... Now there are all sorts of judgments coming up. I will be too slow. I will go meandering all over the place, and nothing will happen.

This first reassurance seems to have worked, and now the Confuser's other fears come out.

C: I'm telling the Confuser that I can understand its concerns, but I don't think that will happen. We've tried things like this before, and I have shown myself to be helpful when given the chance. And you (Jay) are there as well to offer support, so I suggested to the Confuser that it's a chance to find new territory where it can relax and not have to work so hard.

Christine suggests that the protector has something to gain by allowing us to proceed—it would be able to relax.

J: Good. How is it responding?

C: Okay, these images are so funny. The Confuser sort of sat back in a lawn chair and crossed its legs to watch what happens next. It's so funny. Oh goodness. (laughing)

The Confuser's sitting back tells us Christine's reassurance has worked and it is giving permission to proceed with the exile.

Getting Permission from Fran's Protectors

This is a segment of a session with Fran, who was a student in one of my IFS classes. In that day's meeting, we were learning about unblending from an exile. Fran volunteered because she knew about an exile that she was afraid to work with, and she wanted help with it.

> **Fran:** I'm feeling trepidation because I think there's a very big exile, but I want to take this opportunity to work with it.
>
> **Jay:** Ask if there are any protectors that don't want you to work with this exile. Ask them to come forward if they are there.
>
> If you start a session working with an exile, it is always a good idea to do this check before going ahead.
>
> **F:** Oh gosh, I can sense these angry parts marching up and down. "You think you're going to get past this line and talk to this exile. You've got to be kidding." They're making faces and trying to scare me.

> **J:** Before we go any further, let's take a moment to access as much Self as possible.

Here I lead Fran in a short centering/grounding meditation like the one in Chapter 5. The actual meditation is not included here.

F: Okay. I feel I'm in Self, but it feels very fragile. I see those figures in a parade shaking their fists at me, but now I feel more detached from them, more observing, rather than being so scared as I was before.

J: Okay, good. And how are you feeling toward them right now?

F: I feel curious, and I do feel calm.

J: Ask those protectors what their concerns are.

This is a way of checking to see what they fear about working with the exile.

F: There's a sense of sadness. They say: "You're not going to be able to handle it, so don't even start. You started this before and then you abandoned us."

J: Do you know what that means?

F: It means that I start to be attentive to the parts that are hurting and then I don't follow through. I go away and exile them again.

This is a competence fear. They are afraid she won't be consistent in her relationship with the exiles.

J: I see. So it means that you will abandon them after the session. Do you have a sense of whether or not that's true?

F: I think it is. At times, I've been there for myself and started to feel the pain or witness the story, but then I don't know what to do. Later, I feel overwhelmed and then shut them out again. I don't stay with it long enough to develop a relationship with the part.

J: So today's class should help. Probably the reason you couldn't stay with the exile is because it blended with you. If you can stay unblended, you're much more likely to stay with it because you won't be flooded.

F: I didn't realize until now that that was the problem.

J: You might tell that line of protectors that if they let you practice unblending, you will be more likely to stay with the exile.

The idea here is that there was a reason why Fran "abandoned" her exiles — she was getting flooded. She wasn't just being irresponsible. Once she addresses this, she will be able to stay with them more consistently.

F: Well, they seem Okay with that idea. But now I see a part sheltering or hovering over a young child part and seeing me as a punishing god. It doesn't trust me. It's kind of like a parental protector that sees me as dangerous.

Parental protector keeps Fran from accessing the exile.

The group of protectors were reassured about their fear, and now a second fear comes up.

J: So it's afraid that you're going to hurt the exile?

F: Yeah, that I won't be gentle. I'll be harsh. And I'll have expectations of the exile that are unrealistic. I'll want it to be more grown up than it can be. Here's where I start to feel shaky and lack confidence. I'm afraid that I will be harsh.

It looks as though Fran does have a part of her that could make demands on the exile, but the important question is whether that part is blended with her right now. If not, she can reassure the protector about that, and it will let her in.

J: So check to see if you feel that way right now.

F: No, I don't at the moment. I feel warmly toward this child.

J: Yeah. So let the protector know that, and see if it will give you permission to work with the child.

F: ... That feels good. More peaceful now. There is a thin veil in front of a cave where the exile is. But it's not unwelcoming. I can open the curtain. And there are nursemaid figures there now to support.

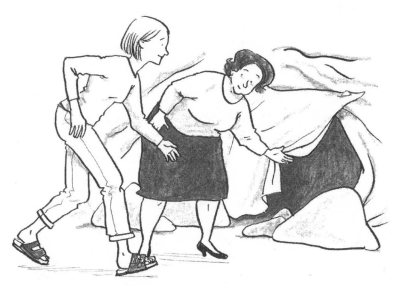

Parental protector allows Fran in to be with the exile.

J: So it is kind of giving you permission?

F: Yes. It is bowing out of the way and opening a space for me to walk in.

The second protector has now also given permission, so Fran can now begin to work with the exile.

We will see the rest of this session in Chapter 11.

Exercise: Getting Permission to Work with an Exile

Do a session in which you practice getting permission from a protector to work with the exile it guards. If possible, choose a protector that you have already become acquainted with. Re-access the protector, make sure you are in Self, and finish discovering its positive intent and developing a trusting relationship with it, as covered in Chapters 7 and 8. Then recognize who the exile is and work on getting permission to contact it, as covered in this chapter. Once you have permission, invite the exile to tell you or show you what it feels. Take notes on what you discover:

Protector _____

Positive intent _____

What it is afraid would happen if it didn't play its role _____

_____

Exile _____

What the protector is afraid would happen if you contacted the exile ____

_____

What the exile feels _____

Summary

In this chapter, you have learned how to ask permission from a protector to work with the exile it shields. You know how to identify this exile, and you understand the kinds of fears that keep protectors from letting you in and how to reassure them so they will give permission. You have learned how to offer hope for a new role to a protector and what to do if protectors keep jumping into to derail your work with the exile.

Chapter 11

Uncovering Your Pain

Getting to Know an Exile

———————————— • ————————————

This chapter explores Step 3 in the overall IFS procedure—getting to know an exile. However, first it would be useful to understand exiles more fully, so let's discuss how they affect our feelings and behavior on an everyday basis.

When an Exile Gets Activated

In Chapter 4, we discussed what it means for a protector to become activated. Something disturbing or threatening happens in your life that prompts a protector to take over in order to keep you from being harmed in some way. For example, in that chapter, Julie's boyfriend was acting needy, and that activated Julie's Tin Man protector, which closed her heart to prevent her from staying involved with him.

Exiles can also become activated by events, people, or situations in your life. However, very often when an exile is activated, its protector will be too. For example, John meets a woman he is attracted to, which triggers an Insecure Exile that feels unsure and socially awkward and is afraid of being rejected. In response to this exile, a protector also crops up to keep

John away from this woman so the exile isn't rejected by her. Let's call this the Withdrawn Protector.

Most of the time, we don't notice the exile because exiles are pushed out of consciousness. If we notice anything, it is the behavior of the protector because it is the protectors that control our behavior. So John might be aware that he stayed away from this attractive woman but might not realize that the Insecure Exile was behind this. If John didn't withdraw but instead forced himself to interact with the woman, then he might actually feel nervous and awkward, thereby becoming consciously aware of the Insecure Exile. Of course, if John is aware enough, he might feel the exile anyway.

To summarize: In most situations that trigger us, at least two parts are involved. The exile is usually triggered first and then the protector, which pops up to guard it. However, the protector may pop up so quickly that we don't notice the exile at all. In fact, that is usually the protector's mission—to prevent us from feeling the pain of the exile.

Sometimes when an exile is activated, a protector doesn't jump in front of it, and we experience and act directly from the exile. For example, John might just interact with the woman he is attracted to, all the while feeling scared and inadequate, and he would probably act in ways that are consistent with that—awkward, self-effacing, halting in his speech, and so on. In this case, the exile is blended with John.

Here is another example of an exile taking over. Jane has been involved with Ralph for four months, and while she was very excited about the relationship at first, she is beginning to see that Ralph is too absorbed in himself to treat her well. A number of her parts are ready to break up with him. However, she has an exile who desperately needs to be connected to a man, which I will call the Needy Part. This part is terrified of losing Ralph and being alone. The Needy Part wants to avoid feeling lonely at all costs. So it hangs onto the relationship with Ralph. It blends with Jane and won't let her break up with him.

There are two ways that exiles can affect our behavior and feelings. (1) They can take over, as with Jane's Needy Part and John's Insecure Exile. (2) Or they can trigger protectors that take over, such as John's Withdrawn Protector. When a protector takes over, you may not be aware of the exile at all, but it is there underneath, prompting the protector's behavior. Therefore, when you are exploring an issue, it always involves an exile, either directly or indirectly.

Getting to Know an Exile

Now let's return to the IFS process. In the last chapter, you obtained permission from the protector to get to know the exile it was guarding (Step 2). In this chapter, we deal with Step 3, getting to know the exile. This involves five sub-steps, E1–E5, which are analogous to the five steps you already learned for getting to know a protector, steps P1–P5. First you access the exile experientially (E1). Then you make sure you are in Self because this is required for getting to know the exile successfully, just as it was with protectors. When you are in Self, you aren't flooded with the exile's pain (E2), and you are able to feel compassion for it (E3). This allows you to get to know it (E4) and develop a trusting relationship with it (E5).

Step E1: Accessing an Exile

Last chapter in Step 2, you discovered which exile was being guarded by the protector and got permission to work with it. Now you must contact this exile experientially in order to get to know it. You sense the exile in your body, or feel its emotions, or get an image of it, just the way you learned to access a part in Chapter 4.

In some cases, the exile may already have emerged experientially while you were working with the protector. For example, you may have felt its emotions or seen an image of it. In this case, access has already happened. However, it might be useful to broaden your access to the part by using an additional channel. For example, if you already feel its emotions, you might see if an image arises that represents the exile.

Step E2: Unblending from an Exile

When working with childhood wounds, there are two dangers. One is that you will be flooded with pain; the other is that you will avoid the exile because you are afraid of the pain being too excruciating. Exiles want to be heard and healed, but unfortunately they sometimes try to be heard by flooding you with their feelings, which means blending with you. This is all they know. Blending can be frightening because it draws you into the exile's vortex of helplessness, and you might become increasingly buried in the pain or chaos. The intensity of reliving a trauma in this way could actually be harmful, and, if this begins to happen, protectors will usually react by stepping in and blocking access to the exile. Keeping you from this suffering has been their job for years, so they will react automatically. You will find yourself going numb or spacing out; you might become distracted or angry. These and other reactions all come from protectors that are afraid of the pain, and for good reason; it really might be difficult for you to cope with.

IFS has discovered a way to explore an exile's pain safely. You stay in Self and *relate* to the exile; you don't *become* the exile. If you merged with the exile and lost contact with the Self, the pain really could be overwhelming. However, the Self, when it is differentiated and separate from the exile, can deal with anything. When in Self, you sit in a calm, grounded place, and therefore you aren't threatened by pain and trauma. If you start to be overpowered by the exile's emotions, which means that the part is blending with Self, IFS has effective techniques for unblending and returning you to a grounded place.

This approach is workable because, in most cases, it isn't necessary for you to directly feel the exile's pain. IFS has discovered that witnessing is usually enough to set the stage for the rest of the healing steps.

There are a number of benefits to this approach. Besides avoiding being retraumatized, you aren't confronted with an armory of defenses to keep you from the exile. Since you aren't threatened by the exile's pain, protectors don't feel the need to interrupt the process. This saves time, and sometimes it is the only way to work with an exile because, otherwise, protectors continually throw up obstacles and may permanently block the process. Furthermore, by remaining in Self, you can be a compassionate witness to the exile's pain and the agent of healing and transformation for the exile. In addition, from Self, you have the perspective to direct your own therapy process successfully.

The Unblending Process

Once you have accessed the exile, if you start feeling his[1] emotions strongly, you need to work on unblending immediately. Even if you're not exposed to too much emotion at first, be on the lookout for the beginnings of blending, which could be the beginning of a downhill slide. When this starts to happen, it is best to catch it as soon as possible. That way you can come back to Self before you become overwhelmed with emotion. If you let the pain grow too intense before you try to return to Self, it will be more difficult to do so. In fact, if you sense that the exile is carrying a lot of pain or trauma, it can be a good idea to negotiate an unblending agreement with him right at the start. If the exile will unblend, you can be there for it. This is the safest route.

Here is the best way to unblend from an exile or to negotiate an unblending agreement. Ask the exile not to flood you with his emotions and pain so you can be there for him and help him. Alternatively, you can ask him to contain his feelings, or to not overwhelm you, or to stay separate from you. Explain to the exile that you will be able to hear his story and help him if you remain in Self. You are not asking the exile to block his feelings; you aren't suggesting that he shouldn't feel his emotions. You are simply asking him to keep those feelings separate from you so you can be in a solid place to help. This is one of the most powerful innovations of the IFS method. Schwartz discovered that exiles have the capacity to cooperate in the healing process and contain the intensity of what you experience, if they want to. If you ask in this way, by explaining that it will help in the healing process, most exiles are willing and able to keep their pain separate from you.

When you ask the exile to contain his feelings, sometimes he says no or you don't notice any change in the intensity of the emotion. Then ask the exile what he is afraid would happen if he *did* contain himself. In most cases, he will say that he expects you to ignore him because he fears that if he doesn't flood you, he will be exiled again. This is completely

---

[1] Up until now, I have referred to a part using the indefinite pronoun "it." In actual sessions, people vary in terms of how they refer to their parts, sometimes using "it" and sometimes "he" or "she." From now on in this book, because of the especially personal nature of the relationship between the Self and an exile, I will often refer to the exile using "he" or "she."

understandable. Most of us alternate between walling off our exiles and being flooded by their pain. So the exile's experience is that the only way he can be heard is to take you over. No wonder he doesn't want to stay separate! He expects to be dismissed if he does. Explain to the exile that, because you are using IFS, this time you will be different. You really do want to know about his pain and witness his story.

However, you must be in Self in order to do this. That way, the exile will experience you as a kindly listener, a caring presence, or perhaps a nurturing parent. Once he understands that he won't be dismissed, he will probably be willing to stay separate. He will see that his cooperation will lead to his being heard, which is what he most wants.

If this approach doesn't work, there are other ways to unblend from an exile, many of which are similar to the ways of unblending from a protector (from Chapter 5). You can internally feel yourself stepping back from the exile. You can do a short grounding/centering meditation. You can visualize the exile at a distance from you.

If you use this visualization technique, later you will want to move closer to the exile. As you get to know him (E4) and the threat of blending recedes, you can visualize yourself moving gradually nearer, making sure that he doesn't flood you, and backing up if necessary. This symbolizes both how you are separate from the exile and how you are becoming more connected with him (E5). The goal is to feel very close to the exile emotionally while still remaining separate. It is like walking a tightrope but is entirely possible. People often visualize this as picking up the exile and holding him close.

Once you have unblended and come back to Self, take a minute or so to experience Self more fully so you solidify the experience. Notice how you feel the qualities of Self in your body. You may experience a fullness or solidity in your belly. You might feel calmness and relaxation throughout your body. You might feel grounded in your feet. You might feel a gentle, loving quality in your heart. Let yourself *be with* this experience so that it becomes more fully felt and embodied in you. This will help to keep you from being flooded by the exile in the future. Once you feel that Self is more fully established in your experience, come back to the exile and get to know him. It can also be useful to anchor your experience of Self in this way before you start working with the exile.

Christine Unblending from the Little Girl

This is a short section of the transcript of Christine's session from Chapter 3, which illustrates unblending from an exile. At this point she has gotten permission to contact the exile.

> **Christine:** So here is the exile. She is very little and skinny, and quite frail. It's interesting because I'm tall and strong. But she is in a little dress, and she is quite vulnerable in her small, light, little body. She's all knotted up in her throat, and she's watching and on the edge of panic.
>
> **Jay:** Mm hmm. You might ask this part what she would like to be called.
>
> **C:** I guess just the Little Girl.
>
> **J:** Okay, ask the Little Girl what she is so frightened of.
>
> **C:** That she is going to be left alone in the dark and nobody will be there. It is so interesting. But now she is panicking, and it's too much for me.

*The Little Girl's panic is blending with Christine
and pulling her out of Self.*

> **J:** Let her know that it is Okay for her to be scared, but ask her not to flood you with it.
>
> **C:** Okay. I'm Okay now. I don't feel too scared anymore. It's good that *she* is allowed to feel the panic, because otherwise she would go away.
>
> *This shows the importance of making it clear to the exile that asking it to separate doesn't mean it can't feel its emotions. If this exile felt that her emotions weren't allowed, she wouldn't have trusted Christine enough*

to stay around.

C: She likes that I'm here now. She actually sees that there is someone (Self) here, and she is surprised. And as soon as that happens, she calms down and just wants to talk to me. She's not charged.

J: Mm hmm. She is more relaxed and open to you.

Now that the part isn't flooding Christine with her panic, Christine can be in Self, and the Little Girl has someone to rely on, which allows her to calm down.

C: Yes, that's right.

Conscious Blending

There is an exception to the need for unblending. Sometimes it is all right to feel an exile's pain. If you don't feel thrown off by the experience and it doesn't keep you from being grounded, you can allow yourself to experience it. In fact, sometimes it will feel right to you to sense this pain. And the exile may want you to experience her pain directly because this helps her to feel fully witnessed by you.

Experiencing the exile's pain in this way means that you are simultaneously in Self and consciously blended with the exile. The exile is showing you her emotion by having you feel it. That is fine as long as you can tolerate this experience and you remain centered and able to be there for the exile, and as long as this doesn't trigger any protectors. Often it is all right to experience the exile's suffering up to a certain limit. Let her know if it gets to be too much, and ask her to contain the rest.

In some cases, you may be able to feel the pain fully and even express it. You will know how far you can go in this direction. This approach is similar to some cathartic therapy methods. However, in IFS, we only move in this direction if it is both safe and productive.

I call this *conscious blending* because you are aware that you are blended and are purposely choosing to allow it. This is very different from being blended without realizing it or being overwhelmed emotionally. By blending consciously, you know that, even while you experience the exile's emotions, you are grounded in a presence (Self) that is much larger and stronger than she. This gives you the opportunity to tolerate how much of her pain you take on.

If you check inside, you will know whether conscious blending is the right thing to do—whether to unblend from an exile's pain or allow your-self to feel it. The main criterion is whether or not you can tolerate the pain. The more fully you are in Self and the more compassion you feel for the exile, the more likely it is that conscious blending will be possible. How-ever, remember that conscious blending is not always better than staying separately in Self. Most of the time, exiles don't need us to take on their pain; witnessing is enough.

Step E3: Unblending from Concerned Parts

In order to get to know an exile successfully, it is important for you to be in Self, just as with protectors. To check for this, notice how you are feel-ing toward the exile. If you are feeling curious, accepting, connected, or compassionate, you are in Self and can proceed. If you are feeling judg-mental, angry, or scared of the exile, or if you want it to go away, you aren't in Self. You are blended with a concerned part (see Chapter 6), which is a protector that is worried about your working with the exile. You have already obtained permission to work with it from the protector that was your original target part, but there may be other protectors that don't think it is safe to open up the exile. This concerned part is one of these. Ask the concerned part to step aside so you can be in a position to help transform the exile. Often that will be enough for it to relax and let you return to Self. Then you can go on to get to know the exile.

If the concerned part isn't willing to step back, ask it what it is afraid would happen if it did. This will uncover the protector's fear that is block-ing you from being open to the exile. It will most likely be one of the protec-tor concerns that we covered in Chapter 10—fear of the exile's pain; belief that change can't happen; concern that the protector will be eliminated or that you aren't competent; or fear that the exile will be harmed, a secret will be revealed, or a dangerous protector will be triggered. Once you know the protector's concern, you can reassure it (as you learned to do in Chapter 10) so it can step aside and allow you to be in Self.

Sometimes a protector isn't afraid of your working with an exile, but it has negative feelings toward the exile, which blocks your ability to listen to it from a caring place. Here are the two most common reasons for this, and how to respond to the protector so it will step aside.

(1) The protector may be upset with the exile because she has caused

problems in your life. For example, the exile's fears have kept you from taking risks to move ahead. Or the exile's feelings of worthlessness have made you depressed. Therefore, it isn't surprising that there would be a protector that doesn't like the exile and wants to eliminate her in order to solve this problem. However, this attitude will not lead to healing. Explain to the protector that you won't let the exile take over. Your goal is to help the exile unburden herself of the fear or insecurity she carries so that she *won't* disrupt your life anymore. Ask the protector to step aside and allow you to relate to the exile from a loving place so this unburdening can happen. Since this responds directly to the protector's concern with the exile, it is likely to agree.

(2) The protector might feel judgmental towards the exile because she is scared or insecure or weak, or just because she is too emotional. These judgments usually mirror the attitudes your parents had toward you when you were young, since protectors sometimes model themselves after your parents. (In psychotherapy, this is called internalization.) Explore with the protector where it got these judgments so it realizes that they aren't actual truths about the exile but rather parental attitudes it took on. You can also explain that the exile is only feeling scared or insecure because of what happened to her when you were young and vulnerable, so it isn't really her fault. This may also help the protector to relax its judgments. Then ask it to step aside so you can heal the exile.

The Importance of Compassion

There is one additional issue involved in working successfully with exiles. You must not only be separate from an exile—you also must feel compassionate and connected to her. It isn't enough to be curious and open with an exile the way you would with a protector because compassion is vitally necessary for healing an exile's suffering. To be fully in Self with an exile requires compassion and connectedness. It is fine to *start out* feeling only curiosity about the exile, but as you listen to her feelings and story, you are going to be witnessing pain, often excruciating pain. This will naturally open your heart to compassion as long as nothing is blocking it.

Let's look at the difference between compassion and empathy and, in addition, how they are related. Empathy is a way of resonating with another person's feelings (or with an exile's feelings). Compassion is a feeling of loving kindness toward someone (or an exile) in pain. Empathy often leads to compassion; you resonate with someone's pain, which stimulates your compassion for him or her. Therefore, the two often occur together. However, it is important to understand how they are different, especially in relating to your exiles. If you feel empathy for an exile without also feeling compassion, there is a danger that you will become too blended with her (because of the resonance) and lose contact with Self. In a state of compassion, you are separate from the exile while still feeling caring and loving, which helps you to stay in Self.

Compassion is crucial for work with exiles. Their pain can be so formidable and tortuous that it may be hard for them to open up to you without this tender, gentle quality. When we feel held by the compassion of a friend, we feel safe enough to reveal our most vulnerable places. Our exiled parts feel the same way. They need our compassion to be ready to come out and be seen. Not only do they carry pain from childhood wounds, they often feel hurt and rejected by us because we have pushed them away and excluded them from our inner family for years. This adds insult to injury. They were injured when young, and then they were dismissed by us because we couldn't handle their pain. So they have been in eternal exile.

Luckily, compassion is the natural human response to someone who is suffering, as long as one is in Self. In an IFS session, the Self is there to give the exile the gift of being seen after years of being locked away in the basement. When the Self witnesses a child part's pain and suffering with compassion, the exile feels touched and grateful for being seen, often for the very first time. Finally it isn't alone.

When you check to see what you feel toward the exile, sometimes you may just feel neutral. You may feel separate but not particularly caring or connected. This is probably because you are blended with a concerned part that wants to stay distant from the exile or with a part that wants to remain intellectual or guarded. Ask that concerned part to relax and allow your natural connectedness and compassion to arise. If it won't, ask it what it is afraid would happen if it did, and work with its concern as discussed earlier for other protectors. Once it has relaxed and allowed you to feel your natural caring for the exile, you can proceed to learn about her pain and negative beliefs and form a loving bond with her, providing a firm basis for the healing steps to follow.

Peter's Concerned Parts

This transcript shows part of a session in which Peter is beginning to work with an exile and must deal with a couple of his parts that don't like the exile. He has already gotten to know a protector and discovered the exile it was protecting.

> **Peter:** Okay. Now I am in touch with the exile. It looks like a toddler who is very upset about something.
>
> *Peter has accessed the exile (E1).*
>
> **Jay:** Ask that protector if it will give you permission to work with the toddler.
>
> **P:** It says yes. Wow, that was easy.
>
> **J:** Good. Are you concerned about being flooded with the upset feelings of the toddler?
>
> **P:** No. That doesn't seem to be happening at all.
>
> *Blending with the toddler doesn't seem to be an issue, at least not now (E2).*
>
> **J:** Okay. Now check to see how you are feeling toward the toddler.
>
> *This check is to see if Peter is in Self with respect to the toddler (E3).*
>
> **P:** Well, I guess I feel Okay about it … Wait, I can sense some judgment—actually, it is quite a bit of judgment toward the toddler. I really don't like it.
>
> **J:** So that is another part of you that judges the toddler and doesn't like it. Ask that part what it doesn't like about the toddler.
>
> **P:** It doesn't like the way the toddler is weak and emotional, like a baby. This part is invested in my being strong and together, so it feels contempt for this babyish part.
>
> **J:** You might explain to this concerned part that the toddler is very young, so it can't help being emotional and weak. That strength will come as it matures. It is fine for this part to want you to have it together, but you can be strong and still have a young part of you that feels intense emotions. You are the adult, not this part.
>
> **P:** Well, Okay. That makes sense to this part, so it seems to be receding.
>
> *Because the concerned part has been reassured, it has stepped aside.*
>
> **J:** Good. Check to see how you are feeling toward the toddler now.

P: Oh! Now another part is coming up that really hates the way the toddler screams and yells and gets out of control when it is upset. It can't stand that kind of behavior.

J: Okay. What is it about that behavior that the part hates?

P: I lost it many times when I was a child, and I really got punished for it. And this has also happened a few times since I became an adult. Those were really bad times. I got very upset and alienated a bunch of people. This toddler has caused me a lot of grief.

Now that we know what this concerned part is upset about, we can reassure it.

J: Well, it is certainly understandable that a part of you would be unhappy about that and wary of the exile. But remind that part that what we are aiming to do here is to help this toddler unburden the pain it carries. Once it releases that pain, it will be much less likely to spin out of control. Ask that concerned part if it would be willing to step aside and allow you to connect with this toddler from your heart so you can help to heal it.

P: It is considering those ideas ... Okay. It is willing to step aside now, but it wants to make sure that the exile doesn't get loose in my life and screw things up again.

J: That's fine. We just need it to step back for the remainder of this session.

P: Yeah. It's willing to do that.

Now that this one has relaxed, we check again.

J: Okay. So check to see what you are feeling toward the exile now.

P: (pause) I can see that it was really hurt a lot, and also betrayed, and that is why it is freaking out and yelling. I am starting to feel some caring about it, some warmth toward it, like I want to help it feel better.

J: Great. So ask the exile to tell you or show you more about what it feels.

Peter is now beginning to relate to the exile from a compassionate place, which means he is in Self (E3). Therefore, we can move on to get to know the exile.

Steps E4 & E5: Learning about an Exile and Developing a Trusting Relationship with It

Once you are solidly in Self, you can proceed to learn about the exile. You are mainly interested in understanding what emotions it feels and also what types of situations trigger these feelings. With exiles, you may not need to ask many questions—you can just invite them to tell you about their feelings or whatever else they would like you to know. Exiles want to be heard; they want to have their pain witnessed and understood. You just need to be open to an exile and invite it to reveal itself to you, and it will most likely be happy to do that. You could ask it what makes it feels so sad (or whatever emotion it is experiencing). As you learn about the exile, further questions may crop up. Don't hesitate to ask them because this will help fill out your understanding of this child part. You can also feel into the exile through your body or emotions and learn about it in that way. In fact, some exiles are so young that they can't communicate in words, and you must learn about them through your body.

As you learn more about the exile, keep checking to see how you are feeling toward it, especially whether you are compassionate and caring. Make a point of communicating your compassion to the exile. This can be done in words, but it is even more effective if you communicate it though your heart directly. Take a moment to feel the actual body sensations that go with your feeling of compassion. You may feel a soft, warm, glow in your heart, for example. Then let your loving kindness radiate from your heart to the exile. Often you will feel the exile in a certain place in your body; you can allow the compassion to flow from your heart to that place.

Then check to see how the exile is responding to your caring. If it doesn't seem to be taking it in, first check to see if it is even aware of you. You may have to ask it to notice you, just as you learned to do with protectors in Chapter 8. Once it is aware of you, communicate your compassion again. Then it will be able to take it in. If the exile doesn't trust you enough to do this, work with its trust issues as you also learned to do in Chapter 8. If at any point you're not sure about the state of your connection with the exile, you can ask it if it trusts that you care about it. Your connection to the exile will deepen throughout the process. In future chapters, I will discuss steps you can take along the way to enhance this relationship.

How Fran Connects with an Exile

This is a continuation of the transcript from Chapter 10, where Fran got permission to work with an exile. It shows each of the steps in getting to know an exile.

Jay: Let me know when you have a sense of the exile.
Fran: It looks like a child with leprosy. It is in a cavern and light is slanting in. The exile has sores and wounds, very skinny.

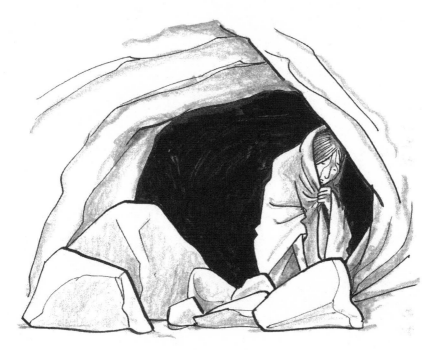

Fran has definitely accessed the exile (E1).
J: Ask that part if it would be willing not to flood you with its pain so you can be there for it.
F: I say to the part: "I'm asking that you not overwhelm me so I can feel enough of the pain to know and validate it, yet not so much that I feel overwhelmed and go away myself. I really want to stay here with you."
J: And how is the exile responding to your request?

211

F: It says "Okay, we'll see." Now I feel sad in my belly. That's Okay. I can feel that amount of pain.

The exile seems to have agreed not to blend with her too much. The sadness is coming from the exile. She is saying that she is ready to blend consciously with the exile to a certain extent. She can tolerate feeling this much of the exile's pain, so we have completed step E2.

F: The exile is stuck over in the corner and I'm feeling kindly toward it.

Since Fran feels kindly toward it, this indicates that she is in Self (E3).

J: Let it know that.

F: I'm moving closer to it, though it's not turned to me. I'm synchronizing my breathing with it. It doesn't feel right to touch it, but I'm within a foot or so.

This is a good way to approach an exile. Moving closer to it gradually serves two functions here. (1) Keeping some distance helps to ensure that Fran isn't flooded with the exile's pain. (2) It gives the exile a chance to learn to trust her before she moves in too close and scares it.

J: Is it aware of you?

F: Yes.

J: Is it taking in your caring?

F: Yeah. I think so. I'm filling the whole cave with a sense of gentle presence.

J: Nice. Invite the exile to let you know more about what it feels.

Now that there is clearly a connection between them (E5), the exile may feel safe enough to show more about its feelings (E4).

F: It just turned its face toward me, and I see a tear going down its cheek, and I feel the sadness … I don't feel like I can quite touch it, but I'm putting my head above the place where the tears are and I'm stroking … Some of the pain is like moving in waves through my body. And I feel like I'm still in Self.

Fran soothes the exile.

J: So it's Okay to be feeling that much?

F: Yeah.

I have her check again to see if this level of conscious blending is tolerable.

F: I'm watching it as a wave. It's delicate.

J: I'm glad you're aware of that in such a sensitive way.

F: If I can be with the wave, I can be more present ... There's a very diffuse light in the cavern ... As I feel the waves of pain, it feels like I'm taking them in and dissipating them in a way ... It seems like I just want to hang out and monitor the waves and the pain, being present with the light coming through from Self, having a smoothing-out effect on the exile.

Fran has found a way to feel the exile's pain while remaining solidly in Self. She seems to do this partially by dissipating the pain so it doesn't overwhelm her. I imagine that this is possible because the exile agreed earlier to not overwhelm her. This allows her to soothe the exile with the presence of Self, symbolized by the light.

J: Is the exile aware of you?

F: Yes. In a low-key kind of way.

Here I'm just checking again to make sure that the connection between them is consciously being experienced by the exile.

What a lovely piece of work! The session had to end here because of time constraints. We don't know much yet about the exile's pain, so when Fran continues the work in a later session, she might want to ask about that. Or she might just be ready to move on to Step 4 in the next chapter.

Exercise: Getting to Know an Exile

Do a session in which you get to know an exile. If possible, start with one that you already have permission to work with, and then proceed through Steps E1-E5. Use Help Sheet 2 below (along with Help Sheet 1) to guide you through the steps. If such an exile isn't ready, start with a protector. Go through the steps to get to know it, discover the exile it is guarding, and get permission before proceeding through the exile steps. Then fill in the answers below that are relevant to your work.

Exile _____

What the exile would be afraid of, if it separated from you _____
_____

Concerned parts and their fears _____
_____

Exile's feelings _____

What situations cause it to feel that way _____
_____

How you feel toward the exile _____

How the exile is responding to you _____

The next page contains Help Sheet 2, which is a summary of the steps for getting to know an exile. It is meant to guide your steps while you are working on yourself or partnering with someone. I recommend you use it in conjunction with Help Sheet 1 from Chapter 6 in your future practice.

Help Sheet 2: Getting to Know an Exile

2. Getting Permission to Work With an Exile

If necessary, ask the protector to show you the exile.

Ask its permission to get to know the exile.

If it won't give permission, ask what it is afraid would happen if you accessed the exile.

Possibilities are:

- The exile has too much pain. Explain that you will stay in Self and get to know the exile, not dive into its pain.
- There isn't any point in going into the pain. Explain that there is a point—you can heal the exile.
- The protector will have no role and therefore be eliminated. Explain that the protector can choose a new role in your psyche.

3. Getting to Know an Exile

E1: Accessing an Exile

Sense its emotions, feel it in your body, or get an image of it.

E2: Unblending From an Exile

If you are blended with an exile:

- Ask the exile to contain its feelings so you can be there for it.
- Consciously separate from the exile and return to Self.
- Get an image of the exile at a distance from you.
- Do a centering/grounding induction.

If the exile won't contain its feelings:

- Ask it what it is afraid would happen if it did.
- Explain that you really want to witness its feelings and story, but you need to be separate to do that.

Conscious blending: If you can tolerate it, allow yourself to feel the exile's pain

E3: Unblending Concerned Parts

Check how you feel toward the exile.

If you aren't in Self or don't feel compassion, unblend from any concerned parts. They are usually afraid of your becoming overwhelmed by the exile's pain. (make these sentences all one paragraph, not two lines)

Explain that you will stay in Self and not let the exile overwhelm.

E4: Finding Out about an Exile

Ask: What do you feel? What makes you feel so scared or hurt (or any other feeling)?

E5: Developing a Trusting Relationship with an Exile

Let the exile know that you want to hear its story.

Communicate to it that you feel compassion and caring toward it.

Check to see if the exile can sense you there and notice how if it is taking in your compassion.

Exercise: Noticing an Exile in Real Time

Choose an exile that you have already gotten to know. Over the next week, notice when this exile becomes activated. To help you with this, think of the kinds of situations that usually trigger this exile._____

_____

When are those situations likely to occur this week?_____

_____

Each time you are in one, pay careful attention to see if the exile is triggered. If it is, what does it feel? _____
Does a protector become activated to guard against this exile? If so,
which protector and how does it act? _____

_____

If there is no protector, how does the exile act? _____

_____

Summary

In this chapter, you have learned Step 3 in the IFS process and its sub-steps
E1-E5. You know why it is important to be separate from an exile's pain
or trauma and how to unblend, if necessary. You have seen that conscious
blending with an exile's emotions can be useful under certain circumstances. You understand the importance of compassion in working with
an exile and how to unblend from any concerned parts that judge it. You
know how to get to know an exile and develop a trusting relationship with
it. You also understand how exiles can be triggered in your life and how
they activate protectors.

Once you understand the exile and it trusts you, you can move on to
Step 4, which is covered in the next chapter.

Chapter 12

Finding Where It Started

Accessing and Witnessing Childhood Memories

One of the major forces behind our psychological issues is the pain we carry from childhood. The IFS perspective on this is that our exiles carry *burdens*. A burden is a painful feeling or negative belief about yourself or the world—for example, abandonment, worthlessness, fear of being hit, or shame. An exile ends up carrying a burden into the present because a harmful incident or relationship from the past, usually from childhood, was not metabolized. For example, you weren't picked up and held very much when you were little. You were teased a lot by the kids at school. You were hit by your uncle with his belt. You were punished whenever you tried to speak your mind or assert yourself. Your mother gave you the message that you were responsible for her happiness. Your father called you stupid.

217

Let's carry the father example further. Because of being judged by your father, you have an exile that carries the burden of believing you are stupid. Now, in your present life, something happens that reminds you of that relationship from childhood. Someone treats you in a way that is similar to how your father treated you. Perhaps your boss tells you that your work has mistakes. This triggers a Little Boy exile who feels ashamed.

Activation of a Part from a Memory

External Situation

The Little Boy is activated because the external situation reminds him of his childhood Memory.

Boss points out mistakes.

This incident triggers not only the Little Boy's shame but also protectors to guard against feeling the shame, causing you to go numb, become defensive and fight with your boss, or get drunk, for example. This scenario shows how our childhood memories affect our current behavior and feelings.

One of the major goals of the IFS process is to help exiles let go of their burdens so they are free of pain and fear. This then releases protectors from their compulsion to engage in extreme and rigid behavior to safeguard the vulnerable exiles. However, before an exile can release a burden, the origins of that burden must be experienced and witnessed. This opens up the exile for the healing steps that follow.

Therefore, once you have gotten to know an exile and connected with it (Step 3), the next step is to access and witness the original childhood situation that created the burden. This is Step 4 in the IFS process, which is covered in this chapter. Exiles know where their burdens come from, and they will usually reveal this to you when asked. This makes it easy and natural to access even deeply buried memories.

Metabolizing Childhood Experiences

Whenever you endure a painful or difficult experience, it must be fully processed and metabolized for your psyche to stay healthy. You must fully feel the experience, make sense of it, and integrate it into your notion of who you are in a way that doesn't leave you with a negative, inaccurate view of yourself. Even experiences in adult life must be metabolized in this way. For example, suppose you lose your spouse to cancer. You need to feel the grief and other emotions that it brings up, think it through, discuss it with friends, and work through any guilt or self-blame that you feel. This will occur repeatedly over many months until you have come to terms with it.

A threatening or traumatic experience puts your body into a fight-or-flight stress reaction. For example, suppose you are threatened with a gun by a robber. Your body goes into hyper-alertness and fear. Later, when you talk through what happened and feel the fear, this will help your body to complete its physiological response and return to a normal relaxed state.

A difficult experience can also make you feel bad about yourself or mistrust people. For example, suppose you are fired from your job for poor work performance. This makes you feel incompetent and, after stewing over it for a while, you come to believe that the world is unfair. You need to take the time to think this through with outside support and figure out what, if anything, *you* did poorly and how much of this resulted from office politics. This will help you integrate the experience into your psyche and sense of self, and learn from your mistakes without taking on a negative view of yourself.

When you have a problematic experience as an adult, you usually have the resources to metabolize it properly. You know how to articulate the problem, you are intellectually and emotionally mature, and you may have support from friends, family, or a therapist. As a child, you often don't have the resources to metabolize difficult incidents. You can't do it on your own, so you need a great deal of sensitive support from your parents or other adults. The more painful and traumatic an experience, the more you need support to be able to metabolize it. And this support often isn't available, either because your parents don't realize you need it or because they don't have the capacity to provide it. Or, worst of all, because your parents were the source of the traumatic incident.

An experience that isn't metabolized creates a burden for the exile that experienced it. In order to heal that child part and help release its burden, the memory must be re-experienced and processed to completion. Having the experience witnessed by the Self is an important aspect of this.

Step 4: Accessing the Childhood Origin

As you get to know an exile, he first shows you what he feels and what situations in your current life tend to trigger him. After you have gotten to know him and connected with him, ask him to show you what caused the burden in the first place. (Sometimes the exile will show this spontaneously, in which case you don't need to ask.) You might say one of the following:

- Please show me an image or a memory of what happened to make you feel this way when you were a child.
- Please show me a time when you first took on this role in childhood.
- Please show me how you learned to believe this when you were little.

It is important to allow this memory to come from the exile. Don't try to figure it out yourself. Don't start rummaging through your memories and trying to decide which one to work with. That uses an intellectual process that probably won't be of much help. Just ask the exile for the memory and wait to see what emerges. Usually a memory will spontaneously arise. You might even see an image of an incident or relationship that you didn't consciously remember.

If you ask and the exile doesn't show you anything, there are a number of possible reasons for this. These are listed below, along with the way to handle each one.

1. You are looking for an explicit memory that is very specific (see Types of Memories below), which is limiting what the exile can show you. Let go of that expectation and be open to implicit memories, fragments of images, body memories, and so on.

2. You don't have full contact with the exile yet. In this case, continue getting to know the exile through witnessing his emotions and inner state. Once you have more intimate access to him, ask again for a memory. Now it is likely to arise.

3. The exile doesn't want to show you the memory. Perhaps it involves a secret that he is afraid to reveal, such as the information that your father was having an affair. Reassure the exile that you are an adult now and this information is no longer dangerous. Perhaps the memory itself isn't a problem, but the exile thinks you can't handle the emotions that go with it. Ask him what he is afraid would happen if he allowed you to see the memory. Then reassure him that you will stay in Self, where the emotions won't overpower you.

4. There is a protector that doesn't want you to see the memory. This could be for any of the reasons listed above. Ask the protector that same question: What is it afraid would happen if it allowed you to see the memory? Then reassure it about its fears.

Types of Memories

Sometimes when you ask the exile for a memory, he will show you a specific situation that you clearly recall. For example, you were eight and came home from school to find your mother lying in bed seriously depressed.

This is called an *explicit memory*. It is a clear recollection of a specific situation. However, not all memories are like this. The mind doesn't just store movie reels that can be played back. Some memories show up as vague body sensations or fragments of images from early childhood. Memories that aren't so clear are called *implicit memories*—for example, a vague sense of imminent attack; a fragment of a mental picture, such as a fist coming at you; an awareness of reaching out with your arms for nurturing and feeling smothered.

With implicit memories, there is more to the original event than you can see or feel; you are only presented with a partial sense of it. There are number of possible reasons for this.

1. The rest of the incident hasn't yet been accessed. For example, if you have a vague image of a hand coming at you, this might come from the fact that you were hit a lot by your mother. If you stay with this image, the full memory might emerge.

2. The full memory is blocked from recall by a protector—for example, one that is afraid of the amount of pain you would feel if you re-experienced being hit.

3. The memory might originate at a time when you were so young that your brain wasn't developed enough to lay down an explicit memory, just vague images and sensations. Instead, you have a preverbal body memory.

Though you may believe that implicit memories aren't important, they can be just as useful for healing as explicit ones. When one arises, witness it and encourage the exile to let you know more about it. Just be open and interested. Additional information is often forthcoming as you develop greater access to the exile and as he feels ready to reveal more. However, don't push for clarity because this could interfere with the spontaneous unfolding of the process. Revealing pain and suffering is a sensitive process for an exile; allow him to open up in his own time. And it isn't crucial to get complete clarity and understanding of what happened. Though it is helpful to know the details of the memory, you can still proceed to the next steps in the healing process without this knowledge.

There are other types of memories. Some arise as generalized images that represent your relationship with a parent (hostile, controlling, distant) or a certain way you were treated in your family (ignored, blamed), rather than a specific incident. For example, you may have an image of your father scolding you for doing something wrong in which your age and the "something wrong" aren't clear. This is a *generic memory*, which represents something that happened many times. Your father probably scolded you with the same voice and expression on his face hundreds of times over the span of your childhood. A generic memory stands for all of these incidents, and, therefore, when you heal it in the course of your IFS process, you are healing all these memories. (You will see in subsequent chapters how to do this.)

Sometimes one explicit memory will stand for a whole raft of them. For example, suppose you see one particular incident, when your father got upset because you couldn't understand your seventh-grade math homework. This memory will usually serve to represent all the other times he yelled at you.

The exile might also show you a *symbolic memory*, which is an image that represents in symbolic form something that happened to you, just as a dream can signify something psychological. For example, Juan had an image of a sea plant floating in the water. It was supposed to be anchored to the ocean floor, but it was floating away in the current. When he explored this, he realized that it represented the way he felt insecurely attached to his mother early in his life. The sea plant represented his infant self and the ocean floor his mother. The sea plant wasn't attached to the ocean floor the way it should have been, which represented his disconnection from his mother. If you are shown a symbolic memory, receive it gratefully and be present with it to see what evolves over time. You can also ask the exile to show you more about what it means. However, it is important not to grill the exile for clarity; just be open to seeing what unfolds.

Witnessing the Childhood Origin

Once the exile shows you the memory, ask her to fill in as much of the details as she wants. She may do this through images or tell you what happened, or you may sense it in some other way. Be there for the exile as a compassionate witness. She may show you very painful experiences, so it is crucial that you receive them with deep caring and respect for her and what she went through. For the most part, allow her to lead the way by showing you what she wants you to know of what happened to her. Exiles want to be witnessed and understood.

There are two primary aspects to any memory—what happened and how that made the exile feel. Make sure she shows you both, if possible.

If she only shows you what happened, ask her how that made her feel. If you only get feelings, prompt her to tell you what happened to cause those feelings.

Stay with the exile as she gradually reveals more and more about the memory. Let the information unfold at whatever speed she is ready for. It may take some time for all the details of the memory to come forth. As this is happening, your contact with the exile will also become deeper, allowing more to emerge. Often at first you see the childhood situation and have some sense of how it made her feel, but as you stay with the experience, her feelings become much clearer, and the depth of her pain becomes apparent. Usually by then you can witness more pain without becoming blended because you have made a greater connection with the exile and are feeling compassion for her. The more fully the pain is felt by her and witnessed by you, the deeper the healing can go.

The exile may also feel anger about what happened, or even rage. These feelings should be witnessed as well as the pain. Just encourage the exile to show you her anger. She may even want to express the anger, usually through internal imagery. While a protector might use anger as a way to defend against deeper pain, exiles often carry anger as well. An exile's anger isn't a defense and needs to be fully witnessed.

If the exile shows you a series of memories, that is fine. However, make sure that the memories are all related to one feeling or issue. For example, if the issue for the exile is feeling judged by people, all the memories should be incidents in which she was judged as a child or something happened to contribute to her feeling bad about herself. If some memories pertain to unrelated issues, ask the exile to focus more specifically on the one primary issue. Let her know that you will come back in a future session to deal with those other memories, but you can only heal one issue at a time.

Feeling Understood

From time to time, ask the exile if she has shown you everything important related to this memory or if there is more she wants to show you. When she has finished fleshing out the memory, check to see if you really understand how painful this was for her. If you don't, ask her more questions until you really get it.

Then ask the exile *if she feels that you understand how bad it was*. This is a crucial question. Before you move on to the next step in the process, the exile must not only tell her story, she must also take in the fact that her pain has been truly seen and heard. If she doesn't feel that you understand, ask her if she needs to show you more or if she doesn't believe that you really emotionally get it.

It may be that the exile has a hard time believing that *anyone* could understand what she went through. Or she may have a hard time trusting anyone. In this case, explore what happened to her in childhood that makes it so difficult for her to trust anyone now, and sympathize with her about that. In addition, explain exactly what you *do* understand about her experience. This will go a long way toward helping her trust you. Of course, it is also possible that you aren't in Self and aren't empathizing enough with the exile's pain. Then you need to unblend from the concerned part that is blocking you so that you are fully open to the exile. This way, she will feel heard.

Benefits of Witnessing

There are a number of important benefits to be gained from this witnessing process.

1. It opens up hidden memories so they can be healed. When an exile and her memories are deeply buried in the psyche, complete healing isn't possible. A wounded part needs the light of day. If you have a purely intellectual understanding of the memory, that probably won't lead to healing. The memory must be opened up emotionally *and* intellectually so it is both felt and understood. However, this doesn't mean that *you* need to feel the exile's emotions. It is usually enough for her to feel them, as discussed in the last chapter.

2. The memory is metabolized under the guidance and support of the Self, so the experience is completed and integrated, and the physiological stress reaction can subside, as we discussed earlier.

3. The exile gets to be fully understood by the Self. There is a crucial difference between what happened originally and what the exile is experiencing now as she relives and shares the memory. This time, the exile is not alone. The original incident was especially difficult because the exile had

to deal with it all by herself with no help or understanding from another living soul. I hear this all the time from exiles; they feel completely alone, having a reaction that they cannot share. Now in the therapy session, the Self is there to witness the experience and provide understanding. This is healing for the exile and creates a greater bond between her and the Self, which sets the stage for the Self being the agent of further healing as we progress in the IFS process.

Self Witnesses Childhood Memory

The Self witnesses the Little Boy's shame in the original situation. This time the boy doesn't feel alone because he is connected to Self.

4. The exile understands that the burden she is carrying is from the past and not intrinsic to her. For example, a child part who feels worthless learns that she was made to feel that way in her family. In this way, she can see that her feeling of worthlessness isn't the truth; it is a burden that she took on in childhood that doesn't really belong to her. Therefore it can be released, and she can experience her intrinsic worth.

Witnessing the Childhood Origins of a Protector

Exiles aren't the only parts that carry burdens from painful childhood experiences. Protectors carry them as well. When something harmful or traumatic happens to you as a child, an exile takes on the pain, and a protector often takes on the role of stopping the pain. Its goal is to keep the incident from happening again or to stop you from being overwhelmed by the pain. The protector's role *is* its burden, in contrast to the exile, whose burden is the pain (or negative belief). It is important to note that not all protectors take on their jobs at the time of a childhood trauma; some do it later in life. For example, an intellectual part may develop years later whose job is to keep you away from all emotional pain. However, many protectors carry a burden that is directly tied to the original childhood harm, so it can be helpful to witness the origins of their burdens. Other than that, you work with both types of protectors in the same way.

In the flow of the IFS process, once you have discovered a protector's positive intent and developed a relationship with it, the usual procedure is to get permission to work with the exile it is protecting, as you learned in Chapter 10. However, sometimes you can ask the protector to show you the childhood memory behind its protective role. Instead of getting to know the exile first and then asking for the memory, you can ask the protector for the memory directly. You do this in the same way you would with an exile.

Let your intuition guide you about when to ask the protector. If it seems to be very concerned about protecting against the reoccurrence of an old wound, you might ask for the memory of that wound directly. For example, suppose you are working with a protector that tries to soothe and placate anyone who raises their voice and seems to be getting angry. Let's call it the Placater. You ask the Placater what it is afraid would happen if it didn't try to pacify people. It says it is afraid they would scream and yell at you and maybe even get violent. You could ask the Placater to show you an image or a memory of what happened when you were little that caused it to be so frightened of this. It will probably show you a memory of being yelled at and physically abused.

As you witness this memory (in the way we discussed above), it will naturally lead to the exile that experienced this anger and abuse. You can then witness the exile, which will have a different experience of the incident than the protector. When something traumatic happens like this, both the exile and the protector hold the memory, though in different ways, and either one can lead you back to the original incident.

Christine Witnesses Her Exiles

Let's look at the next section of Christine's session with her Little Girl exile to see how she accesses the childhood origins. This is the exile that was all alone in the dark. At this point, Christine has unblended from her and is ready to get to know her.

Jay: What does she want to tell you?

Christine: How hard it has been for her. How she's had to do it all on her own, and she's really frightened. She didn't know what was happening. Nobody was there.

You can tell from Christine's use of the past tense that the Little Girl is already in a childhood environment and Christine realizes this. But we don't yet know what happened back then, so it is useful to ask.

C: My impulse is to ask her what the situation was.

J: Sounds good.

C: … I can see how my mind jumps in and says it was in the hospital when I was a baby, but I'm not sure. I want *her* to tell me.

Christine has an intellectual idea of where the exile's fear comes from in her childhood, but to be sure it's accurate, she needs the information to come from the exile experientially, so she asks her. This also allows the work to proceed in the alive, embodied way that it needs to.

J: Good.

C: She is telling me it is dark and the lights are out. And nobody loves her. Nobody's there, so that means nobody loves her. There's no one to take care of her.

This is the childhood experience that created the burdens of fear and panic, and the belief that no one loves her. This is an implicit memory since it doesn't refer to any specific incident. Now she goes on to witness it more.

C: And so from the point of view of Self, when I hear that, I want to hold her. I want to sit her on my lap.

J: Go ahead and do that.

Christine has a wonderful, spontaneous impulse to comfort the Little Girl, thus deepening their bond.

C: I'm struck that the little body doesn't have tension in it. It's a very soft, undefended little body. And there's a weight, a heaviness in the heart, that she is carrying around … Okay, the heaviness in the heart comes from hopelessness that nothing is going to get better. And she has to carry this burden all by herself because nobody else is there. (pause)

There it is. I can see the thread now. When nobody is there to pick her up, there is a contraction, a closing off, a walling off. There is fearful watching in the cells of the body. This heavy heart has formed over time. It's not one event that does it. It sort of chips away. The heaviness comes from her inability to change anything.

This is a generic memory, a representation of many events over a number of years in Christine's early childhood when no one was there for her when she needed comfort or holding, and this part took on a burden of heaviness and closing off.

J: And the thing that formed in the cells of the body, what was that?

C: The watchfulness, the alertness, guarding, protecting, and the closing off from the world. It's like a defense. It's a felt thing. Almost like a catch in the tissues. (pause)

C: Now there is a sense of being frightened, caught in the dark by herself. That feeling is much younger; it goes way back. I'm getting a specific memory. She's flailing her arms and legs. Somebody is supposed to come and pick her up, but they don't come.

This memory comes from a younger part, an exile that I will call the Baby.

C: Now I'm getting some vague memory of something dangling in a crib … a hollow sound. There's a sense of trying to get somewhere, to get picked up. But no one is there.

This memory is both implicit and generic; it is vague, and it probably represents many other similar times when she wasn't taken care of.

J: She desperately needs to be picked up, but no one comes.

Christine has now witnessed the important aspects of these memories and can move on to the next step in the IFS process.

Melanie Witnesses a Shame Exile

This transcript shows more about how to witness an exile. Melanie had already done several IFS sessions in which she gained access to an exile that holds a lot of shame. She had previously received permission from the protector to work with this Shame Exile, so we can start right in.

Jay: Focus on the Shame Exile, and let me know when you have a sense of it.

Melanie: I have contact with the Shame Exile. It's a sunflower with its face looking down on the ground.

J: And how are you feeling toward that part?

M: I don't know if I feel anything, but I have the attitude of being supportive. I understand that the exile is a bit embarrassed that we're addressing her story.

J: So invite her to tell you or show you more about what she feels, and ask her not to flood you so you can remain in Self to be supportive of her.

Here I check to see that Melanie is in Self with respect to this exile, and I include some insurance to guard against her becoming blended with the exile.

M: She feels this chronic despair. It's always there, this despair, like a nowhere place. It's a void, a nothingness, an emptiness. It's like falling and falling and never coming to a bottom. And she's now showing me a memory of how she used to feel this a lot as a little girl. It's a black hole, and she would fall in and there would be nothing of her, just the black hole.

As Melanie is getting to know the exile, a generic childhood memory is spontaneously revealed.

M: I remember those time when I experienced this black hole, just a space of nothingness. There was no meaning, no substance, nothing to be connected to.

J: You might ask her how she feels emotionally in that place.

M: She can't tell me. It's a place of such dread and such meaninglessness that ... She feels pretty much dead there.

J: So there are two feelings—dread and deadness.

It is worthwhile to name the feelings the exile has expressed.

M: Yes, that's right. Now I'm feeling quite sad that I didn't have this kind of awareness until now. That's pretty serious. That's a very heavy … I don't have a word for it.

J: So let her know that you get how heavy this is.

Since Melanie understands how the exile feels, I have her communicate this to the exile because it builds their connection.

M: She says, "So what? So you get it, so what?"

J: So she's feeling hopeless?

Exiles generally want to be heard and understood, so when this one seems not to care about this, I assume it is because she is hopeless about anything improving her plight.

M: Yeah. She is also feeling powerless. Yeah. "I shared this with you, and I shared my internal nonexistence with you." Yeah, it could be hopeless. She thinks, "What's the use of even trying to explain it?"

J: So let her know that if she keeps going with us, we can help her release these feelings.

I say this to give the exile some hope that she can feel better. This helps ensure that she won't put up roadblocks to the work.

M: Well, I let her know that. She's not resistant, but she doesn't have any kind of expectations.

J: She doesn't have to. That's fine.

The part doesn't have to believe in what we can do; it just needs to allow the work to proceed.

J: So ask her to show you a memory or an image of what happened when you were little that made her feel this way.

Even though the exile already showed us a memory, it included only the emotions, not the events that caused them.

M: She says there are many memories of lack of forgiveness from my parents. Once I made a mistake or did something wrong, I was punished over and over and over again for the same mistake. That seemed to be a pattern, a very solid pattern.

J: Ask her to show you how her parents punished her.

M: I see one time when they really yelled at me for spilling something. She's feeling very scared and bad about herself.

J: So that really frightened her.

M: Yeah. And she felt like there was something really wrong with her. (pause) Now she's showing me a time a little later when there are people visiting, and my dad tells them the story of my spilling whatever it was. Oh, I guess it was some kind of liquid on my dress. And he's making fun of me about that, and everyone is laughing at me.

Melanie's dad makes fun of her Shame Exile.

J: Oh. And how is that making the little girl feel?

M: Mortified. She just wants to disappear. (pause) And there is some sort of implication that she is not just clumsy but sort of … dirty, I guess. At least that's what she felt.

J: That's terrible.

M: And they keep doing this, over and over again, telling this same story to different people, as if it is really funny for them to keep humiliating her like this.

J: So ask her how it made her feel to be punished like that over and over again.

M: Like she was a piece of dirt. That's the best description.

This is very powerful. Christine has gotten to the depth of the exile's experience.

J: Yeah. Check with her to see if that is everything she wants to show you about this or if there is anything else she wants you to know.

M: She is really angry about this.

J: Encourage her to let you know about her anger in any way she wants.

M: She's screaming and yelling at them.

J: Yeah. (pause)

Anger is a feeling like any other that exiles need to be able to express. Often they couldn't feel or show anger at the time they were wounded, and it is very satisfying to be able to do it now.

J: Anything else she wants you to know?

M: That seems to be all. (pause) I feel very sad.

J: Does that mean you're experiencing her sadness or feeling compassion for her?

M: I do feel a lot of compassion for her because it's the first time I've heard that "piece of dirt" thing. Even a piece of crap would be something, but to feel like just a piece of dirt, that's really bad. I get the message loud and clear.

J: Communicate to her your compassion in some way. (pause)

Now that the little girl has shown Melanie what she needed to, it is important for Melanie to send her compassion. This helps build their connection.

J: And check to see if she feels that you get how bad it was.

M: She knows that I've heard her. She's glad that I've heard her finally.

This was the final check to see if the exile feels fully understood emotionally. Now that she does, Melanie can go on to the next steps in the IFS process, which are revealed in Chapters 13 and 14.

Exercise: Accessing and Witnessing a Childhood Memory

Do a session in which you access the childhood memory of an exile and witness it. If possible, start with an exile that you already have permission to access and have worked with to some extent. If you don't have one this far along, start with a protector and go through the steps to get to know it, discover its exile, and get to know her. Then access and witness the childhood origins of her pain as you have learned to do in this chapter.

Exile _____

Exile's feelings and beliefs _____

_____

What happened in childhood _____

_____

How that made the exile feel _____
How you feel toward the exile now _____
Does the exile feel that you understand how bad it was? _____

Summary

In this chapter, you have learned how to access the childhood memory that was the origin of the burden an exile carries. You know what a burden is and the different kinds of memories that can be accessed. You have seen how to witness what happened in that childhood situation and how it made the exile feel, which is Step 4 in the IFS process. You understand the benefits of this witnessing process and how to check to see if the exile feels heard by you. This prepares the way for the first explicit healing step in the next chapter.

Chapter 13

Caring for an Inner Child

Reparenting and Retrieving an Exile

———————— • ————————

This chapter and the next deal explicitly with healing exiles, so let's discuss what healing really means. Our parts take on burdens because of painful or traumatic experiences in childhood that we can't metabolize at the time. We can't change those experiences; they have already happened. However, *we can change their effect on us*. It isn't the experiences themselves that determine how we feel and behave in our adult lives; it is the residue of those experiences in our psyches, which IFS refers to as *burdens*. Your current issues are caused by the way your psyche was structured by your childhood to hold certain beliefs, body tensions, and emotions. So while you can't change the past, you can change the way the past is codified in your mind. This is what I mean by healing.

IFS uses the term *exile* to refer to what has often been called the *inner child*. However, people often talk about *the* inner child as if there were only one. In IFS, we recognize that there are many inner child parts or exiles, each carrying its own burden. Every exile must be healed in a way that is unique to it because each one has its own feelings, burdens, and memories.

Once an exile's pain has been witnessed, as you learned to do in the last chapter, you can move on to Step 5 in the IFS process, reparenting, and Step 6, retrieval, both of which are covered in this chapter.

Step 5: Reparenting an Exile

The Self can provide the exile with a new positive experience to replace the original painful one. During the witnessing step, the exile showed you a memory. Whether it was explicit, implicit, or generic, and whether it was clear or vague, the exile showed you a certain situation or relationship from the past in which it took on pain and negative beliefs. If it showed you a number of related memories, let the exile choose one of these to focus on for the reparenting step and those that follow.

Here is how you reparent the exile: In your imagination, you join the exile in that original childhood situation. For example, if the memory involves being ridiculed by your mother for the way you are helping her in the kitchen, you imagine yourself in that kitchen with that child part and your mother. Make sure that you enter the situation *as the Self*—with all your adult knowledge and capacities, enhanced by the qualities of the Self, such as compassion and calmness. Be with the exile in the way she needed someone to be with her then. She may need understanding, caring, support, approval, protection from harm, encouragement, or love. Sense what she needs from you in that situation to heal her and redress what happened. For example, she might need to be seen or to be reassured that she isn't bad—that whatever happened wasn't her fault. In addition to *sensing* what the exile needs from you, you can *ask* her.

When you understand what she needs from you, give it to her through your internal imagination, including visual image, body sensing, emotional contact, and talking to her. From Self, you have the capacity to reparent the exile—to be the good parent that she needs. This is very satisfying for the exile and is also rewarding for you because it feels wonderful to provide comfort and safety to a part of you that desperately needs it. It also deepens the bond between you.

The reparenting process actually lays down new neural pathways in the brain. That is why your psyche and your life can change so dramatically. You give that child part a new experience of some aspect of your childhood, an experience that heals or replaces the old one. This time, you, as the Self, are filling the child's deepest needs, which is exactly what didn't happen in that early situation. While it may look as if you are simply pretending the past was different, what you are actually doing is creating a new, wholesome relationship with the exile in the present, which shows her that life can be good and happy. The exile doesn't really exist in the past; she is here right now in the present. She just thinks she is still in that painful childhood situation. Therefore, when she has a new experience and a new relationship with you, you are actually bringing her closer to the reality of the present. She isn't just *imagining* what it would be like to have an ideal parent. You are *becoming* the ideal parent for her. When this happens, the exile is transformed. She feels differently about herself and the whole world.

For example, if the exile wasn't cared for as a child, you might hold her to your heart and tell her you love her. If she is starving because she was bottle fed on a schedule instead of when she was hungry, you might cradle her in your arms and let her suckle at your breast. If she was blamed for your family's problems, you might explain that what happened wasn't her fault and that she is a good child. If she was ridiculed when she was sad, you can give her permission to cry the tears she couldn't shed then. You could explain to her that her sadness was a perfectly natural response to the situation she was in, and there is nothing wrong with her for feeling it. If she was hit by your father, you can enter that scene and protect her from his internalized presence so that she feels safe. If your mother ignored her, you could enter that scene and speak out to the image of mother, telling her that's no way to treat a child. You might also tell the exile that you are really interested in her.

If she had to perform for your parents or be a high achiever in order for them to value her, you could tell her that she doesn't need to do anything for you. You love her and value her just the way she is. If your parents never had the time to really listen to her, *you* could take the time to hear the intimate details of her life. If she was alone a lot, you might be her buddy and playmate and have fun with her. If she never had someone to explain to her how the world works or support her in developing her abilities, you can do that for her now. If she was made to feel responsible for her parents' feelings, you can let her know that she wasn't; they were the adults, and she was only a child. It wasn't her job to take care of them. If she feels ashamed for feeling angry or needy, or for having sexual feelings, you can tell her that those feelings are completely natural for a child to have, and there is nothing wrong with her having them.

Don't try to make the exile change in any way. Don't ask her to feel different or think about herself in a better way. That will naturally result from the reparenting you give her. Just provide her with what she needs, and she will naturally feel free, happy, valued, safe, and confident. If the exile wants something from you in the future (over the next few weeks, for example), that is important, but deal with that later in the session. You don't want to lose touch with her right now; she needs to have her needs met in the moment. So make sure to find out what the exile needs from you *right now* so you can give it to her in this session.

If You Aren't Ready

Reparenting can't be faked. You must genuinely feel love or caring or respect for the exile. You must really feel like giving her what she needs—holding her or encouraging her, for example. And you easily will if you are in Self. Self naturally wants to respond to an exile's needs with exactly the feeling or action that is needed because Self is a place of compassion and love. If you don't feel like giving the exile what she needs, this means that a protector has blended with you and taken you out of Self.

Let's look at how this might happen. Maybe a protector has taken over that wants to keep distant from the exile because it is afraid of the exile's needs or pain. In this case, reassure this part that you are in Self and won't be harmed by the exile's suffering. You might need to work more on unblending from the exile first (see Step E2 in Chapter 11). Another possibility is that there is a protector that judges the exile's vulnerability. Explore where this part got the idea that vulnerability is bad, and ask it to step aside.

There might be a part that fears that you don't have the capacity to take care of the exile because you aren't loving enough or strong enough, for example. Explain that Self is so large, loving, and resourceful that it can handle *anything* the exile needs. If there is a protector that is afraid that you don't know how to nurture a baby or take care of a wounded child, explain that you will know what to do simply by tuning in to the exile. These fears often come from a part that feels inadequate. Ask this part to step aside and trust the Self to handle whatever comes up. The Self always knows what to do. You might also explore where the belief in your inadequacy came from.

A protector might be afraid that the exile's needs are too much for anyone to take care of. Explain that you (in Self) can handle any degree of need. An exile's needs often seem overwhelming because they weren't met adequately when you were young and they've been bottled up ever since, compounded by the fact that the exile has been ignored all this time. This would make anyone's needs rather intense. Once you begin to meet the needs of this child part, the urgency of the needs will quickly calm down and the whole process will become easier.

There might be a part that is afraid that meeting the exile's needs will take too much time out of your busy life. You can explain that this process isn't as time consuming as taking care of a flesh-and-blood baby. An inner child becomes satisfied fairly easily with just a little attention every day. It doesn't take much time at all.

Once you have reassured any concerned parts and they have stepped aside, you can proceed with reparenting the exile from Self.

Reworking the Situation

Sometimes the exile needs you to do something that changes what happened in the original childhood situation. This lays down a new experience on top of the old memory, one that redresses the wrong that was done to her. For example, she might want you to protect her from an abusive parent. If that's what she wants, then do it. Take protective action and rework the situation in your imagination in such a way that she isn't abused. Imagine the situation happening differently. If necessary, you can be just as large and strong as needed to stop even the most powerful parent.

If she wants you to talk to your parents and explain to them that they shouldn't treat her so badly, then do that. You might tell them how she needs to be treated and why it is important to her. Then imagine that they take in what you are saying. After listening to you, they understand that what they did was harmful, and they want to treat her differently because they want the best for her. If the exile wants you to beat up a parent or even destroy him, go along and do that. Even though we obviously don't want to act that way in the real world, sometimes violent fantasies can help an exile to feel stronger and more fully protected.

Whatever the exile needs, your goal is to arrange it for her. And this may mean altering the incident, reworking it so it happens exactly the way the exile needs, the way that will be most healing for her. This doesn't mean that you will forget what really happened, but your psyche will be restructured so that the new experience has the primary influence on the way you feel and behave in the present.

239

Sometimes this change is difficult to imagine. For example, let's suppose you talk to your father image about how the exile needs to be treated, but you can't imagine him responding positively because you have no actual experience of him ever acting that way. Here is how to make this work: Evoke a different father image who *will* respond in a healing way. There are a number of ways to arrange this. One is to evoke a healthy versions of your father, to imagine him the way he would have been if he didn't have psychological problems. Or you could bring up the essence of your father—his spiritual core, his Self. If you can't imagine this, then evoke an ideal father to replace the one you had. Create a father who has exactly the qualities and feelings needed to respond to the exile in a healthy way. Then talk to this father and let him know how she needs to be treated. He will then respond in the right way for the exile to be healed. Let the old situation be reworked to have this new ending. Let the exile really take in this new healing relationship with her father. This will lay down new "memories," new neural connections that will free the exile from the burdens of the past and allow you to feel better about yourself in the present.

So far I have been talking about the original childhood situation as if it involved a parent or parents. However, it can revolve around your brother or sister, or the entire family. It might involve an aunt, uncle, or grandparent. It might even be about the bullies on the playground. That original situation could be an incident in your adult life in which you suffered trauma. (If you're sent to Iraq, for example, you very well might end up with new burdens.) No matter who was involved or when it happened, the principles remain the same. Act in whatever way the exile needs to rework the situation for the better. Make it come out in a way that lays down a new memory that is healing and freeing for the exile.

Taking in Reparenting

As you are giving the exile what she needs, check to see if she is taking in the reparenting you are giving her. For example, does she feel your caring? Is she allowing herself to feel loved and comforted? If you are telling her how much you value her, is she feeling valuable? If she isn't, there are three possible reasons.

1. An exile can be so caught up in that original childhood relationship that she isn't even aware of you. She is simply lost in the past. So first ask the exile if she is aware of you. If not, move closer to her, tap her on the shoulder to get her attention, and ask her to notice you. This can be a big shift for some exiles, because up till now they've been isolated in their own worlds; they might not even know that anyone else exists. Take all the time that is needed for the exile to turn her attention in your direction. If you have a visual image of her, be with her until you see her turn and face you and pay attention to you and what you are offering her. If you feel the exile in your body, take a moment to become her. From that place, turn your attention back towards the Self so you (as the exile) can take in what the Self is giving you.

2. Some exiles have trouble taking in reparenting because they don't trust anyone. An exile may never have had an adult that could be trusted before, so it may be hard for him to trust you. If this is the case, explore where the exile's distrust comes from and empathize with his difficulty in trusting. It is also important to take the time to hang out with the exile for a while without expecting him to trust you right away; gradually, over time, he will learn to trust you.

3. Sometimes an exile can't take in reparenting because he is really fixed on getting what he needs from his real parent rather than from you. He wishes he could somehow reignite his relationship with his mother or father, and this time everything would be right. Or he really needs to receive the reparenting from an obvious parental figure, and for some reason you don't fit the bill. This happens especially when the exile needs nurturing from his mother. He might be so fixed on her that he can't take in what he needs from you, especially if you are a man. If this is the case, evoke an ideal version of the parent or an ideal parent who has exactly the qualities the exile needs, just as was described earlier in this chapter under "Reworking the Situation." For example, you might evoke an ideal nurturing mother figure and let her care for and love the exile.

Once you have worked through any blocks to the exile's taking in the reparenting, spend some time in Self sensing the experience of reparenting the exile. Feel the emotion of love, support, or compassion, for example, and especially how it is experienced in your body. This will ground you in the experience and make it more embodied. You might feel compassion as a warmth in your heart. You may feel your support for the exile as a solidness in your pelvis or strength in your arms.

Then take time for the exile to bask in the good feelings that result from his taking in your reparenting, and feel this in his body. He may experience a lightness and springiness in his step. He may have a sweet feeling in his heart. He may feel a deep relaxation in his body because he now feels safe for the first time in his life.

Christine Reparents the Baby

Here is a transcript of Christine reparenting the exile called the Baby. We have already seen the entire transcript in Chapter 3. There was also another child part called the Little Girl who appears in this transcript. They both felt scared and abandoned, and the Little Girl felt heavy and hopeless.

Jay: Focus on the Baby, and bring yourself into that place where she is all alone. See what she needs from you.

Christine: She wants me to pick her up.

J: Go ahead and do that.

C: She cries louder and then she just clings. Now I'm nuzzling her around the ears and she's clinging to me. I see her bald head. She's quite young and doesn't have much hair, just soft down.

J: Can she sense you there?

I ask this question to make sure that the Baby is receiving the reparenting Christine is giving her.

C: Very much so.

J: And how is she responding?

C: Softening, and now she's not crying. She's feeling into me and resting into me. And now there's a little burp. You know when a baby has been crying and there's a little aftershock going through her. I can feel it in her back.

Clearly the Baby is taking in Christine's reparenting.

C: Well, Okay, I don't know if this is right or not, but what happened is that the Little Girl, with the little body and the heavy

heart, wants to hold the Baby. So I'm going to let her do that.

J: Okay.

C: It's so sweet! The whole thing has now just shifted to this beautiful playtime. I just feel so much love. Not just from me to these little ones, but both of them are bathed in love. They're totally relaxed. (Sigh)

The Little Girl has become involved in giving to the Baby. It sometimes happens that parts want to give to each other. And in the process, the Little Girl seems to be participating in the healing; she is receiving love as well as giving it. Just lovely!

Step 6: Retrieving an Exile

One of the things the exile may need is to be retrieved—taken out of that childhood situation altogether, especially if she is being abused or if she feels very threatened or trapped. This is an optional step that is not always needed. The exile may not think of this on her own, so if it seems appropriate, ask her about being retrieved. Ask her if she would like you to take her out of there and bring her to a safe, comfortable place where she can be with you. If she wants this, there are a number of options for places to take her.

1. You can bring her into a safe, pleasant place in your present life, such as a room in your home.

2. You can bring her into your body—for example, next to your heart.

3. You can take her to an imaginary place where she will feel safe, cared for, recognized, listened to, or whatever else she needs. For example, she might want to play in the ocean or go to a forest clearing by a stream. This should be a situation where she can be with you in the way she needs and perhaps even with other people as well. One exile wanted to be with a group of kids who accepted her and played with her.

Once the exile is ready to be retrieved, let her decide where she would like to go, and take her there. You can also check to see if any other parts would like to come, too. (Some parts will be aware of the session as it happens.) In the new place, be with her in whatever way she needs, and let her enjoy her safety and freedom. Take some time for her to revel in the new environment and to interact with you or other people in whatever way she would like. Check to see if she is taking this in and feeling the positive emotions it brings up for her.

Even after being retrieved, exiles are sometimes afraid that they will be forced back into that original terrifying situation again, the one they were helpless to leave in childhood. Even though they may love the place where they are taken, some of them don't believe it is permanent. They are so used to being in the old situation. So it is often useful to reassure the exile that she *never* needs to go back to that wounding place again. She can stay with you in this new place forever. This is very comforting and encouraging. While it may seem that retrieval is just another way of pretending that the original incident didn't happen, remember that the exile is not actually in the past; she just thinks she is. She actually exists in the present, just like all of your parts. Therefore, retrieving her brings her closer to present reality.

If the exile doesn't want to be retrieved, this may simply mean that retrieval is not necessary. Remember that it is optional. However, there can be another reason. Odd as it sounds, sometimes an exile doesn't want to be retrieved because she is attached to the painful childhood environment. There are a number of possible reasons for this.

1. She might be afraid of losing her parents if she is taken out of there. In this case, you can explain that she can take with her any aspects of her parents that she wants and leave the rest behind. And reassure her that she won't become an orphan; you will be her parent.

2. She might feel responsible for her younger brother. In this case, she can bring him along, too.

3. She might also feel that the family would fall apart without her. This is a burden in itself, so it will probably be necessary to go back to the previous step and witness the memories where she was taught that she was responsible for the family. Then, after she has unburdened that belief, she will probably allow herself to be retrieved.

Sometimes it can be helpful to retrieve an exile temporarily. You might come to the end of a session in which you haven't yet completed the witnessing or reparenting steps, but you don't want to leave the exile in that awful, harmful childhood situation any longer. Even though you haven't done enough work for a permanent retrieval to make sense, you can do a temporary one. Ask the exile if it would like to be taken to a safe place where it can hang out until your next session. Then you will take it back to the childhood situation to finish witnessing and reparenting. After that, the exile can be permanently retrieved.

The Exile Is in Charge of What Happens

Notice that in both reparenting and retrieval, we always check to see what the exile needs or wants. This guides us in deciding exactly how to do the reparenting or retrieval. It isn't a good idea to assume that you know what she needs. You can suggest options to the exile that she might not think of, but don't you decide what she needs without checking with her. She knows best. You may be very surprised to discover what she wants. The exile can sense more truly than you what would be most healing for her. In addition, it is healing for the exile to be in charge of what happens to her. In the original childhood situation, it was just the opposite. She had no say in how she was treated, even though it caused her considerable pain. This leads most exiles to feels powerless and helpless. Now you can redress this by having her be in control. This will empower her and help her feel safe.

Melanie Reparents and Retrieves the Shame Exile

This transcript shows reparenting and retrieval with Melanie's Shame Exile from the last chapter. This is the child part who was ridiculed by her parents in front of their friends. At this point Melanie has finished witnessing this.

Jay: Okay. What I'd like you to do is bring yourself into that childhood situation where she's getting punished over and over again, and she's feeling like a piece of dirt. See what she needs from you to help her feel better or to make that situation come out differently.

Melanie: This is very weird. She says she needs freedom. I'm trying to understand what that means.

J: You might ask her what she needs from you to help her have freedom.

M: Well, hmm. When she is treated like that, she needed to be able to get away from incidents, but they were happening every day.

J: So I can think of two possibilities. One is for you to protect her and stop her parents from punishing her, and the other is for you to take her out of there.

M: She needs both of those things.

J: Okay. Let's start with protection. How does she want to be protected from her Dad, when he is making fun of her in front of other people.

M: Well … She wants me to stand up for her, to tell him to stop. Actually, she wants me to explain to him that what he is doing is cruel and it's making her miserable.

J: Good. Go ahead and do that.

M: Okay.

J: How is he responding?

M: He is very surprised. He doesn't really want to embarrass her. He is agreeing to stop.

Melanie protects the Shame Exile from her dad.

This type of reparenting involves protecting the exile by reworking the situation.

J: Make sure that he agrees to never do it again.

M: (pause) Yes. He is agreeing to that. He doesn't really get it, though. He doesn't understand how much he hurt her.

J: Does she need him to really get it, or would she prefer to have you take her out of there, now?

M: That's what she wants, for me to remove her from there.

It is always important to ask what the exile wants so that she is in charge of what happens.

J: Alright. So let's do that. You can bring her into some place in your current life, or into your body, or anywhere that she would feel safe and comfortable.

M: We're just experimenting with my body, carrying her or holding her, we're just figuring that out … It seems to me that I could carry her on my back between my shoulders. That would be Okay, and I could move quickly. It would be kind of a protection and a getaway.

J: So put her there right now. And see how she likes that.

M: It's a little awkward. It doesn't seem to be working.

J: So see what would work.

I think Melanie took the idea of bringing the exile into her body too literally. It isn't necessary for the exile to be carried in a way that you would with a real child.

M: We're running in the forest.

Melanie brings her Shame Exile into a forest.

Melanie has switched to an imaginary place, and this seems to be working well.

J: And how is she feeling there?

M: She's feeling free.

J: And what does that feel like in her body?

M: She feels light and bouncy, and exuberant.

J: Great. Check and see if there is anything else she needs from you, or if that does it for now.

M: She wants some sort of guarantee that this freedom is going to last.

J: Is it enough for her to be in the forest with you, or does she need something else?

A guarantee like this is something that can only happen over time, so I check to see if there is anything else that Melanie can give the exile in this session.

M: She likes to have fun and laugh. She wants more of that. I'm not sure I can laugh right now. She thinks its funny that she got out of there.

J: She's amused by that?

M: Yeah. She thinks that's really funny. "Ha ha. I got out of there."

J: Is she satisfied now?

M: Yes.

Exercise: Reparenting and Retrieving an Exile

Do a session in which you give an exile the reparenting and retrieval it needs. If possible, start with an exile that you already have worked with to some extent. If you don't have one, start with a protector, get to know it, get permission to work with its exile, and witness the childhood memory. Then reparent the exile as you have learned to do in this chapter, and also retrieve it if appropriate. Use Help Sheet 3 below (along with 1 and 2) to guide you in this session.

Exile _____

What happened in childhood _____

_____

How that made the exile feel _____

_____

What form of reparenting you gave the exile _____
If the exile needed to be retrieved, where did you take it? _____
_____

The next page contains Help Sheet 3, which is a summary of the steps for healing an exile. It is meant to guide your steps while you are working on yourself or partnering with someone. I recommend you use it in conjunction with Help Sheet 1 and 2 in your future practice

Help Sheet 3: Healing an Exile

4. Accessing and Witnessing Childhood Origins

Ask the exile to show you an image or a memory of when it learned to feel this way in childhood.

Ask the exile how this made it feel.

Check to make sure the part has shown you everything it wants to be witnessed.

After witnessing, check to see if the exile believes that you understand how bad it was.

5. Reparenting an Exile

Bring yourself (as Self) into the childhood situation and ask the exile what it needs from you to heal it or change what happened; then give that to the exile through your internal imagination.

Check to see how the exile is responding to the reparenting.

If it can't sense you or isn't taking in your caring, ask why and work with that.

6: Retrieving an Exile

One of the things the exile may need is to be taken out of the childhood situation and brought into a place with it can feel safe and comfortable.

You can bring it into some place in your present life, your body, or an imaginary place.

7. Unburdening an Exile

Name the burdens (painful feelings or negative beliefs) that the exile is carrying.

Ask the exile if it wants to release the burdens and if it is ready to do so.

If it doesn't want to, ask what it is afraid would happen if it let go of them. Then handle those fears.

How does the exile carry the burdens in or on its body?

What would the exile like to release the burdens to? Light, water, wind, earth, fire, or anything else.

Once the burdens are gone, notice what positive qualities or feelings arise in the exile.

8. Releasing the Protective Role

Check if the protector is aware of the transformation of the exile. If not, introduce the exile to the protector.

See if the protector now realizes that its protective role is no longer necessary.

The protector can choose a new role in your psyche.

Follow-Up Reparenting with an Exile

Reparenting and retrieving an exile in a session aren't usually enough by themselves to effect complete healing. They involve forming a relationship with the exile, which is a crucial aspect of healing and transforming her, but this relationship must be kept up after the session. This will fortify your connection with her and integrate the relationship into your psyche and life. At the end of the session, ask the exile what she wants from you over the next week or two. Most likely, she will say that she wants you not to forget about her, to stay connected with her. This is very important. Check in with her every day over the next couple of weeks. Make a note to yourself to do this so that you don't forget. If you do, it could undermine the good work you have just done.

Each time you check in, first re-access the exile. The best way to do this is to remember how you accessed her during the session. Did you have an image of her? Did you feel her in your body? Did you feel her emotions? Call up the same image or body sensation or emotion that represented the exile for you in the session.

Then check in to see how she is feeling now. Does she still feel connected to you? Does she still have that positive feeling that came from the reparenting or retrieval? Or has she slipped back into the pain she felt in childhood? Perhaps something is happening in your current life that is disturbing her. Take a brief moment to witness what the exile is feeling. Then repeat the reparenting that you gave her in the session. Hold her in your arms or tell her that you love her, for example. Give her anything else she needs from you in that moment. This whole check-in process doesn't need to take very long. It usually takes only a few minutes a day—five or ten at most.

This will help you get to know each other better and deepen your relationship. She will gradually come to feel that you truly care about her. This is especially important for exiles that were abandoned or betrayed as children. What they're most afraid of is trusting someone and being left again, and if you forget about them, you are repeating that wound. One session of connection can't heal them completely. They need to know that you will be consistently connected to them over time.

In addition to checking in with the exile on a daily basis, you can also reparent her at those times when she is triggered in your life. This will also enhance your connection with her and solidify her healing. Here is an exercise for doing this.

Exercise: Reparenting an Exile in Real Time

Choose an exile that you have already given reparenting to.

Name of exile _____

Original childhood situation _____

How you reparented the exile _____

You will continue to reparent this exile in real time over the next week. In order to be aware of when the exile is likely to be triggered, answer the following questions:

What kinds of situations or people tend to activate this exile? _____

_____

When are these likely to occur during the next week? _____

_____

Set an intention to be aware of whether this part becomes activated during those times. There are also other ways to notice an exile. What body sensations, thoughts, or emotions will let you know she is triggered?

_____

When you notice that the exile has been triggered, take a moment to tune into her and find out what she is feeling and what she needs. Most likely, she will need the same form of reparenting that you have already given her in a session. This makes it easy to do because you already know what she needs. Give the exile the reparenting in the moment. Notice how she responds to this. _____

Summary

In this chapter, you have learned how to give an exile the reparenting she needs to heal what happened in the original childhood situation. This is Step 5 in the IFS process. It sometimes involves reworking that situation so that it turns out differently. You have learned how to unblend from any parts that might keep you from being able to reparent well. You also know how to make sure the exile takes in what you are giving.

Furthermore, you have learned how to find out if the exile needs to be taken out of that situation to a safe place and how to do this. This is retrieval—Step 6 in the process. Once these steps are completed, you are ready to go on to the final healing step, unburdening, in the next chapter.

Chapter 14

Healing a Wounded Child

Unburdening an Exile

———————— · ————————

At this point in the IFS process, you have accessed and witnessed the childhood origins of an exile's pain, and you have reparented and retrieved it
(if appropriate). The next major step is unburdening, which is covered in
this chapter. The burden is not intrinsic to the exile; that's why it can be
released. The IFS perspective is that the *exile* itself wasn't created by the
childhood incident—the *burden* was.

The Origins of Parts and Burdens

This brings up fundamental questions: Where do parts come from? How
are burdens created? Let's examine this from the beginning of life. When
babies are born, they exhibit certain natural characteristics—sweetness,
aggression, playfulness, sensitivity, quietness, vibrancy, contactfulness,
and so on. Each baby has its own unique set of characteristics, which are
natural differentiations of the newborn psyche/body. (And there are other
characteristics that only emerge as the child, and later the adult, develops—responsibility, mature love, wisdom, creativity, fortitude, and so on.)
In IFS, all these qualities can be seen as parts. At this early stage, however,

the parts don't yet have burdens. It takes a painful experience that can't be metabolized to create a burden. Therefore, these parts aren't considered either exiles or protectors—they are simply healthy parts.

As the child grows, when a painful or traumatic incident occurs, there is usually one particular part that experiences the incident. The other parts avoid the experience, while one gets stuck having it, because *someone* has to experience it. For example, suppose you repeatedly reached out for hugs from your mother, but she was distracted and ignored you. A Loving Part might be the one that reached out and that part will therefore experience those incidents and take on hurt as a burden.

Sometimes a part will actually be a hero and intentionally step up to absorb a harmful experience, taking the bullet, so to speak, for the whole system. For example, if you are being struck by your father, a tough part might step up to the plate. It takes the hit in order to protect the Self from the trauma. In a young person, the Self is not yet fully developed, so it doesn't have the strength and groundedness to be able to handle a trauma. So parts hide the Self away to keep it safe. They keep it out of consciousness so it isn't damaged by the harmful experience. This way, the Self remains pure and whole throughout life, but, unfortunately, it may stay hidden into adulthood and therefore be difficult to access.

The part that experiences the traumatic incident in place of the Self can't really handle it either, and it ends up wounded. It is left with a burden, a painful emotion or negative belief that tends to persist until it is healed. In the example above, the Loving Part experienced hurt that was so intense that it couldn't be metabolized, so this part took on the burden of hurt. From then on, it won't appear to be the Loving Part; it will simply look like a Hurt Exile. However, beneath the hurt, that part's original love is still there, and once the burden is released through therapy, its true nature will again be revealed.

So far we have been discussing parts that experience harm and take on painful burdens. These, of course, are the exiles. As we know, there are also protectors, which try to guard the vulnerable psyche from the intolerable pain of these harmful events. Their burdens are not the original pain but rather the protective roles they adopt. To continue the above example, suppose the Loving/Hurt Exile is hurt so many times that a Self-Sufficient Part eventually decides that there is no use continuing to reach out because each time you do, you are wounded. It cannot make your mother give you what you need, so its only solution is to close down the need itself to prevent continued wounding. The Self-Sufficient Part has now become a Shut-Down Protector. Shutting off your needs is its role and its burden, especially shutting off the needs of the Loving/Hurt Exile.

The Shut-Down Protector has exiled the Hurt Part. While exiles are burdened with feelings and beliefs, protectors take on active, purposeful roles. When the Shut-Down Protector is finally able to unburden its protective role, it can return to its original nature as a Self-Sufficient Part.

By the time you reach adulthood, you will have a number of exiles, quite a few protectors, and some parts that haven't taken on burdens—the healthy parts. They simply manifest their original qualities of joy, playfulness, strength, intelligence, and so on. The goal of IFS is to help all the exiles and protectors—all the burdened parts—release their loads so they can again become who they truly are and manifest their natural positive qualities.

Step 7: Unburdening

The unburdening step, which is the culmination of the exile work, is done through an internal ritual in which the exile lets go of its burden and is transformed; then it can manifest its natural qualities. This is Step 7 in the IFS process. The releasing of the burden is given a specific form (which is described in detail below) that symbolizes the letting go of pain and negative beliefs. This process is similar to some external rituals, such as the practice of writing negative beliefs on a piece of paper and throwing it into a fire. However, here it is all done in your imagination. This often has a profound impact on people.

At this point, you may be thinking, "How could a simple ritual cause such a major change? That sound like unrealistic magical thinking. I don't believe it." This is a reasonable question, which will be addressed later in this chapter.

First we name the burden or burdens the exile is carrying as the result of the childhood scene you witnessed in Step 4. Though the exile has undoubtedly talked about these before, it is helpful to make them explicit now. The exile might be carrying an emotional burden such as shame, fear, or hurt. He also might be carrying a negative belief, such as, "I am worthless," or "No one cares about me." You aren't looking for all the burdens the exile carries—just those that he took on as a result of the childhood situation you are working on in this session.

Checking if the Exile Is Ready

Next, ask the exile if he wants to give up or release the burdens. You can also ask the exile if he is *ready* to release the burdens. If he says yes, move on to the ritual, which is described below. If he says no, there could be a number of reasons.

1. Something else may need to happen first—for example, more witnessing, more trust of Self, fuller reparenting, or retrieval. Suppose that, earlier in the session, you witnessed a memory of your parents dismissing the exile as not worthy of their attention. You learned how hurt the exile felt, but in that session, he didn't show you all the ramifications—how alone he felt, how hopeless about ever having any one to turn to. He wasn't hiding them; they just didn't come up. These aspects of his experience may have to be processed and witnessed before he is ready to release the burdens he's carrying. Go back to Step 4 and spend more time fully witnessing the new feelings; then return and attempt the unburdening.

2. The exile doesn't want to unburden because he is attached to his burden. In this case, ask what he is afraid would happen if he let it go. Then you can reassure the exile by explaining how you will handle whatever he fears. For example, suppose the exile carries the burden of making his mother happy; he feels close to her by being responsible for her well-being. He may be afraid that if he lets go of this, he will lose his connection with her. In this case, you can reassure him that he can still keep his connection with her, and let him know that he also has a connection with you now.

3. There might be a protector that doesn't want the exile's burden to be released. In this case, find out what the protector is afraid of and reassure it. For example, suppose the exile has a burden of worthlessness. A protector is afraid that, without this burden, you will have enough confidence to step out and go after your goals in the world, but it believes this will lead to your being shot down, just the way it happened in your family. Explain to the protector that you are no longer a child at the mercy of your parent; now you have adult capacities to deal with whatever results from taking risks.

4. A protector may be afraid that if the exile releases the burden, you will be attacked by someone in your current life whom you are close to, such as a parent or spouse. For example, suppose that the exile carries a belief that he is nuts because when he was exuberantly expressive as a child, it scared his parents and they told him he was crazy. Perhaps they didn't mean it literally, but he took it that way. A protector may be afraid that if the exile releases this burden, you will become expressive now and be judged or ridiculed by your wife. There are two possibilities here:

a. If this is just a fear carried over from the past, reassure the protector that it won't happen now. You wife would never do that.

b. If your wife is indeed likely to ridicule you for being exuberant, it wouldn't be safe for the exile to release this burden. Don't even try to do the unburdening. Instead, put your energy into working things out with your wife so that she can accept your being more expressive. Sometimes inner work can't go further until you make external changes in your life, even though this might be difficult. Once you have cleared up this danger from your wife, see if that protector will allow the exile to release his burden.

Any hesitation about the unburdening must be resolved before the ritual can take place. Don't proceed with it until the exile and any relevant protectors are completely ready for this particular burden to be released. You can tell this because, when you ask the exile, he says he is ready to be unburdened, and you hear no objections from other parts.

Sometimes the exile doesn't need to do an unburdening ritual. The previous steps of witnessing, reparenting, and/or retrieval may have already healed and transformed him. Meeting his needs may have allowed him to let go of the pain and negative beliefs he was carrying. This is called *spontaneous unburdening*. In this case, there is no need to perform the unburdening ritual. Ask the exile, and he will tell you whether or not the ritual is needed. If there is doubt, go ahead with the ritual. If the unburdening isn't necessary, you can move on to Step 7.

The Unburdening Ritual

Once the exile is ready, check to see how she carries the burdens in her body or on her body. This could mean an actual physical problem in the body, such as a clenched muscle or ball of anxiety in the stomach, or a physical posture that the body takes when this exile is activated, such as ducking the head. The burden may also be seen visually. For example, a burden of responsibility might look like a heavy sack on the shoulders, or one of loneliness might be pictured as an empty hole in the heart.

Once it is clear how a burden is carried in the exile's body, ask her what she would like to release the burden to. IFS has found that it is particularly meaningful to release a burden to one of the natural elements (air, light, water, fire, or earth), because that signifies that the burden is being carried away or transformed by something elemental and powerful, and therefore is permanently gone. There are a number of options to offer the exile. A burden can be:

1. released to light,
2. washed away by water,
3. blown away by wind,
4. put in the earth,
5. burned up in fire,
6. or anything else that feels right.

If you are religious or spiritual, you may want to release the burden to God or the divine. Let the exile decide or intuit what seems best to her. Then picture that situation so the exile can release the burden in exactly the way she wants. She can do this herself, or you can help her if she would like. For example, the exile might wade into the ocean to have the tightness in her solar plexus washed away by the water. You might create a great bonfire, take the heavy sack of responsibility off her shoulders, and throw it into the flames to be burned to ashes. A brilliant shaft of white light could shine down from the heavens, and the empty hole in the exile's heart could be released into it and be carried up and away.

Allow as much time as needed for this ritual to be completed until all of these particular burdens are completely gone from the exile's body or as much is gone as can be released at this time. In my experience, this usually takes only a few minutes. While the burden is being released, sense what it feels like as it leaves the exile's body. This helps to make the experience more palpable and to ground it in your tissue.

Even after all your careful preparations, the ritual still may not work. Or at some point during the ritual, the unburdening might stop working. This is simply an indication that the exile wasn't completely ready. She seemed to be, but actually engaging in the ritual reveals that she wasn't.

This could be for any of the reasons listed previously in this chapter under "Checking if the Exile Is Ready" and should be dealt with in the same way.

Sometimes the exile may be ready to release only part of the burden at this time—say 50 percent. That is fine. Release as much as will go now, and then come back to unburden the rest in a future session. You can also check to see what is preventing the rest of it from being released. For example, the exile might not be ready to release all of the burden because she needs time to see if the Self will continue to be with her and help her over the next few weeks. This is a strong indication that follow-up with the exile is necessary. Once she sees that you won't abandon her, she will be ready to release the rest of her burden.

After the Ritual

Once the burden is unloaded, the exile is free to become more of who she truly is. Notice what positive qualities or feelings arise in her now that the burden is gone. These qualities are natural to the exile; they were buried or blocked from expression because of the burden. Now these qualities will spontaneously arise. The exile might feel joy, strength, playfulness, freedom, love, or lightness, for example. Take some time to really enjoy these experiences and to feel how they manifest in the exile's body, which is also how they manifest in your body. (At this point, it is all right to be blended with the exile and feeling her experience because it is healing for you and your whole internal system.)

For example, if the exile was carrying a burden of worthlessness, when that is released she might feel a sense of lightness and joy because she is freed from that oppressive belief. You might experience this as an uplifting, buzzing feeling in your head. If the exile was carrying the burden of feeling weak and at the mercy of hurtful people, when that is released she is likely to feel strong and powerful. You might experience this as an upright position in your spine and fiery energy in your arms. Allow yourself to really *be with* these experiences, to embody them, and to integrate these new feelings and qualities into your sense of who you are.

As you stay with an experience like this, notice how it unfolds. These manifestations aren't static. For example, the lightness might develop into feeling playful and energetic. The natural energy of the exile, which was held down by that negative belief, is now free to manifest. As the experience continues to unfold, she may begin to realize for the first time that she is all right just as she is, which leads to a natural feeling of high self-esteem and a sense of being valuable. This feeling is not a bonus; it is your birthright. You deserve it, but until now it was blocked because of the burden of worthlessness. Now that the exile has thrown off this burden, she is transformed. She can feel really good about herself, and so can you.

What Is Required for Unburdening to Succeed

At this point, you may be wondering: "Can it really be this easy to change a long-standing pattern of behavior or feeling? I can't believe that all you have to do is have a fantasy of letting go of the pain. It can't be that easy." And, of course, it's not. The unburdening ritual doesn't achieve transformation all by itself; it only caps off the process. All the previous steps in the process are necessary and must be completed before the unburdening ritual will have the desired effect. You must work with the protector(s) to obtain unimpeded access to the exile. You must develop a trusting connection with the exile and witness the original childhood incident. She must feel understood by you. You must reparent her and, if necessary, retrieve her. And the exile must be ready to release the burden. Only after all this has been accomplished can the unburdening ritual work. This ritual is really the culmination of this entire sequence of steps; it solidifies the whole IFS transformation process.

In addition, you must do the entire sequence of healing steps for each exile and each important painful memory. When you carry out the unburdening ritual, it is for a specific memory and the burdens that came from it, not for every burden that exile might be carrying. The exile releases the burdens specific to that memory, which effects a certain amount of transformation. However, if the exile carries other burdens related to other memories, its healing won't be complete until they are also processed and released. You must go through the healing steps for each important memory the exile carries. Furthermore, when these are complete, that particular exile will be transformed, but there will be other exiles that must be treated separately. IFS is efficient and powerful, but it isn't a quick and easy cure-all. You must take the time and energy to do the hard work of witnessing each important memory and healing each exile.

You must follow up with the exile over the next few weeks after the session to consolidate the unburdening. As we discussed in Chapter 13, it is helpful to check in with the exile every day or so to reaffirm your connection with her. If you don't do this, the burden may return.

Burdens can return for a variety of reasons. Therefore, in the session after an unburdening, make sure to re-access the exile and check to see if the burden is still gone and the exile has really been transformed. If so, take a moment to enjoy the sense of freedom and the positive qualities of the transformed exile and to celebrate what happened. If the burden has come back, explore to see why that happened. Usually it is because your internal system wasn't fully ready for the unburdening for one of the four reasons listed earlier in this chapter under "Checking if the Exile Is Ready." Ask your parts questions to find out why the burden came back; then address that issue in one of the ways discussed previously. Then do the unburdening again, and it should stick.

Even when an exile is truly unburdened, more is often needed to change a behavior pattern. After unburdening the exile, you must go back to the protector you started with and help it to let go of its protective role. Then your problematic behavior will shift. This is explained in the next chapter.

Unburdening Melanie's Shame Exile

Let's look at an example of unburdening by visiting the rest of Melanie's session with her Shame Exile who was ridiculed by her parents in front of guests. At this point, those memories have already been witnessed, and Melanie has protected the Shame Exile from her parents and taken the exile for a safe, enjoyable walk in the forest. We take up the transcript from there.

Jay: Let's check and see what burdens the Shame Exile took on because of all those times she was punished by your parents. Clearly she felt like a piece of dirt. And she took on shame. Anything else?

Melanie: I think at some level she agreed that it was her fault.

J: A belief that it was her fault.

M: Also a belief that she was non-human, that she was flawed. Also she believed to some degree that she was evil, and that's why she was being punished.

J: Yes … So ask her if she would like to release those feelings and beliefs.

M: She's Okay with it, but she is a bit skeptical.

J: Ask her if she feels ready to release them

Since the exile was hesitant, I checked to see if she was really ready.

M: Yeah. She is because she really values freedom.

J: Check to see how she is carrying those burdens in her body or on her body.

M: She carries them in her joints and on the left side of her chest.

J: Any particular form those burdens take?

M: It's like sludge over her chest and in her joints.

J: All right. She can release it to light, or have it blown away by wind, or washed away by water; or she can put it in the earth, or burn it up in fire, or anything else that seems right.

M: Well, she really wants light, shining down on her.

J: So see that light shining down, and the sludge being taken up. And feel it leaving her body. Stay with it as long as you need to, until all the sludge is taken away. Let me know when it's all gone.

Melanie's Shame Exile releases her burden to light.

M: (pause) Mm hmm. She's turning pink. Yeah. She's feeling quite light and free.

262

J: Good. So take a few minutes to feel that sense of lightness and freedom or anything else that emerges. Take it in and let it permeate her body and yours.

M: She's starting to glow brightly. She's feeling pretty delightful. (pause) She's giggling, so that's good. That was quite a transformation from a speck of dirt to a brilliant entity.

This is quite a remarkable change in the Shame Exile and in Melanie. She reported that this change lasted long after that session.

Christine Unburdens the Baby and the Little Girl

We return to Christine's session, which was included in full in Chapter 3 and continued in later chapters. At this point, Christine has witnessed the Baby and the Little Girl being left alone, and she has lovingly held the Baby.

Jay: The Baby has taken on certain feelings like panic and loneliness as a result of being left alone in the dark. If it's appropriate, we can now do an unburdening where she releases those emotions she took on. It's possible that some of them have already been released during this process, but it might be helpful to conduct an internal ritual to release them further. Check with the Baby to see if she would like to release them.

Christine: (laughs, cries) Okay, goodness.

J: What's happening?

C: There was a rush of sadness and pain, and then when I asked that question, she wanted to grow up so she could be with the Little Girl. It's like an accelerated growth thing without any blocks in the way. I felt a big rush of emotion coming up; it moved through my heart.

J: And was that Okay?

C: Yeah. It felt good.

J: Good.

C: The Baby is happy.

This is very sweet. It seems that the Baby has had a spontaneous unburdening that came from my simply mentioning the possibility of the ritual.

Of course, this could only happen because of all the good work that had previously occurred in this session.

J: I offered to do an unburdening ritual, and then this feeling moved through you. Now check to see if that is all that is needed or if the ritual would still be helpful.

C: The Baby is fine now, from whatever that rush was, but the Little Girl seems to need an unburdening ritual.

J: Okay, what burdens is that Little Girl carrying?

C: The heavy heart, the despair, the sense that things will never change, that she'll always have to carry the panic and fear of the baby.

J: First check to see if she is aware that the Baby is happy now.

I want the Little Girl to really take in that the Baby has been unburdened because that might allow her to let go of her hopelessness and her need to protect it.

C: Yeah. She wants to play with the Baby. That's interesting. Even though she's playing with the Baby, there's still a belief that she's got to look after it and carry that burden. Even though she's seen with her own eyes that the Baby is happy, she still thinks she can't let go of the heaviness and hopelessness.

J: Okay. Ask the Little Girl if she would like to release that heavy heart she is carrying and the belief that things will never change.

C: That's disorienting because she believes that is who she is. Without that belief, she wouldn't be there.

J: Let her know that if she lets go of that belief, she can be whoever she wants to be and take on any other role she wants.

As I've said, parts aren't defined by their burdens. They have their own potential that is intrinsic to them. That is why they can let go of a burden and take on a new role in the psyche.

C: Yeah, she wants to let go of that so she can play. She can see that that would be fun.

J: Good. Check and see how she is carrying that heavy heart and the hopeless belief—where she carries those in her body or on her body.

C: There is a weight around her heart, and the rest of it is almost like a heavy mantle that she wears over her head and back and shoulders. And she's not allowed to be joyful.

J: Okay. She can have those washed away by water, or blown away by wind, or she can give them up to the light, or put them in the

264

earth, or have them burned up in fire, or anything else that feels right to her.

C: She wants them to be transformed so nobody else has to carry them. So … burning.

J: She wants to burn them in fire. So arrange that.

C: She wants to burn her little dress, as if that is the burden. That is so weird, but that is what she is saying. She wants another dress.

Clearly, to the Little Girl, this dress symbolized the weight around her heart and the mantle on her back and shoulders.

J: As you see the dress burning, feel that burden leaving her body, and take as much time as she needs until it's all gone.

C: That's interesting. She felt quite disoriented and scared in the moment it was changing, but then I held her hand, and now she's got a new dress.

J: Are all those burdens gone now?

C: Yeah.

265

J: So notice what positive qualities are emerging in her now that the burdens are gone.

C: She's grateful. The two of them are actually looking up at the smoke from the burning dress as it blows away. So bizarre. Somebody in here is a bit embarrassed by all this, but these images are coming, so I'm just going to say them anyway ... They're playing footsie with each other. I mean, I couldn't make that up. It's really happening. It's sweet. All the little feet.

Both of Christine's exiles have now released their burdens, which allowed sweetness, playfulness, and connection to arise, qualities that are evidently intrinsic to the exiles, and, of course, to Christine."

Exercise: Unburdening an Exile

Do a session in which you unburden an exile. If possible, start with an exile that you have already worked with. If you don't have one, start with a protector, get to know it, get permission to work with its exile, and proceed through the steps, culminating with the unburdening you have learned to do in this chapter. Use the Help Sheets to guide you.

Exile _____

What happened in childhood _____

_____

How that made the exile feel _____

What form of reparenting you gave the exile _____

_____

If the exile needed to be retrieved, where did you take it? _____

_____

Burdens the exile carries _____

_____

Where it carries the burdens in its body _____

What element the burdens were released to _____

Positive qualities that emerged _____

_____

Summary

In this chapter, you have learned how to see what burdens a particular exile carries and whether she is ready to release them. You know how to conduct an internal ritual of unburdening in which the burdens are released to one of the natural elements. This allows the exile to experience those positive qualities and feelings that are natural to her. You understand what issues might keep an exile from being ready to unburden and what might cause a burden to come back afterwards, and you know how to resolve these blocks so the unburdening can be successful. In the next chapter, we will go back to the original protector to help it release its protective role.

Chapter 15

Transforming a Protective Role into a Healthy One

Unburdening a Protector

—————•—————

We are now ready for the last step in the IFS process. Since the exile has been transformed and is no longer in pain or in danger, its protector may be free to change as well. This chapter describes how to help the protector release its role, which is Step 8 in the IFS process, and how to integrate these changes with the rest of your internal system, thereby completing this segment of your work.

Checking with the Protector

Since the protector views its role as crucial in guarding the vulnerable exile or defending you from the exile's pain, the protector must be aware of the exile's transformation before it can let go of its role.

First, re-access the protector by calling up the image, body sensation, or emotion that you used to contact the protector before. If it is no longer easily accessible, ask it to come forward. Once the protector is there, check to see if it is aware of the work you have just completed. Does it realize that the exile has been transformed? Sometimes protectors have been paying attention and are aware of what has happened, and sometimes they haven't. You want the protector to see that the exile is no longer vulnerable and in pain. You want it to be aware of the exile's new qualities, whether they be strength, joy, or playfulness.

If the protector doesn't know what has transpired, introduce the transformed exile to it. This means bringing them together in the same internal space so they can be aware of each other. You might visualize them together in a room shaking hands. You might bring them into the same place in your body. Now the protector will be able to see the changes in the exile.

Ask the protector how it feels about what has happened to the exile. Is it happy to see her feeling joyful and free? Is it relieved that she is no longer in pain? Ask the protector if it now feels that its protective role is no longer necessary. Would it like to let go of that role? Often it is happy to let go once it sees that the exile is all right.

If the protector isn't ready to let go of its role, ask what it is afraid would happen if it did. It may still believe its role is necessary because it also guards other exiles that haven't yet been unburdened. In this case, you must unburden them before the protector can let go. There could be other reasons why it is hanging onto its role. For example, it might believe that it is protecting the exile from being harmed by someone in your current life. We discussed how to handle this in the last chapter. Or the protector might see that the exile has changed but is afraid that the change won't last. In this case, let it know that you will continue to work with the exile to make the change permanent. Whatever the protector is worried about, reassure it by explaining how you will resolve its concern. Once its fears are assuaged, it will let go.

Step 8: Releasing the Protective Role

Protectors have burdens too, but they are not the same as the exile's. An exile's burden is pain, whereas a protector's burden is its protective role. That role is not natural to the protector. It was taken on because the protector perceived a great danger to you. Once that danger is no longer there, the burden of this protective role can be released.

If the protector is now ready to let go, usually it will simply do so. However, sometimes it is helpful for the protector to go through an unburdening ritual of its own. Ask it if it would like to do an unburdening. If it hasn't completely let go and needs a little extra help, it may choose to go through the ritual. If it would like to do an unburdening, follow the same procedure that you learned in the last chapter for unburdening an exile. Find where it carries the burden in its body, and then release it to one of the elements.

A New Role

Once a protector lets go of its job as a defender, a new role for it in your psyche might emerge spontaneously. If not, let it know that it can choose whatever role it would like. For example, suppose you had a protector that was judgmental about your not working hard enough. It might decide to take the new role of encouraging you and cheering you on with your work endeavors instead of judging you to make you work harder. This is a healthy, non-extreme version of its old role.

However, sometimes protectors want to be the opposite of the dysfunctional way they were before. For example, suppose you have a protector that was very disdainful of the exile it was guarding. It might decide instead to be a loving supporter for that exile. Another possibility is that a protector will choose a role that is neither of these—that has nothing to do with its old role. For example, a protector that worked very hard to keep you spaced out might decide that it just wants to play. Let the protector choose its new role. Don't decide yourself what you think it should be. This might not fit what the protector wants, and it violates the spirit of cooperation that is at the heart of IFS.

Sometimes, instead of the protector choosing a new role, certain positive qualities (such as clarity, strength, or love) will naturally arise in it now that the burden is gone. This is similar to what happens when an exile is unburdened. The protector doesn't *need* to do anything at this juncture. Choosing a new role is just an option. A new role may just emerge gradually over time. What's important is that the protector let go of its old dysfunctional role.

Integrating with the Rest of the System

Once you have unburdened an exile and its protector, it is important to integrate these changes with the rest of your internal system. Since your parts are related to each other, a significant change in one or two of them will affect many of the others. Remember, this is an internal family. Just as with an external family, if a brother or sister suddenly starts acting very differently, it will affect everyone.

Ask all your parts if any of them are upset by the work you have done and the changes that have occurred. A protector might feel that these changes make the internal family too vulnerable because a defense mechanism has been eliminated that it believed was keeping you safe. Reassure it that you (in Self) can handle whatever might occur, and you can care for any exile that gets triggered. Other protectors may feel threatened by the embodiment of certain positive qualities that weren't safe to show in the past. For example, if the work has released love, spontaneity, or strength, there might be parts that are scared of this. *You* know that these are positive, healthy qualities that can only bring joy to your life. However, if you were punished in childhood for being spontaneous, there may be a protector who thinks this is dangerous and wants to block it. When this part speaks up, listen and then reassure it that you aren't a child anymore and can't be punished. If that isn't sufficient, plan to do a session with it soon. Work with any concerned protector to help it adjust to the changes in the system. Otherwise, it may sabotage the transformation that has occurred.

Testing Against the External Situation

If you have time, it is a good idea to test these changes against the trailhead that usually activates the protector. Before encountering this situation in your life, you can try it out in your imagination right here in the session. Suppose the protector always tried to please authority figures in order to get them to approve of an exile that has felt unloved. You can test this as follows: Imagine yourself in a situation with an authority figure in your life now, and notice if the unloved exile gets triggered and if the pleasing protector comes forward. This will give you an idea of whether these parts have been fully unburdened. In addition, you can see if other parts also react to authority figures. This internal testing process will prepare you to face that situation in real life and will also let you know what further work might need to be done.

If the exile and protector don't get triggered, notice how you do feel in the situation. You may notice an unusual feeling of relaxation and ease. Or you might feel clarity or strength. Let yourself take some time to enjoy this experience. Celebrate the changes that have occurred.

If either the exile or the protector does get triggered, investigate to find out why. If the exile is triggered, it means the burden is not completely gone. Investigate what is interfering with the release of the burden, as we discussed in the last chapter, so you can redress that. If the protector is triggered, explore what is keeping it in its protective role, as you learned to do in this chapter.

What Is Required for Behavior Change

It is hard to predict ahead of time how much unburdening will be necessary to produce a significant change in your behavior. Sometimes one session will do it. Sometimes it takes a series of sessions culminating in the unburdening of an exile and its protector. Sometimes much more is needed. Here's why.

As we discussed in the last chapter, in order for an exile to be fully healed, you must witness each significant childhood memory that created a burden for this exile and then do the reparenting and unburdening that are needed for that memory. In most cases, it takes even more than that for your behavior to change. Most of our behavior comes from our protectors, since they push our exiles out of consciousness and don't allow them to control how we act in the world. Therefore, to change a particular problematic behavior pattern, such as eating too much, you must unburden the protector that is responsible for it—the one who was protecting the exile. And if this protector is guarding more than one exile, each of them must be healed before the protector will completely let go of its role and change its behavior. For example, the overeating protector might be protecting one exile that is starving because you were schedule-fed as an infant. It might also be protecting you from the pain of another exile that was abandoned by your mother when she got depressed. And it might be protecting you from a third exile that gets enraged when it believes you have been lied to. For the overeating behavior to truly disappear, you might have to heal all three of these exiles and then, finally, unburden the overeating protector.

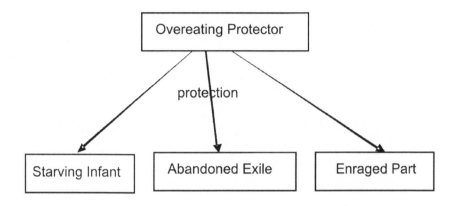

The Sooty Demon Lets Go

Remember the Sooty Demon part, that wanted to attack Lisa's sister in order to protect Lisa's heart from her sister's occasional harshness? Let's look at what happened at the end of a series of sessions in which Lisa worked with this part and its exile. We saw segments of a session in Chapters 6 through 8 in which Lisa got to know the Sooty Demon and made a good connection with it. After that session, Lisa did some additional work with the vulnerable exile (called the Heart Part) in sessions that do not appear in this book. She healed the exile so it became less vulnerable to being hurt by her sister. We pick up the work in the last of those sessions:

> **Jay:** Let's now go back to the Sooty Demon. Check to see if that part is aware of the work we have just done with the Heart Part.
> **Lisa:** Yes, it is aware of what's happened. It says it is very pleased.
> **J:** Ask it if it still feels the need to attack your sister or other people who are harsh or judgmental, now that the Heart Part is no longer in danger.
> **L:** Well, it is thinking about that ... It seems to be saying that it doesn't need to do that anymore. Yes, it feels much more relaxed about guarding me.

J: Great! Would it like to do a ritual in which it releases that attack role, or is that not necessary?

L: It doesn't seem to be necessary.

The Sooty Demon realizes that its attack role isn't needed and is ready to release it, even without an unburdening ritual.

J: Okay, see if the Sooty Demon would like to choose a new role in your psyche.

L: It says it would like to just be playful. I can actually see it buzzing around and jumping up and down. It's doing this in a sort of aggressive way even though it doesn't want to attack anyone. It's just having fun.

J: Good. Take some time now to enjoy this playful part. By the way, do you want to change the name of the part at this point?

L: Yes. That part wants to be called Zappy.

Parts sometimes need new names to reflect how they have transformed.

J: Okay. Take a moment to sense what Zappy is feeling in its body.

L: High energy, a lot of freedom. There's strength in the movement. There is a vibrant, electric feeling, especially in my arms and legs. It's really fun!

Embodying the transformed protector in this way helps to integrate the changes in a permanent way.

J: Would you like to test out this transformation?

L: Sure.

J: Imagine that you are with your sister, and she says something harsh to you.

L: Okay. I imagine her making a crack about my appearance.

J: Notice how you feel in response to this. How is that part reacting?

L: Well, I don't notice the usual resentment. I'm just not that affected by the crack she makes. It just seems like her stuff. And Zappy is not feeling like attacking the way it used to.

J: I guess that means that the unburdening is solid.

This not only confirms the transformation, it helps to solidify it.

J: So we can stop there. Thank Zappy for its willingness to let go.

L: Okay. It is happy.

J: See if there is anything that any of your parts want to say, or if you want to say anything to them before we stop.

L: Zappy is just buzzing around and showing off. He doesn't need to say anything.

J: Good. Make sure you keep checking in with the Heart Part over the next week to continue your connection with it.

Whenever an exile is transformed, it is important for Self to continue its relationship with the part so the change is maintained.

This now completes Lisa's work with the Sooty Demon (Zappy) and the Heart Part.

Art's Protector

Let's see an example of a protector that *isn't* ready to let go after an exile has been healed. This transcript also illustrates how to re-access a part from a previous session. In that work, Art had unburdened a Teenage Exile who was afraid of rejection. The Teenager released those fears into the ocean. However, Art wasn't sure who the original protector was.

Art: The exile is the Teenager, and we got as far as the unburdening on the beach. But I started that session working on the Teenager directly, so there wasn't a protector involved.

Jay: We can work with that. Sense into that exile and see if you can re-access it and where it is now. Let me know if you need more help doing that.

A: Well there's a little bit of confusion because the image of where we ended up on the beach is very present for me. That's the re-access point. I'm having an experience in my body of spaciousness, so it seems like the Teenage Exile is still transformed. But I'm not sure if that spaciousness is just where I am at the moment or if that actually is the exile's feeling.

J: Well, I have an idea. Let's do that testing step to see. What types of situations come up in your life in which this exile is triggered?

This testing step is normally done after unburdening the protector, but here I use it to see if the exile is still unburdened.

A: Social situations. This is an exile that tends to hide out in my room.

J: Okay. Describe a typical social situation in which this exile gets triggered, because I also want to get a sense of the protectors that are operating here.

A: Parties, family events, networking events, and retreats.

J: What protectors are active in these situations?

A: One is a protector that tries to keep me from going to them. It comes up with a lot of reasons why I shouldn't go and negative projections about what it would be like to be there.

J: What shall we call this protector?

A: The Stay-Away Part.

J: Have you worked with it before?

A: Not much.

J: Okay, imagine yourself in one of those situations.

A: I'm imagining going to a retreat, because I'm actually leaving tomorrow for one. My feeling is very different than it was before we did that session with the Teenage Exile. I'm feeling very open and looking forward to seeing people. To me that indicates that some kind of transformation is holding.

J: So we will assume that means the exile is still transformed. Now access the Stay-Away Part.

A: It starts coming up with reasons to spend time in my room when I'm not in meetings at the retreat. There will be a party Friday night, and it is saying to me, "Don't go to that." It's like an automatic no.

J: Take a moment to connect with the Stay Away Part. Check how you're feeling toward it, and acknowledge that it has been trying to protect this exile.

Since Art hasn't worked with this protector previously, I want him to make a connection with it before we go any further. Otherwise, it may not cooperate.

A: I'm feeling very compassionate toward it, and I'm also getting a sense of an exile that's even younger than the Teenager I worked with in the previous section. I'm able to appreciate what the Stay Away Part has been doing and why.

J: Ask the protector if it's aware of the work you did in the last session with the exile, and how the exile is now transformed.

A: Yes, he is.

J: And how does he feel about it?

A: He appreciates what's happened, but he'd like to see the transformation in action. He's not sure if it's safe to go to this party.

276

J: So he's still afraid that the exile will be upset at the party or feel shame?

A: Yes, shame is a very good word. Feeling bad about himself, not knowing what to do. The protector is making a blanket statement, "Don't even think about going there."

J: Let's try something. Introduce that Stay Away Part to the exile right now.

A: They're together.

J: Is the Stay Away Part aware of the transformed exile?

A: Mmm. This is getting tricky. Yes, that does seem to be true, but I'm now flashing on a memory from a much younger exile. It's a very powerful memory that I'm being shown that has to do with being pushed into a party by my mother. I don't know how that relates to the Teenage Exile.

J: Ask the Teenage Exile if this is its memory or if it's another part's memory.

A: It seems to be another part's memory, but it's related to the Teenage Exile, too.

The younger exile is related to the Teenage Exile because they both experience fear in social situations, and they are both guarded by this avoidant protector.

J: I think the Stay Away Part is saying that he can't let go yet because this other younger exile hasn't been healed. Let him know that you will work with the younger one in a future session.

Since the Stay Away Part isn't ready to let go despite the healing of the Teenage Exile and Art was shown a memory from a younger exile, it makes sense that this protector still needs to stay in its role because it feels it must guard the younger exile. Nothing more needs to be done in this session with the Stay Away Part.

When the younger exile is also healed (and any others being guarded by this protector), it will probably relax and let Art go to social events. We can show this graphically as follows:

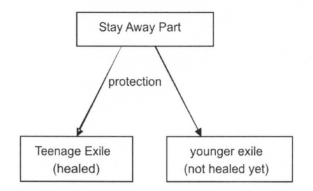

Exercise: Releasing a Protector

Choose an exile that you have already unburdened, if possible. If you don't have one, choose one that you have worked with to some extent, and carry the IFS process through to unburdening. Then re-access the protector of that exile and help it to release its protective role as you have learned to do in this chapter.

Protector _____

Protector's role _____

Exile _____

Exile's burden _____

Is the protector now ready to let go of its role? _____

_____

If not, why not? _____

_____

If so, what new role would it like to play? _____

_____

Are there any parts that are uncomfortable with these changes? What are their concerns? _____

_____

How did you reassure them? _____

_____

When you imagined the external situation, what did you feel? _____

_____

Were any parts triggered? _____

Does any future work need to be done? _____

_____

Healthy Part vs. Self

Now that you are getting a sense of the healthy roles and qualities that parts manifest after they are unburdened, you may wonder how these relate to the qualities of Self. Can one of these transformed parts manifest a Self quality? Suppose that, after unburdening, a part manifests calmness, which is a quality of the Self. What if a part wants to choose a new role of being compassionate? How do you tell the difference between a part like this and the Self?

You make this distinction in the same way that you tell one part from another—by a felt sense of identity. For example, if you feel a sense of calmness, there are two possibilities.

1. You may sense that this is coming from a particular part of you, perhaps one called the Meditator, which brings you that quality as one of its gifts.

2. It might feel as if the calmness is coming from your core Self—who you naturally are. If you can't tell the difference, don't be concerned. In practical terms, it doesn't matter which way you see it, as long as you have access to that positive quality when you need it.

Exercise: Follow-Up with the Protector

Choose a protector that has released its protective role. You will be checking in with it during the week, whenever it is triggered.

Preparation

To help yourself be aware at those times, answer the following questions: What kinds of situations or people tend to activate this protector? _____

When are these likely to occur during the next week?_____

What body sensations, thoughts, behavior, or emotions will let you know it is triggered? _____

During the Week

In those situations in which the protector is usually triggered, notice whether or not it becomes activated. If it doesn't activate, notice how you feel and act that is different than before. _____

Appreciate the changes you have made. Celebrate your success.
If the protector does become activated, check in to see what triggered it
and what it is afraid of. _____

_____

Keep track of this so you know what additional work is needed in a future
session to complete the transformation of this protector.

Summary

In this chapter, you have learned how to introduce a protector to the transformed exile it was protecting and see if the protector can now let go of its
guardian role. You know what to do if the protector isn't ready and how to
unburden it if needed. The protector can now choose a new role to replace
its old one. You know how to check with other parts to see if they are comfortable with the changes and how to test this transformation against the
external situation that usually triggers the protector. This completes the
IFS process for this particular protector and exile.

Chapter 16

Supporting the Therapy Process

Tips on Working Alone, with a Partner, or with a Therapist

─────── • ───────

Tips on Working with a Partner

To get the most out of this book, you need to practice IFS on a regular basis. Each chapter suggests exercises that bring home the concepts, making them relevant to your psyche and your life. For most people, it works best to do these with a partner; the two of you take turns working on yourselves with the other as witness and facilitator. If you are one of the few people who prefer to work by themselves, skip on to the section of this chapter with tips on that.

We human beings are social creatures. Even when we are doing deep inner work, we yearn to be seen and understood. When doing IFS work on yourself, it feels supportive if you have someone listening to you who cares about your feelings and concerns, and is interested in your personal journey to wholeness. It isn't easy to open up deep places of pain in yourself, even with the powerful and respectful IFS method. When someone is there to witness you, it makes the whole exploration more inviting. It provides a holding environment for your wounded and defended parts. Even a silent witness provides presence and support that is very helpful for most people.

There are usually a number of protectors that don't want to deal with your inner world of pain and difficulties. Without a witnessing presence, it is easy for them to take you away from the focus of your work without your even realizing it. Working with a partner will help to keep you on track. And if some of these protectors want to avoid doing inner work altogether, it helps to schedule sessions with a partner. That way, you can't easily put them off; they are on the schedule.

Throughout the rest of this chapter I will refer to the person who is working on him or herself as the *explorer* and the person who is listening and sometimes facilitating as the *witness*. When doing an exercise or session, set aside enough time that the two of you can take turns. When it is your turn to be explorer, engage in the exercise while the witness listens and helps, and then afterwards take about five minutes for the witness to give you feedback and for both of you to discuss what happened.

While you are the explorer, describe out loud what you are experiencing and what questions you are asking your parts so the witness knows what is happening. For example, "I feel a tension in my shoulders." "I am asking the part what it is afraid of." "It says that I will make a fool of myself."

Responsibility for the Work

When you are the explorer, you are in charge of the session and responsible for what happens. This is different from being in psychotherapy, where the therapist has more responsibility for the work. When you are working with a friend in peer counseling, she can be helpful to you, but she doesn't know any more about IFS and therapy than you do. Therefore she can't take on responsibility for what happens in the session the way a therapist would. It is up to you to conduct the session in a way that works for you. It is your job to judge how fast or slow to take the process and how deeply to explore certain issues. You are in charge of keeping track of what is happening in the session and where you are in the IFS procedure. You are responsible for choosing what parts of yourself to explore and how far to go into painful or vulnerable places in your psyche. Though the witness has an important role to play, it is your show.

When you are the witness, you may offer suggestions, but it is up to the explorer to decide whether or not to take them. If he gets stuck or lost, it is *his* job to figure out how to proceed. He might be confused for a while and have to work it through. You can help in any way that seems right, but you aren't obligated to "fix" him or remove his pain or get him out of a stuck place.

The transcripts in this book do not model this principle because, as an experienced IFS therapist, I took a more active role in facilitating those sessions. I was there to demonstrate new IFS concepts that the client couldn't be expected to know. However, remember in your sessions that the witness isn't expected to do this.

Stage 1: The Silent Witness

As a witness who is new to the process, I recommend that you be silent for the first four sessions. You will gradually be able to participate more as you gain experience and learn how to be helpful. To make this clear, I have divided this learning process into three stages. For the first four sessions, in Stage 1 of this process, don't speak unless the explorer asks for your help. This helps to cement the idea that the explorer is in charge and responsible for the session. It helps him to learn how to work on himself, and it encourages you to be free of any sense of responsibility for what happens. You will, however, have an opportunity to give the explorer feedback after each session. Starting with the fifth session, which begins Stage 2, you are allowed to do active listening (described below). Beginning with the ninth session, Stage 3, you may do full facilitation. Starting out slowly like this gives you the leeway to become comfortable with the process before you take an active role. You will gradually learn to be helpful without having the burden of knowing what to say thrust on you too soon. Remember that your presence and full attention are very helpful to the explorer's process, even if you don't say a word.

During the first four sessions, if the explorer asks you for help at a particular moment in the session, it is all right to provide it; otherwise, don't say anything until feedback time at the end of the session. Even if the explorer seems to be stuck or doing the process incorrectly, don't jump in to help unless he asks you. Let him struggle. This forces him to learn how to facilitate himself. And you may always not be seeing things clearly. Your attempt to help could actually be detrimental to his process. Explorer: If the witness says anything without your asking, remind her about being silent.

There is one exception to this guideline: The explorer has the option of asking the witness to facilitate the entire session. When you are the explorer, if you want that kind of detailed help from the witness, you can ask for it. If the witness feels ready to provide this facilitation, the two of you can agree to this active format from the start.

Witness: For those first four sessions, even though you won't be saying anything, your presence and listening are very helpful. It is important that you be in Self as much as possible. This helps the explorer to be in Self as well, and it helps him to feel supported. Follow along with the explorer's process, so that you understand exactly where he is and what is happening. I recommend that you use the Help Sheet so you can track which step he is engaged in.

Being silent also gives you an opportunity to pay more attention to your own experience while the explorer is working. Notice whether you are in Self and what parts become triggered. Work on staying in Self as much as possible, which means being open, interested, and compassionate. Ask any activated parts to step aside and allow you to be there for the explorer. This is much easier to do if you are a silent witness. You have the opportunity to find your way back to Self without the explorer having to know about this and without his having to endure a comment of yours that has an edge to it because a protector is interfering.

Feedback after Sessions

After each session, the witness gives feedback to the explorer, and the two of you discuss what happened. Remember that the explorer may be in a vulnerable place, so it is important to present feedback in a way that is sensitive and supportive. The last thing a vulnerable person needs is to be criticized or judged.

Here are some possibilities for feedback. You can:

Talk about any personal responses you had to the explorer's work, For example, "When that lonely exile of yours came up, I felt very sad. I think it tapped into something similar in me." "I also have difficulty standing up for myself." This helps the explorer to feel understood and to know that her experience isn't weird or unusual. Keep your response brief and make sure it is directly related to the explorer's work. Don't go into details about your feelings or issues.

Offer any positives responses you had to the work. For example, "I was really moved by your courage and vulnerability." This helps the explorer to feel valued.

Ask questions that might further her understanding of her work or help her see something she might have missed. "I wonder if there was an impatient part operating during the last half of the session."

Mention any steps of the IFS process that she skipped over. "I don't think you finished witnessing the Child Part before you started to reparent her."

Mention any way in which she deviated from the instructions for the exercise. "I think you were supposed to focus on a protector in this session."

Make sure that your feedback is not just on the content of the work or the explorer's psychological issues. Give feedback on how she used the IFS process so you can help each other learn the method. Do this in a gentle, almost tentative way, since she is in charge of her work. It isn't your job to make sure she does it correctly; you are just offering possible help. For example, you might say, "It seemed to me that you didn't check how you felt toward that protector before getting to know it." Or, "I wonder if the sadness was really coming from a different part, not the one you started with. What do you think?" Wording it as a question is less likely to feel challenging or demanding.

Explorer: If you feel uncomfortable or judged by the witness's feedback, it is good to say something to prevent this from happening in the future.

Stage 2: Active Listening

After four sessions being a silent witness, it is time for Stage 2. For the next four sessions, I recommend that you reflect what the explorer is feeling or experiencing. This is sometimes referred to as *active listening*. It entails feeding back to the person what she tells you she is experiencing or what a part is experiencing, so she feels seen and understood. You can do this with the exact words the explorer used, or you can paraphrase. Strange as it may seem, it can sometimes be useful to reflect what a person says in exactly the words she uses. For example, if she says, "I am feeling tired and upset," you say, "You are feeling tired and upset." You might also reflect what a part is feeling. If she says, "The critical part says it is trying to protect me from failure," you might say, "It is trying to protect you from failure."

It can also be helpful to rephrase what the explorer says to reflect the meaning as you hear it. For example, suppose she says, "The part is feeling tired and lonely. No one appreciates or understands it." You might reflect, "It feels alone and unseen." By paraphrasing you may bring out something that was implicit in what the explorer said that he didn't consciously realize was there. Often the explorer will say a whole paragraph, but you might reflect just the essence of what you heard. Here is an example of this from Lisa speaking about the Sooty Demon: "It seems like a little Tasmanian Devil, and when I allow it to show itself, it starts whirling, like a little attack thing. It says 'Grrr' and latches onto my sister's leg tenaciously." You might reflect, "This Tasmanian Devil Part wants to attack your sister."

When you are rephrasing what the explorer says, it can be tempting to do this in a way that leads her in a direction that you think is useful by inserting things she *hasn't* said. Or you may think you are helping her go deeper by making subtle guesses about her underlying motivation or pain. This is not good active listening. It is much better just to be a good mirror. Remember, you aren't her therapist. You are only there to facilitate. For example, let's look at another part of Lisa's transcript:

> **J:** Okay. You might ask the Sooty Demon what it is trying to accomplish by attacking your sister.
> **L:** It seems like it does this to protect my heart. It's a protective action. It fearlessly throws itself into the fray. Specifically with my sister, it does this because my heart has no defense against her. It can't close itself off to her because I love her.
> *Suppose I reflected in the following way:*
> **J:** It is trying to protect your heart from the pain of losing your sister's love.

Notice that I have added something here. Lisa didn't say that the part was afraid of losing her sister's love. In fact, it turned out that she was afraid of her sister being sharp with her and wounding her, which is not the same thing. Try to refrain from sneaking in interpretations in this way. Reflect as cleanly as possible what your partner means based on what she actually says. The IFS process will naturally help her go where she needs to without your influence.

Don't try to reflect everything the explorer says or even most of it. That would be inserting yourself too strongly into her work. Just speak up occasionally, when it seems to you that it will facilitate her process. Here are some reasons why it might be helpful to reflect a given statement:

1. It can help the explorer to go deeper or become clearer, especially when she is struggling to understand an experience that is still a little vague or unformed. For example, if she says, "The part feels sort of jittery and pushy," you can simply say, "It feels jittery and pushy." Hearing her words spoken aloud can help the explorer to reflect on her experience more fully. Then she might say, "Yes, I see. It is in a hurry and annoyed that things aren't moving faster."

2. It can reassure the explorer (or one of her parts) that she is being heard and understood. When dealing with delicate, emotional issues, it is very important for us to feel that someone hears and cares, especially when there is shame involved. This allows us to take the risk to reveal our experience, even if it isn't always something we are proud of. It is especially important for exiles to know that they are being witnessed and understood because they carry wounds.

3. If the explorer says something you don't fully understand, it sometimes means that she doesn't either. So reflect what you think she meant, but phrase it as a question. This may help both of you to get clearer on her experience. For example, suppose she says, "The part feels tough as nails, like it doesn't allow a way through." You might say, "Did you say that it is tough and won't allow you to get through to something?" This gives the explorer a chance to get clearer on what she means. She might say, "Oh, actually, it isn't allowing other people to get through to me." If you don't understand enough about what your partner is saying to reflect it, you can ask a clarifying question. You might say, "I'm not quite clear. What doesn't it allow through?" Or just say directly, "I don't understand what you mean by that."

Use these tips to help you decide when it might be useful to reflect what the explorer says, but don't try to figure it out intellectually—just allow your intuition to guide you.

You can also reflect what you observe in the explorer, even if she doesn't mention it. You might notice her tone of voice, facial expression, posture, or gestures. You can give her direct feedback on what you see—for example, "I notice that you are clenching your fists." Or you might get a sense of what she is feeling. Feedback on this is most useful when phrased as a question: "Are you feeling touched by what happened?" Or, "Is that part really annoyed at him?"

Correcting Reflections

Reflecting your partner's feelings can be helpful even if you are inaccurate. When you feed back her meaning, it encourages her to consider her experience. If your reflection is a little off, it is still useful because she will need to feel into her experience even more carefully to get clear on what she really meant. For example:

Explorer: "The Child Part feels heartbroken and totally alone, as if the world is not a safe place."

Witness: "The Child Part feels sad and lonely and in danger."

Explorer: "The Child Part doesn't feel in danger. (considering) The lack of safety is more about feeling lonely and abandoned. No one is there to make her feel safe, to make her feel like she will be taken care of. She feels totally neglected."

Notice that when the witness offered a reflection that was somewhat inaccurate, it gave the explorer a chance to explore more deeply what she meant by the world not feeling safe.

When you are the explorer, it is very important that you feel free to correct reflections that aren't completely accurate. This will help you to explore yourself more clearly. Don't worry about making the witness feel bad if you correct him. He knows that he is still being helpful to you. Your corrections will also help him understand you better and enable him to become more proficient at active listening.

In Stage 2, it is best if you stick to reflecting and asking clarifying questions, as I have just discussed. You will be allowed to become more active in Stage 3. For explorers: If your partner says anything other than a reflection, remind him of this guideline. And if he says anything at all that isn't helpful to you, let him know. This will help ensure that you have a productive session, and it will help the two of you to develop the best working partnership.

Active Listening Exercise

Pick an issue in your life with some emotional juice that you would like to talk about. As you talk about it, your partner should occasionally reflect what she hears or ask clarifying questions. Spend fifteen minutes on this. Then take some time to discuss how this worked. How did it feel to the witness to be actively reflecting? How was it received by the explorer? Was it too much reflection or too little, or just right? How did the reflections affect your process of sharing your feelings about the issue? Then switch roles and perform the exercise again.

Being in Self as Witness

The most important aspect of being a witness is to do it from Self. This ensures that you feel connected to your partner and want the best for him in his self-exploration. As Self, you are curious about what he will discover and what his parts will reveal. This is an open curiosity; you have no agenda about what is supposed to happen. If you do have an idea about where his exploration is headed, you also recognize that it might *not* go there. It could lead in an unexpected direction at any moment. You aren't invested in the work arriving at a certain insight or achieving a particular result. For example, suppose the explorer is working with a protector that doesn't want him to get re-involved with his girlfriend because of the pain that was triggered in a previous breakup. You have a sense that this protector is guarding an exile that was hurt by her. However, you are open to discovering which exile is really there. It might turn out that a part feels guilty for hurting her, and that is the one being protected.

In Self, you empathize with the explorer's feelings, which means you have enough emotional resonance that you can sense what he is feeling, not just recognize it intellectually. When pain arises in him or one of his parts, compassion will naturally arise in you. You feel caring toward your partner and his parts. No matter how destructive or difficult his parts are, you are open and accepting toward them. You don't judge them or want them to go away. You aren't overly invested in fixing them quickly. You can allow his process to unfold at the pace that is best for him and his parts. The explorer may encounter some intense feelings during his work. Even though you are empathizing with him, you stay calm and grounded in Self. You don't get overly caught up in his emotions.

Self is the best place to be, whether you are the explorer or the witness. However, it isn't always easy to stay in Self when in the witness role because you can't work with yourself out loud the way the explorer can. Here are some suggestions for how to maximize your ability to stay in Self.

Working with Your Parts

When you are the witness, start out each session by taking a little time to access Self. See "Self Meditation" in Chapter 5 for a way to do this. As the session progresses, focus some of your attention on your own state as well as that of the explorer. Set an intention to notice when your own parts are triggered. If a part blends with you and takes you out of Self, spend some time silently working with that part so you can re-access Self. Say, "I hear you, but now is not a good time." See "Helping a Protector to Relax in Real Time" in Chapter 7. If the part is so blended with you that you can't get back to Self quickly, don't say much until you can because your words may not be helpful. Take some time after the session to work with that part so you will be more able to stay in Self in future sessions.

There are two common reasons why a part may become activated when you are in the witness role: resonance with a part of the explorer or concerns about being a good witness. Let's look at each in turn.

While the explorer is talking about an issue, accessing her parts, and getting to know them, she may be dealing with emotionally charged material. As a good witness, you will be listening in an open way and empathizing with her. For example, if she is ashamed about something she did, you would resonate with her shame just enough to know what she is feeling. If you have a similar issue in your life, a part of you that feels shame might become activated. This could trigger a defense from one of your protectors, leading you to feel cold or angry or intellectual, to prevent you from experiencing your own shame. If this happens, take a moment silently to see which of your parts is triggered. Then work with them to allow you to return to Self. Tell those parts you will work with them more at a future time.

When in the witness role, it is common for a part that wants to be a good helper to be triggered. Maybe it can't stand to see your partner in pain and wants to take it away as quickly as possible. It might want to fix her because it is frustrated with her being stuck, or it can't stand the difficulties in her life. It might become judgmental toward her "resistant" part and try to push past it prematurely.

One of your parts might be overly concerned about your partner doing the IFS process properly—for example, always following the steps in order. Though it can be useful to remind her of a missed step, a perfectionist part might be correcting her too often, which would interfere with the natural flow of her process and make her feel judged.

Sometimes a part is invested in being useful and helpful, not just for the explorer's sake, but because of its need to feel valuable. It might take too much control of a session and not allow the explorer to be in charge of her own work. It might need to show how smart and insightful you are. It might expand your reflections into interpretations, interfering with your partner's process. It might want to be heard or to make a contribution to her work, which could lead it to jump in before a reflection or facilitation is really needed. Any of these reasons could lead you to over-facilitate.

When you notice one of these helper parts, take a breath, step back, and relax into Self. Don't judge yourself or the part. Just ask it to let go and allow you to respond from a relaxed place. Remind it that you aren't responsible for the explorer's work; she can take care of herself.

Feedback with an Active Witness

When you are working in Stage 2 or 3 with an active witness, leave ten minutes for feedback after each person works, if possible. During the first five minutes, the feedback focuses on the work that was just done, as usual. The witness gives feedback to the explorer, and the two of you discuss what happened. During the second five minutes, the feedback focuses on the witness's experience. Witness: Reflect on what the experience was like for you. How much were you able to stay in Self? What parts came up, and how did you handle them? How did you feel about doing active listening? Share this with the explorer. Explorer: Give feedback to the witness about your responses to his facilitation. What was helpful? What got in the way? What would you like more of in the future? Discuss together any improvements that are needed for the partnership to work better.

Stage 3: Full Facilitation

Once you have done eight practice sessions, the last four using reflection, you can move on to Stage 3, full facilitation. Now there are no restrictions on the kind of facilitation you may use as the witness. However, even though you are taking a more active role, remember that the explorer is still in charge and responsible for the session. You are there to help at times, but you are not required or expected to always know what to do. Please facilitate only when it feels right, not because you think you have to do something. You aren't obligated to fix the explorer or remove his pain or get him out of a stuck place. You are there as an equal, not as a trained professional. Remember the importance of the supportive holding that comes from a silent witness.

It will be valuable to follow along on the Help Sheet so you know where the explorer is in the process. The following are possibilities for facilitation:

1. Point out when it seems that a new part has emerged without your partner realizing it. For example, you might say, "You have been talking to a distant part, but now it says it is angry. You might check to see if this is a new part."

2. Mention when you think a concerned part is getting in the way. For example, "It seems to me that you're feeling judgmental toward that protector. You might check to see if you are still in Self."

3. Mention when you think the explorer is blended with the target part. For example, "You seem pretty annoyed. You might check to see if that angry part has blended with you."

4. Suggest questions for the explorer to ask the target part. It is better to *suggest* rather than *telling* the explorer what to say. I recommend using the phrasing, "You might ask the part ... " This leaves him room to not take your suggestion.

5. Suggest which step the explorer might take next. This can be in the form of a question to ask the part. For example, "You might ask the part what it is trying to accomplish by judging you." Or it could be done by mentioning the step explicitly. For example, "Maybe it is time to check for blending now."

6. Point out when you think a part is an exile or a protector if that will influence what happens next. Sometimes explorers don't recognize which type of part they are working with. For example, "It looks to me like that part is an exile. Shouldn't you check for protectors before working with it?"

7. When the explorer is working with concerned parts, keep track of the original target part so you can help him to return to it when it is time.

8. Keep track of concerned parts and protectors that have stepped aside. At the end of the session, you can remind the explorer of them so he can check in with them and thank them.

Creating a Successful Partnership

When working with a new partner, take a few minutes before it is your turn to be explorer to discuss what you need from the witness once you start. Would you prefer her to be relatively silent and only speak if she feels that you are going in an unproductive direction? Would you prefer her to be quite active by suggesting questions to ask your parts? Would you prefer a lot of reflection of your experience, or very little? Do you want space to try your wings and make your own mistakes? Or would you like a good deal of direction?

After the session, discuss how well the witness followed your desires and how well it worked for each of you. Do you want to try something different next time? Be sure to discuss anything your partner did that wasn't helpful so she can change her way of facilitating. This discussion should be a two-way street. Even though you have the right to the kind of facilitation that works for you, the witness also has the right to her feelings about doing it that way. The more you discuss these issues, the better your working partnership will become.

When you are the explorer, one of your parts may be triggered by something the witness says or by the way she is responding to you. The part might not feel seen by your partner. It might even feel judged or dismissed. It might perceive the witness as cold, demanding, intrusive, or controlling. It may not be obvious at first that your part is reacting to your partner. In fact, you may not realize at first that a part is reacting at all. You may just notice that your work is stalled or a part won't come forward, or you can't get permission to work with an exile. If anything like this occurs, the source of the problem might be a part that is reacting to your partner rather than something purely within you. You may be reluctant to recognize this or to mention it because you're embarrassed about having a negative reaction to your partner. However, it is very important that you do so.

If you discover a part that is reacting to your partner, there are two possibilities.

1. The part's perceptions of the witness aren't accurate, or they are strongly colored by the part's fears. For example, the part could be perceiving your partner as your mother. If this is the case, you have a chance to explore this part, discover where the perception comes from, and heal the part. This will allow you to see your partner more clearly.

293

2. There is some truth to the way your part perceives the witness. For example, she *was* being distant or pushy. Then she will need to change her behavior or demeanor so that it works better for your part. If she can't or won't change, you will need to find a different partner.

No matter what ensues, it is always a good idea to bring up your part's reaction with your partner. Bring it up from Self, which means you describe the part's feelings in a neutral way; you don't dump them on your partner. You might say, "There is a part of me that doesn't trust that you are really interested in me." Don't judge or attack her, even though that may be what the part would like to do.

As in any ongoing relationship with some depth, conflicts will inevitably arise. You may not feel safe to reveal your pain because your partner isn't showing hers. It may seem that your partner really isn't in Self while you are working. When she is giving feedback, you may feel she is judging you. You might wish that she were a more active, confident facilitator. And so on. As soon as you are aware of problematic feelings toward your partner, bring them up with her. Treat this as an opportunity to enhance your partnership, not as a fatal flaw that will end the relationship or as a problem to be swept under the rug. Ask her to set aside some time for the two of you to talk about the conflict. Endeavor to be in Self for this interaction so that the way you express yourself comes from wisdom and compassion, not anger and hurt. Own your feelings by identifying the part of you that is having the reaction. Speak *for* that part rather than allowing the part to attack your partner. Then listen to your partner's responses from Self, asking any parts that get triggered to step aside and let you lead. This is good practice in applying IFS principles in real life.

There is much to learn about how to communicate well that is beyond the scope of this book. If you would like to explore this further, the book *Non-Violent Communication* by Marshall Rosenberg describes a very good approach. I teach a class on "Communication from the Heart" that uses IFS principles. Remember, the most important attitude when dealing with conflicts is to be in Self. Then you can work with any parts that became reactive. If you have difficulties in communicating with your partner, invite a third person to help you.

Tips on Working Alone

Even though it is easier to work with a partner, it is valuable to learn how to do IFS sessions on your own, since a partner (or therapist) is not always available. This allows you do a session on the spur of the moment whenever an important trailhead comes to the fore. And it is empowering to know that you can engage in successful healing by yourself. Working on your own, however, requires a greater degree of Self in order to stay focused and direct the work effectively. No one else is there to point out that you've lost track of the thread of your work or to recognize that you are blended with a part. Therefore, I recommend that you *learn* IFS by working with a partner, if possible. As you gain more facility with the work, you can begin to practice on your own as well.

It is a challenge to stay focused while working on your own. Without someone to be present with you and witness your work, it is easy to space out and lose track of where you are. Here are some tips to counter this tendency. Before you start a session, be clear about what part or trailhead you want to focus on, and make a written note about this. If at any point you decide to change your target part, make another brief note. This will fix your intention in your mind.

It can be helpful to do your work out loud, as if you were speaking to someone. That makes it similar to working with a partner and serves to keep you focused. You can even go a step further and record your sessions. This will not only help you stay focused, but the recordings can be played back for additional learning. The tape recorder serves as a witnessing presence; knowing that your work is being recorded for posterity will help you to stay alert. Another possibility is to do the session in writing. Write out each step of your session as it happens, or type it into a computer. This *forces* you to keep focused and leaves you with a complete record of your dialogues with each of your parts. The possible downside is that writing can make it harder to go deep inside experientially because opening your eyes and writing can take you away from your experience.

The other major difficulty in working alone is that you must be both the explorer and the witness who is facilitating. It is easier to do this in IFS than in many forms of therapy because IFS sessions are conducted from Self. In order to lead yourself, the Self must not only be the curious, compassionate healer for your parts, it must also keep track of where you are in the IFS process and decide what needs to happen next. Use the Help Sheet to keep you attuned to where you are in the process. After you complete each step, briefly open your eyes and check the Help Sheet to see what to do next. This will aid you in facilitating your own sessions, and it will also help you to stay focused while working alone.

Another way to arrange self-direction is to have a "therapist part" that facilitates your session. This is a healthy part of you that is monitoring the steps of the process, looking for blending, watching for unexpected parts arising, keeping track of the thread of your work, and performing other facilitator tasks. Ideally, you would be able to enter your therapist part when direction is needed and then return to Self for the actual therapy.

Tips on Working with a Therapist

Sometimes it is necessary to work with an IFS therapist. If you're having a very difficult time accessing Self or you encounter trouble with extreme or chaotic parts, seeing a professional may be the only viable option. For people who have serious trauma in your history, I recommend that you go into therapy with an IFS therapist rather than trying to work on your own or with a partner.

However, even if an IFS therapist isn't necessary, it can still be beneficial to work with one. You will benefit from her expertise and experience with the model and her ability to help you stay in Self. There are a variety of ways to arrange this. You could do an occasional session with a professional to develop your ability to go deeper in your work or to help you get unstuck from an impasse. Perhaps you will do a series of sessions on a particularly troublesome cluster of parts. You might even decide to engage a therapist for the complete therapy process. None of these options exclude working on your own or with a partner. In fact, your ability to work successfully outside the professional setting will only enhance the effectiveness of your therapy.

Since an IFS therapist is an expert on the human psyche, therapeutic healing, and the IFS model, she will see many things that you might miss, and she has years of experience with the practical details of how to actually make sessions successful. She may catch blended parts, subtle protectors, and other dynamics that you can't see and even a perceptive partner might miss. She knows more advanced IFS techniques that can help you out of a jam or take you deeper into your core issues. Your therapist will also provide a caring, attuned presence, which can be very comforting and healing in its own right, especially when your exiles emerge from their dungeons.

However, one of the dangers of working with a therapist is that you could give over too much power to her. You might get lazy and assume that she is going to fix you. You might fail to take responsibility for your work, for example, by not keeping track of your parts or following up with your exiles. This could seriously detract from the benefits you get from therapy.

Even when you are working with a therapist, it is still *your* work and your psyche. There will be times when the therapist doesn't fully understand what is going on or makes a suggestion that isn't on target. Even the best therapists aren't omniscient. It's very important to tell her whenever she makes a suggestion that isn't right for you at that moment or whenever she seems to misunderstand your experience.

Whenever my clients tell me where I am off, I welcome it because it helps me to understand them better and makes our sessions more productive. After all, my clients are on the inside; they are directly experiencing the subtleties of their inner experience and their interactions with their parts in each moment. I am only hearing their reports. A client who is in touch with herself can tell me much about what needs to happen. Of course, I also have a crucial part to play because of my expertise, experience, and caring. The best approach is for us to work together in a partnership or dance.

The other crucial aspect of working with a therapist is your relationship with him. From time to time, your parts will have emotional reactions to your therapist. A protector doesn't trust him. An exile feels hurt or frightened by something he says. Another part idolizes him and desperately needs his approval or love. When these reactions happen, don't be embarrassed or feel that you are doing something wrong. In fact, talking about them will only enhance the therapy process because you are using your relationship with your therapist as part of the healing. These feelings are commonplace in therapy. It is important to bring them up as soon as you become aware of them.

It is especially important to talk about negative reactions. If you push them underground—if you don't let yourself be aware of them or don't talk to your therapist about them—they can poison your therapeutic relationship and undermine the whole process. Pluck up your courage and tell your therapist about hurt or angry feelings. This will lead to productive work with your parts and a chance to work through the problem with your therapist, thereby restoring trust and safety. Having a therapeutic relationship that is open and trusting provides a crucial support for the therapy. Bring up whatever needs to be worked through in order to keep this relationship clear.

Summary

In this chapter, you have learned a framework for doing sessions with a partner successfully, including guidelines for giving feedback to each other. You know that the explorer is always responsible for the process, and you understand the role of the witness. You have seen how to be an active listener and a facilitator of IFS work. You have explored how to remain in Self as a witness despite the various ways that your parts might be activated. You understand how to create a successful working partnership and how to work through conflicts that may arise with your partner.

You also understand how to stay focused when working by yourself and how to facilitate your own work. You know the importance of telling your therapist when a suggestion isn't right and bringing up any reactions you have to her.

You have learned the advantages of working with a partner versus working on your own versus working with a therapist. There is no reason you must choose just one of these modes for your work. Use them in whatever combination is most helpful.

Chapter 17

Conclusion

———— · ————

This last chapter presents an overall view of the IFS process and its application in a variety of contexts. We review what to do when the IFS process doesn't go smoothly and what happens over time as you develop your skills and capacities with the model. We also briefly touch on issues that go beyond the scope of this book—using IFS as a therapist, working with polarized parts, and understanding relationships using IFS. Finally, the chapter looks at IFS in larger contexts—groups and organizations, spirituality, and social transformation.

When the IFS Process Doesn't Go Smoothly

As mentioned in Chapter 9, the human psyche isn't as linear as you might expect from looking at the step-by-step procedure presented in this book. We shouldn't expect the therapeutic process to work out in a straightforward manner most of the time. Our minds are too complex and dynamic for that. Sometimes the psyche can shift intensely and unexpectedly, and at other times it can change so subtly that you may not notice. IFS is aware of these possibilities and has ways of handling them.

At any step of the IFS process, things might not proceed in the ideal way. The following are a few scenarios. A part may not be ready to move on to the next step in the process, even though you think you've done everything necessary. You may not be fully in Self, though you were a few minutes before. An exile may not be receptive to healing from the Self. Protectors may block the therapy from proceeding, despite your paying careful attention to them. A protector may be upset about the results of unburdening an exile and may undo it.

IFS is prepared for all of these difficulties and many more, and it has ways of checking for them, understanding what is happening, and working them through. That is what makes this approach so robust. Once you truly understand the process, you are never at a loss to recognize what is happening at any given moment and how to handle it.

Your Development as an IFS Practitioner

You have now learned the basics of the IFS model. The key to making it work for you and achieving substantive change is *practice*. You must do the exercises in this book and continue to do IFS sessions on yourself after you finish reading the book, preferably with a partner to witness you, aid you, and hold you to your commitment. If you want additional help with the IFS approach, you could take my IFS classes or work with an IFS therapist (see Appendix).

If you practice IFS work seriously, your skills and abilities will develop over time. You will reach a point where you understand the model intuitively, which means you don't need to be bound by the step-by-step procedure in this book. However, you can still use the steps as your base point and improvise when that feels right. Or you can discard them altogether and employ a completely intuitive approach that is based on your understanding of the principles of IFS. Then you only need to return to the steps for guidance if you get stuck.

As you continue to practice, your skills and self-awareness will develop. You will improve your ability to detect parts that arise unexpectedly. More of the time, you will know what to do when your process gets stuck. You will learn how to skillfully perform the IFS steps—unblending from a part, accessing a childhood memory, reparenting an exile, conducting an

300

unburdening, and so on. You will gain greater understanding of how to deal with subtle issues—for example, accessing preverbal exiles, working through trust issues with a part, and differentiating one part from another. You will eventually be able to follow almost any trailhead to a healing conclusion, whether this takes one session or many.

Not only will your skill develop, your inner system will shift in a healthy direction. You will gain easier and more consistent access to Self, including greater ability to return to it when a part floods you. Instead of your parts taking over and controlling how you interact with the world, they will increasingly trust in your Self to take the lead in making decisions and relating to people. You will come to trust the IFS process and your own ability to work through any issue you choose to focus on. Your protectors won't be hesitant to face underlying pain because they will know that you can handle it and that exiles really can be unburdened. Over time, your exiles will be relieved of much the suffering and negative beliefs they carry. Therefore, you won't feel the same underlying anxiety and depression, and your protectors won't be constantly pressuring you to take over and block this out. You will be less reactive to difficult people and situations in your life and more able to stand in a solid place within yourself without becoming upset or angry.

You will also feel more at ease inside yourself and more trusting of your ability to handle problems and conflict. You will experience inner harmony and wholeness, and know your intrinsic worth. Your relationships will become more cooperative and enjoyable because of your greater capacity to be open and loving with people. Your relationships with your spouse and family may grow deeper and more intimate. In all situations, you will be stronger and more assertive, able to stand up for yourself, express your opinions, and take risks when called for. You will have a greater ability to accomplish your life goals, leading to security, pleasure, and fulfillment. You will feel more at home in the universe and connected to all beings. The deeper purpose of your life may become more apparent to you.

Using IFS Professionally

Let me briefly address therapists from a professional prospective on how to use IFS. I only have space to touch on some of the issues involved, not to go into them in any depth.

Being in Self

The most important key to being an effective IFS therapist is to be in Self. Not only do your clients need to be in Self before proceeding to get to know their parts, *you* need to be in Self during sessions. As therapists, we all know the importance of the therapeutic relationship. In IFS, the most important healing relationship is between your client's Self and his parts, but even so, your relationship with your client is a crucial support for this process. When you embody Self and relate to a client from that place, he knows that you care about him and want the best for him. This supports his ability to access Self.

You are a coach who helps the client's Self relate successfully to each of his parts and to engage in the IFS process. To do this well, you must embody Self in a way that your client can perceive. This provides a model for how the client can relate to his parts. You are openly curious and compassionate toward each of his parts. You aren't in a rush to get past his protectors. You don't get annoyed when a protector repeatedly makes him space out or get distracted. Or, at least, that is your goal. It isn't realistic to expect yourself to always be in Self. When you slip up and a part takes over, try to recognize this and take the time to silently unblend right in that moment. Work with the part to help it to step aside and allow you to return to Self. However, this isn't always possible, so when you aren't able to fully return to Self during a session, spend some time afterwards to work with the part that took over. Get to know it and perhaps unburden it so you can be fully present in Self in future sessions with that client.

Occasionally, a client will have difficulty accessing Self early in his therapy. In this case, you must hold Self for that client. You must provide the Self qualities that are needed for the therapy to proceed until the client has progressed enough to access Self and hold it. Until then, *you* relate to his parts from Self. You provide a caring holding environment so that the client's parts can feel trusting enough to open up and reveal themselves. However, you don't want to take on the role of Self to such a degree that the client never learns to take that seat himself. You do it only until the client has developed enough access to Self that he can take over this role.

Trauma

IFS is very effective at working with trauma, just using the regular procedure without any specialized techniques. This is partly because Richard Schwartz developed IFS at a time when a large percentage of his clients had experienced significant trauma.

An important reason for the effectiveness of IFS with trauma is the way it deals with unblending from exiles. The biggest difficulty in working with trauma is the danger of retraumatizing the client when she is accessing and healing the exile that carries the trauma. IFS deals with this in a highly effective manner (discussed fully in Chapter 11). The client stays in Self and develops a relationship with the traumatized exile. She doesn't *become* the exile (blend with it) unless it is safe to do so and there is a clear benefit. If the exile begins to flood her with terror, shame, or other emotions related to the trauma, the therapist helps the client negotiate with the exile to stay separate. This is one of the major innovations of IFS for trauma work. Schwartz discovered that exiles have the capacity to contain their feelings and not overwhelm the client if they choose to. The exile simply needs to understand that it is in its best interest to refrain from blending because then there will be a Self to witness its story and heal it.

IFS continually emphasizes being in Self while working with traumatized exiles, and this is crucial to the success of the therapy. Even clients who *could* retrieve memories of the abuse and deal with them without being in Self *shouldn't* do so because it is unlikely lead to healing. It is only when the client is in Self that true healing can happen because the Self embodies compassion, love, groundedness, and strength, all of which are necessary for the healing process.

The IFS method is also very helpful in understanding the defensive manifestations that constantly crop up in trauma work. Dissociation, for example, is understood as coming from a protector that is trying to keep the client from re-experiencing the trauma. You work with a dissociative part in a similar way to other protectors. You connect with it and reassure it that the client will stay in Self and not be flooded by the traumatized exile.

The Center for Self Leadership is the main IFS organization headed by Richard Schwartz. It offers professional training programs in IFS, which I highly recommend, in cities around the U.S. and in Europe (see Appendix).

Polarization

There is more to IFS than I can describe in one book. Let me briefly discuss one major aspect of IFS that can't be covered in detail in this book—polarization. We often find ourselves in conflict about how to respond to an issue in our lives. One part of us feels one way, and another feels quite differently. One part wants to take a certain action, and another wants to do the exact opposite. Polarization can show up in our lives in a multitude of ways. It can cause us to procrastinate, be indecisive, have "mixed feelings," or vacillate about what action to take. We may judge ourselves and then defend against our own judgments. In these situations, if you really listen inside, you will hear arguments going on between different parts of you. Even experiences like depression, anxiety, and low self-esteem, which at first glance don't look like inner conflict, are often rooted in polarization.

IFS understands that inner conflict results from two parts being polarized, which means they are opposed to each other, feeling and acting in ways that are contrary, like reaching out versus holding back. One part might want something, and another might be afraid of it. One might work hard toward a goal, and the other might sabotage this effort. Each part is convinced that it must take an extreme stand in order to deal with the destructive actions of the other. For example, a Dieting Part becomes very strict to counter the indulgent tendencies of an Eating Part, and the Eating Part feels that it must rebel against the rigid control of the Dieting Part. Polarized parts are often locked in an unending struggle that causes intense emotions and counterproductive behavior. Usually, both polarized parts are protectors that are guarding exiles, and sometimes they are even protecting the same exile using opposite strategies.

With IFS, you get to know each polarized part and develop a trusting relationship with it, just as you would with any protector. This helps you to realize that you don't want to get rid of either side because each of them has something to offer and each is trying its best to help you. Then, you can guide the two parts in having a dialog instead of fighting each other. This helps each part to stop seeing the other as an enemy and to recognize its positive qualities. They learn to cooperate with each other instead of being at war. In some cases, you may have to heal the exiles they are protecting before cooperation is possible. However, since they both want the best for you, this is always achievable. The key is for each protector to trust that the Self understands and cares about its mission. Then they will let you help them learn to collaborate with each other on your behalf.

IFS and The Inner Critic

The Inner Critic is the part that judges you, demeans you, and tells you who you should be. It undermines your self-confidence and makes you feel bad about yourself. Since this is one of the most difficult and tenacious issues that people face, I have collaborated with Bonnie Weiss, LCSW, on a serious study of how to transform the Inner Critic using IFS. Our core understanding is that self-esteem is your birthright, and the Inner Critic is one of greatest challenges to realizing this.

Actually, there isn't just one Inner Critic part; most people have a number of self-judging protectors that operate in different ways. We have identified seven types of Critics with different motivations and strategies for controlling you. Since an Inner Critic part is a protector, it is actually trying to help you, as surprising as that may seem. This makes it possible to connect with a Critic from Self rather than fighting it, and this helps it to let go of its judgments. We have worked out the details of how to transform each of the seven Inner Critics using IFS.

Another exciting and hopeful result of our study: We have discovered that you can develop an aspect of your Self that we call the Inner Champion, which supports and encourages you. It is a magic bullet for dealing with the negative impacts of your Inner Critics. See Appendix B for links and details about our Inner Critic work.

IFS with Couples

IFS has a very insightful way of understanding the dynamics of love relationships. When a couple gets into difficulties, it is because a cycle of "protector wars" has started. Let's say that Henry says something a little judgmental, which hurts an exile of Elaine's that is sensitive to being criticized. This brings up one of Elaine's protectors that feels it must defend this exile. This protector tries to control Henry by telling him exactly how to talk to her so she won't feel criticized. Unfortunately, Elaine's behavior triggers an exile of Henry's that is sensitive to being controlled. One of Henry's protectors then forces him to withdraw from her to keep the exile from feeling as though it is under her thumb. This activates another exile of

Elaine's that feels abandoned. Immediately, her controlling protector tries to get Henry to come back to her by telling him how wrong it is for him to pull away from her. Of course, this further inflames Henry's exile that is afraid of being controlled, which makes the protector withdraw even further. And around and around they go.

Neither Henry nor Elaine has any idea that the conflict is being driven by the exiles that are being frightened and wounded, and they are hardly even aware of the protectors that are fighting. All each partner can see is the hurtful behavior of the other, so they each believe that the conflict is entirely the other person's fault. All the protectors are doing is trying to keep the exiles from being hurt; they have no idea of how much they are harming their partner's exiles and thereby exacerbating the conflict and creating distance in the relationship. This is the kind of dynamic that happens with almost every couple that is having problems. The particular exiles and protectors may be different, but the dynamics are similar.

Using IFS, you can identify the parts involved in the protector war with your partner. Then you work with each of your parts separately. You begin to heal your exiles and help your protectors to let go of their guardian roles. This gradually calms the exiles and makes it easier for the protectors to relax, which makes it possible for you to begin to access Self. Your partner can do the same. Your goal is to relate to each other from Self while recognizing those moments when a part becomes triggered. When this happens, you speak *for* the part in a neutral voice rather than acting it out. For example, instead of yelling, "YOU CONTROLLING BITCH!" you would say, "A part of me is angry because it feels controlled by you." In this way, you take responsibility for your part's reaction, and you don't inflame your partner's protectors by attacking her. Doing this allows you to stay in Self and continue a fruitful conversation with your partner. Dialoging from Self will give the two of you an amazing capacity to work through differences of opinion, past hurts, and other difficulties.

IFS with Groups, Families, and Organizations

IFS originated from Family Systems Therapy, an approach to working with families by seeing them as systems. During the original development of

IFS, Richard Schwartz observed that the interactions among subpersonalities within a person was quite similar to the systems dynamics among people in a family. That's why he called his new approach Internal Family Systems Therapy. Schwartz was applying a *systems perspective* to the psyche. This view shows that the parts of any system aren't just a collection of separate items; they are related to each other in important ways. In the human psyche, some parts protect against other parts; some parts are polarized with others; and some are allied with others. Much of the healing power of IFS comes from its systems perspective because understanding these relationships leads directly to effective technique.

This perspective also allows IFS to be used in working with systems larger than the psyche—families, groups, and organizations. Of course, IFS is powerful in working with families not only because of its origins in family therapy, but also because it helps you discover how the parts of each person in the family relate to the parts of the others.

Groups and organizations are also systems, so IFS insights can be applied to them as well. You can study an organization and ask who are the exiles and who are the protectors. From this viewpoint, an exile isn't a part of a person, it is a part of the larger system we are examining. An exile would be a group of people in an organization who are pushed aside, who are kept from being visible and influential. A protector would be a group of people, usually those in power, who are guarding against certain outcomes that they think will be harmful to the organization. Often this protectiveness is influenced by past events in the history of the organization and is out of touch with the present situation. Polarization is also a crucial dynamic in organizations, where the members divide into two subgroups that are fighting each other for power. IFS-oriented management consultants uncover the dynamics of protection, exiling, and polarization in an organization, which helps them understand how best to intervene.

IFS work is also being used by coaches to help people in organizations heal their parts so they function more effectively. This work is similar to IFS therapy except there is less emphasis on healing the deep pain of exiles and more on understanding and connecting with protectors to modify their problematic behavior.

IFS and Spiritual Development

The central role of the Self makes IFS a spiritually oriented therapy. As we have seen, the Self is the source of love, compassion, and connectedness, which are important spiritual qualities. The Self is connected to the deeper ground of being that the world's spiritual traditions speak of. This ground is referred to in different traditions as God, Essence, Buddha Nature, Atman, Inner Light, or Christ Consciousness. In fact, at its deepest level, the Self *is* that spiritual ground, as Schwartz has noted.

Most schools of psychotherapy deal primarily on the ego level and don't recognize that everyone has a Self underneath their psychological issues. According to these theories, many clients are lacking a Self and must internalize Self qualities from their therapists. IFS, however, recognizes that every single person has a Self, though it may be obscured by parts that have taken over the psyche. This viewpoint is consistent with the understandings of the world's spiritual traditions, which teach that this spiritual ground is, in fact, who we truly are. Thus, IFS makes use of our spiritual nature in its approach to psychological healing. Furthermore, IFS fosters spiritual development by liberating the Self from our extreme parts.

As we have seen, IFS takes the stance of welcoming all parts with acceptance and compassion, even our most dangerous and destructive ones. This is actually a spiritual practice—to open our hearts to every aspect of ourselves and discover that they only want the best for us. This allows us to see that the basis of all inner activity is love. It becomes an even more profound practice when we apply it to other people and their parts. Suppose we understood that everyone's parts are just doing their best to protect against pain, and this is true even for those people and nations that are causing horrible suffering in the world. This challenges our judgmental and separating attitudes and encourages us to experience our inherent connection with all people and all beings. It doesn't blind us to destructive and hateful actions, but it does open our hearts to compassion, loving kindness, and universal love.

IFS provides a way of directly enhancing spiritual development. Most spiritual paths involve the cultivation of specific qualities, such as loving kindness, interconnectedness, joy, spaciousness, peace, and so on. However, these spiritual qualities are often hard to integrate into our lives because they are blocked by protectors. To be more precise, a certain quality will be blocked by a particular protector. For example, compassion may

308

be blocked by a protector that judges people; interconnectedness may be blocked by a protector that keeps you closed off or distant from people.

Though you may engage in a spiritual practice that is designed to open up a specific spiritual quality, for it to truly manifest in your life, you must also work through the psychological issues that prevent it from flowering. For example, though you perform a certain meditation to cultivate loving kindness, you must also transform your judgmental protector so that you can actually relate to people in a loving way. You may feel loving kindness when you are in comfortable, unthreatening circumstances, but if someone dismisses you or attacks you, the judgmental protector will be triggered, interfering with your intention to be kind. To fully liberate loving kindness, you must help the judgmental protector to let go of its role (which usually means first unburdening the exile that is being protected). Once this has happened, you can fully reap the fruits of your meditation practice. Loving kindness can manifest naturally at those moments in your life when it is needed because nothing is in the way. Thus, you can target IFS work to enhance your spiritual development by choosing to focus on those parts that are blocking a particular spiritual quality you want to cultivate.

IFS and Social Transformation

Our world is going through a major historic transition. The many crises we face, from global warming to the current financial breakdown, all stem from deeper systemic problems. Our modern culture and worldview—characterized by rationality, control, competition, individualism, and materialism—is no longer working. Modern society has made many wonderful contributions to humanity, from science to democracy to individuality. However, the combination of advanced technology, population growth, and national competition is threatening our environment and our civilization. This is causing a breakdown in our society and opening the way for a breakthrough into the next stage of our evolution.

A new culture is already emerging, even as the old one is crumbling. The signs of this are everywhere, though there is a long way to go. It involves a shift from an attitude of power-over to one of openness, inclusiveness, and dialog. It involves a change from individualism and competition to connection and cooperation—between people, among groups and nations, and with nature. The emerging culture is based on the widespread adoption of processes for inner awareness and spiritual development that use intuition, emotional awareness, and participation as opposed to rationality and control.

IFS is playing its part. It is not only an extremely effective method of personal growth, but it also embodies the characteristics of the new, emerging culture. IFS teaches us the importance of understanding and compassion for our parts and, by extension, for other people and other cultures. It helps us to heal rifts and end competition among our parts so they can cooperate with each other. This can translate into cooperation with other people and groups because our inner life affects our outer actions. IFS produces personal healing and transformation through emotional openness, intuitive perception, and body awareness, as opposed to rational control and programming. Thus, IFS therapy not only makes us healthier, but it also fosters our capacity to be contributing citizens and co-creators of the new culture and society that is being born.

Conclusion

IFS has enriched my life enormously, both personally and professionally. I hope you find it to be natural, accessible, and powerful, just as I have. I encourage you to practice it regularly so you can reap the full benefits of this amazing model. This will permit you to heal yourself and develop your capacities for love, creativity, achievement, and connection, making your life meaningful, exciting, and satisfying.

Appendix A

Help Sheet for the IFS Process

---•---

This is a summary of all the steps of the IFS procedure. It is meant to guide your steps while you are working on yourself or partnering with someone.

1. Getting to Know a Protector
P1. Accessing a Part
If the part is not activated, imagine yourself in a recent situation when the part *was* activated.
Sense the part in your body or evoke an image of the part.
P2. Unblending Target Part
Check to see if you are charged up with the part's emotions or caught up in its beliefs right now. If so, you are blended.
Check to see how you feel toward the target part right now. If you can't tell, you may be blended.
If you are blended with the target part, here are some options for unblending.
- Ask the part to separate from you so you can get to know it.
- Move back internally to separate from the part.
- See an image of the part at a distance from you or draw the part.
- Visualize the part in a room to provide a container for it.
- Do a short centering / grounding meditation.
If the part doesn't separate, ask what it is afraid would happen if it did.
Explain to it the value of separating and reassure it about its fears.

311

P3. Unblending Concerned Part

Check to see how you feel toward the target part right now.

If you feel compassionate, curious, and so on, you are in Self, so you can move on to P4.

If you don't, then unblend the concerned part:

- Ask the concerned part if it would be willing to step aside (or relax) just for now so you can get to know the target part from an open place.
- If it does, check again to see how you feel toward the target part, and repeat.
- If it isn't willing to step aside, explain to it the value of stepping aside.
- If it still won't, ask what it is afraid would happen if it did, and reassure it about its fears.
- If it still won't, make the concerned part the target part and work with it.

P4. Discovering a Protector's Role

Invite the part to tell you about itself.

The part may answer in words, images, body sensations, emotions, or direct knowing.

Here are questions you can ask the part:

- What do you feel?
- What are you concerned about?
- What is your role? What do you do to perform this role?
- What do you hope to accomplish by playing this role?
- What are you afraid would happen if you didn't do this?

P5. Developing a Trusting Relationship with a Protector

You can foster trust by saying the following to the protector (if true):

- I understand why you (do your role).
- I appreciate your efforts on my behalf.
- I know you've been working very hard.

2. Getting Permission to Work With an Exile

If necessary, ask the protector to show you the exile.

Ask its permission to get to know the exile.

If it won't give permission, ask what it is afraid would happen if you accessed the exile.

Possibilities are:

- The exile has too much pain. Explain that you will stay in Self and get to know the exile, not dive into its pain.
- There isn't any point in going into the pain. Explain that there is a point— you can heal the exile.

- The protector will have no role and therefore be eliminated. Explain that the protector can choose a new role in your psyche.

3. Getting to Know an Exile
E1: Accessing an Exile
Sense its emotions, feel it in your body, or get an image of it.
E2: Unblending From an Exile
If you are blended with an exile:
- Ask the exile to contain its feelings so you can be there for it.
- Consciously separate from the exile and return to Self.
- Get an image of the exile at a distance from you.
- Do a centering/grounding induction.

If the exile won't contain its feelings:
- Ask it what it is afraid would happen if it did.
- Explain that you really want to witness its feelings and story, but you need to be separate to do that.

Conscious blending: If you can tolerate it, allow yourself to feel the exile's pain.
E3: Unblending Concerned Parts
If you aren't in Self or don't feel compassion, unblend from any concerned parts. They are usually afraid of your becoming overwhelmed by the exile's pain.

Explain that you will stay in Self and not let the exile overwhelm.
E4: Finding Out about an Exile
Ask: What do you feel? What makes you feel so scared or hurt (or any other feeling)?
E5: Developing a Trusting Relationship with an Exile
Let the exile know that you want to hear its story.

Communicate to it that you feel compassion and caring toward it.

Check to see if the exile can sense you there and notice how if it is taking in your compassion.

4. Accessing and Witnessing Childhood Origins
Ask the exile to show you an image or a memory of when it learned to feel this way in childhood.

Ask the exile how this made it feel.

Check to make sure the part has shown you everything it wants to be witnessed.

After witnessing, check to see if the exile believes that you understand how bad it was.

5. Reparenting an Exile

Bring yourself (as Self) into the childhood situation and ask the exile what it needs from you to heal it or change what happened; then give that to the exile through your internal imagination.

Check to see how the exile is responding to the reparenting.

If it can't sense you or isn't taking in your caring, ask why and work with that.

6: Retrieving an Exile

One of the things the exile may need is to be taken out of the childhood situation and brought into a place with it can feel safe and comfortable.

You can bring it into some place in your present life, your body, or an imaginary place.

7. Unburdening an Exile

Name the burdens (painful feelings or negative beliefs) that the exile is carrying.

Ask the exile if it wants to release the burdens and if it is ready to do so.

If it doesn't want to, ask what it is afraid would happen if it let go of them. Then handle those fears.

How does the exile carry the burdens in or on its body?

What would the exile like to release the burdens to? Light, water, wind, earth, fire, or anything else.

Once the burdens are gone, notice what positive qualities or feelings arise in the exile.

8. Releasing the Protective Role

Check if the protector is aware of the transformation of the exile. If not, introduce the exile to the protector.

See if the protector now realizes that its protective role is no longer necessary. The protector can choose a new role in your psyche.

Appendix B

IFS Resources

Self-Therapy Companion Books

Self-Therapy Exercise Book. A compilation of all the exercises in this book that involve writing out answers. Download it for free from www.personal-growth-programs.com. Mouse over Self-Therapy on the Books menu, and then click on Support for Self-Therapy.

Self-Therapy Workbook. Bonnie Weiss, LCSW. A companion workbook for Self-Therapy that integrates concept descriptions and exercises for individual exploration, journal-style following of your process, small groups, and classes. Also includes polarization, firefighters, and using IFS with couples.

IFS Courses and Groups

My colleagues and I teach courses for the general public where people learn to use IFS for self-help and peer counseling. This book is based on the first two of these classes. They can be taken by telephone or in person in the San Francisco Bay Area. We also offer courses on polarization and other IFS advanced topics, some of which are for professionals. In addition, we offer courses on specific issues, such as spirituality, the Inner Critic, and eating issues.

I also offer ongoing IFS therapy groups. In the future, I expect to offer a long-term personal growth program based on IFS.

I offer individual and group consultation for IFS therapists, including a telephone group. See www.personal-growth-programs.com for more information and a schedule of classes and groups.

Other IFS Books by Jay Earley

Resolving Inner Conflict. A professional book on working with polarization using IFS.

Working with Anger in IFS. A professional booklet that shows how to deal with the various ways that anger can arise in an IFS session.

Negotiating for Self-Leadership in IFS. How to work with a protector to let go of its problematic role in a specific life situation.

Freedom from Your Inner Critic, with Bonnie Weiss. How to work with and transform self-critical protectors using IFS.

Illustrated Workbook for Freedom from Your Inner Critic, by Bonnie Weiss. Provides illustrations of the concepts and detailed exercises for doing the work.

All of our books are available at our online store at http://www.personal-growth-programs.com/store/.

IFS Books by Richard Schwartz and Others

Introduction to the Internal Family System Model, by Richard Schwartz. A basic introduction to parts and IFS for clients and potential clients.

Internal Family Systems Therapy, by Richard Schwartz. The primary professional book on IFS and a must-read for therapists.

The Mosaic Mind, by Richard Schwartz and Regina Goulding. A professional book on using IFS with trauma, especially sexual abuse.

You are the One You've Been Waiting For, by Richard Schwartz. A popular book providing an IFS perspective on intimate relationships.

Parts Work, by Tom Holmes. A short, richly illustrated introduction to IFS for the general public.

Bring Yourself to Love, by Mona Barbera. A book for the general public on using IFS to work through difficulties in love relationships.

Other Books and Audio Products

The Pattern System. The Pattern System is a systematic approach to understanding personality that can lead directly to psychological healing and personal growth. You can think of it as a Periodic Table for parts. This book is an overview of the entire Pattern System, intended for both people who want to work on changing their patterns and professionals who want to use the Pattern System in the work.

Conflict, Care, and Love: Transforming Your Relationship Patterns. This book helps you to explore and change your patterns around intimacy, conflict, caring, and power.

Books on Single Patterns. I have published five books that deal with single patterns from the Pattern System. Actually, each book covers one pattern and the healthy capacity that transforms it. Each of the five books is connected to a workbook on the web that allows you to actively work with this pattern and develop a practice for changing it and manifesting the healthy capacity in your life. The books are *Embracing Intimacy, Taking Action* (Procrastination), *Letting Go of Perfectionism, Beyond Caretaking,* and *A Pleaser No Longer.*

Activating Your Inner Champion Instead of Your Inner Critic, with Bonnie Weiss, describes the types of Inner Critics and allows you to profile your version of them in detail using a web program. Each of the types has an Inner Champion that is the magic bullet for transforming that particular type of Critic. From this book, you can also access a web program to create and profile your unique Inner Champion for each of the Critics.

Inner Champion Meditations. Each healthy capacity has a corresponding Inner Champion that supports you in developing and manifesting that capacity. Bonnie Weiss and I have produced a series of recorded guided meditations for activating these Inner Champions.

Pattern Meditations. We also have produced a series of guided meditations for using IFS to work on many of the Pattern System patterns using IFS.

All of these books and audio products (and others still to be created) are available at our online store at http://www.personal-growth-programs.com/store/.

Self-Therapy Journey

Self-Therapy Journey, www.selftherapyjourney.com is the first general-purpose web application for users to explore and heal their psychological issues and practice changing their behavior. It is based on both IFS and the Pattern System.

For its initial launch in January 2014, Self-Therapy Journey contains 23 patterns and their corresponding healthy capacities. You can take a quiz to help you determine which patterns you would like to explore. Then you can read about the pattern and use checklists, fill-ins, images, and guided journaling to explore exactly how this pattern appears in your psyche and your life.

You can explore the underlying motivations for your pattern, heal the wounds from childhood that are behind it, and set up a detailed homework practice for changing the pattern into the corresponding healthy capacity, with web support. Self-Therapy Journey includes guided meditations based on IFS to provide experiential work on each pattern.

The Center for Self-Leadership

The Center for Self-Leadership (CSL) www.selfleadership.org is the official IFS organization, created by Richard Schwartz.

Finding an IFS Therapists. If you want to find an IFS therapist to work with, consult the CSL website. It contains a listing of IFS therapists, which can be searched by geographical location. Many of these therapist offer IFS sessions by telephone or Skype.

IFS Professional Training. The Center for Self-Leadership conducts training programs in IFS for therapists and others in the helping professions, which I highly recommend. There are three levels, which can be taken one at a time. Level 1 consists of six three-day weekends. These training programs are held in many different cities around the U.S. and in Europe. The leaders are excellent and the curriculum is well-designed. They are experiential trainings, so you learn about IFS by working with your own parts and practicing doing sessions with others in the training. There is an emphasis on building community in the training group, which fosters personal and professional connection.

The CSL website contains a number of professional articles by Richard Schwartz on IFS. He has produced a number of excellent videos and DVD's of IFS sessions he conducted, which can be purchased from the website. There are also audio recordings of presentations from past IFS conferences.

IFS Conference and Workshops. There is an annual IFS conference in Chicago, which is an excellent opportunity to delve more deeply into the model and network with other professionals. Richard Schwartz leads week-long personal growth IFS workshops open to the public at various growth centers in the U.S. and Mexico. There are other professional workshops and presentations on IFS by Schwartz and other top IFS trainers.

Definitions of Terms

———— • ————

Accessing a Part
Tuning in to a part experientially, through an image, an emotion, a body sensation, or internal dialogue, so you can work with the part using IFS.

Activation of a Part
A part can become triggered by a situation or a person so that it influences your feelings and actions.

Active Listening
When you are the witness for someone doing an IFS session, you attempt to understand their experience and reflect that back to them.

Blending
The situation in which a part has taken over your consciousness, so that you feel its feelings, believe its attitudes are true, and act according to its impulses. Blending is a more extreme form of activation.

Burden
A painful emotion or negative belief about yourself or the world, which a part has taken on as the result of a past harmful situation or relationship, usually from childhood.

Childhood Origin

An incident or relationship from childhood that produced enough pain or trauma that it caused an exile to take on a burden.

Concerned Part

A part that feels judgmental or angry toward the target part. When you are blended with a concerned part, you aren't in Self.

Conscious Blending

The situation in which you choose to feel a part's emotions because doing so will be helpful in the IFS process. You are aware that you are blended and can unblend easily if necessary.

Exile

A young child part that is carrying pain from the past.

Extreme Role

A role that is dysfunctional or problematic because the part carries a burden from the past or because a protector is trying to protect an exile. An **extreme part** is a part that has an extreme role.

Firefighter

A type of protector that impulsively jumps in when the pain of an exile is starting to come up in order to distract you from the pain or numb it.

Generic Memory

An image that represents a kind of incident that happened many times during your childhood.

Healthy Role

A role that is the natural function of a part when it has no burdens. A **healthy part** is a part that has a healthy role.

Implicit Memory

A childhood memory that shows up as a vague body sensation or a fragmented image, giving you only a partial sense of the actual incident or relationship.

Part
A subpersonality, which has its own feelings, perceptions, beliefs, motivations, and memories.

Polarization
A situation where two parts are in conflict about how you should act or feel.

Positive Intent
All parts are playing their roles in an attempt to help you or protect you, even if the effect of the role is negative.

Protector
A part that tries to block off pain that is arising inside you or to protect you from hurtful incidents or distressing relationships in your current life.

Reparenting
The step in the IFS process in which the Self gives an exile what it needs to feel better or to change a harmful childhood situation.

Retrieval
The step in the IFS process in which the Self takes an exile out of a harmful childhood situation and into a place where it can be safe and comfortable.

Role
The job that a part performs to help you. It may be primarily internal, or it may involve the way the part interacts with people and acts in the world.

Seat of Consciousness
The place in the psyche that determines your identity, choices, feelings, and perceptions. The Self is the natural occupant of the seat of consciousness, though parts can take over the seat by blending.

Self
The core aspect of you that is your true self, your spiritual center. The Self is relaxed, open, and accepting of yourself and others. It is curious, compassionate, calm, and interested in connecting with other people and your parts.

Self-Leadership
The situation in which your parts trust you, in Self, to make decisions and take action in your life.

Symbolic Memory
An image that represents a memory through symbols, as in a dream, rather than showing exactly what happened.

Target Part
The part you are focusing on to work with at the moment.

Trailhead
A psychological issue that involves one or more parts. Following it can lead to healing.

Unblending
Separating from a part that is blended with you so that you are in Self.

Unburdening
The step in the IFS process in which the Self helps an exile to release its burdens through an internal ritual.

Witnessing
The step in the IFS process in which the Self witnesses the childhood origin of a part's burdens.

Made in the USA
Lexington, KY
24 August 2019